Proximity Marketing

Proximity Marketing

Converging Community, Consciousness, and Consumption

Rajagopal
Distinguished Professor of Marketing
EGADE Business School
Tecnologico de Monterrey
Santa Fe Campus, Mexico City
Mexico
&
Visiting Professor
Department of Administrative Sciences
Boston University, Boston, MA

ılıBEP
BUSINESS EXPERT PRESS Q
Leader in applied, concise business books

To Arati

Description

This book discusses the emerging concepts and practices of proximity marketing through theoretical foundations, design arguments, and managerial analysis. The concept of proximity marketing has been explained contextual to the social and business ecosystems, while the strategy spinning practices are focused on the business orientation, customer acquisition and loyalty, and market competitiveness of firms. This book converges the business, social, crowd, and behavioral ecosystems with the proximity marketing approaches. Success factors of the proximity marketing in the context of customer-centric companies synchronized with crowd-based business modeling, cocreation, and coevolution initiatives have been explained through people-oriented models. The proximity approach has been critically examined in this book with focus on the changing patterns of consumer interactivity and psychodynamics. Developing "out-of-the-box" strategies for proximity marketing has also been discussed in the book explaining crowd behavior, market competition, consumer needs, preferences, and associated values. Emerging crowd-based approaches as socialization of business as a corporate philosophy to understand customers and stakeholders to motivate the cocreation of value-based business performance through interpersonal experience, values, cognitive reasoning, and interactive communication have also been discussed in this book. Thematic discussions are divided into three sections comprising interactive business design, business socialization, and future perspectives across five chapters explained through the contextual case studies.

Keywords

proximity marketing; business modeling; crowd behavior; collective intelligence; social media; participatory strategies; consumer advocacy

Contents

Preface

The debate on the concept of proximity marketing in business had begun with the growing concern of neighborhood marketing, relationship marketing, and modeling of economic geography. Neighborhood marketing has been practiced since long by consumer products companies like Mary Kay Cosmetics as community approach to marketing. Marketplace for community-centric products in health, food, textile, and sustainability is undergoing remarkable changes in fast-developing countries due to the ongoing major societal changes that reflect in the social and sectoral service system.[1] This has induced companies to make more careful, long-term strategic planning on their neighborhood business orientation and service provision to assure acceptable profit level, empower customers, and cocreate values. In India, Shakti Experiment to empower rural women to sell consumer products of Hindustan Unilever in their neighborhood has been successful in co-creating value chain within the community and supporting community marketing strategy of the company. Therefore, to effectively explore the real needs of consumers for merchants and recommend the right products to consumers at the appropriate time, proximity marketing helps in outreaching consumers.[2] Proximity marketing has evolved as a business model by converging business with philanthropy and has integrated the two domains to improve regional trade and economic conditions in developing countries.[3] The neighborhood business practice has become central to the people's engagement in businesses

---

[1] L. Jokinen, I. Puumalainen, and M. Airaksinen. 2019. "Influence of Strategic Planning on Product Marketing and Health Service Orientation of Community Pharmacies—A National Survey in Finland," *Health Policy* 123, no. 5, pp. 462–467.

[2] Rajagopal. 2021. *The Business Design Cube: Converging Markets, Society, and Customer Values to Grow Competitive in Business* (New York, NY: Business Expert Press).

[3] E. Likoko and J. Kini. 2017. "Inclusive Business-a Business Approach to Development," *Current Opinion in Environmental Sustainability* 24, no. 1, pp. 84–88.

and democratized the organizational design and governance at the bottom-of-the-pyramid market segment. Nestlé in Columbia, Unilever in India, and Mary Kay Cosmetics in Mexico are growing with the inclusive business philosophy by developing design-to-society business model. Inclusive business arguably rose into prominence as a key concept toward inclusive development approach for the people at the bottom-of-the-pyramid segment.[4] Fast-moving consumer goods require proximity to local markets, although economies of scale in certain functions are not effectively achieved and need centralized control. At the same time, a flexible matrix of stakeholder engagement, business leaders, and managers around the world share a common understanding of corporate strategy. Some customer-centric companies practicing proximity marketing approach maintained consistent practices toward engaging high-quality managers and linking decentralized neighborhood groups through the profit-with-purpose goals of marketing.[5]

The concept of proximity in businesses rose into prominence by the end of the 20th century, as crowd workspaces and sharing of experience offered deep and meaningful relationships between customers and employees of the company to increase collective psychodynamics. The activities performed by the firms in developing a new customer relationship are often built around efficient communication tasks to drive interpersonal communications, confidence, and cognitive bonding. Brand marketing is characterized by extensive interpersonal communications not only between buyers and sellers but also between a wide variety of functions performed by the actors at back- and frontstages.[6] Conversational interaction is an important tool to develop proximity and can be achieved by understanding how companies can forge authentic and durable brand relationships with the various segments of consumers when they aggregate

---

[4] J. Hall, S.V. Matos, and M.J.C. Martin. 2014. "Innovation Pathways at the Base of the Pyramid: Establishing Technological Legitimacy Through Social Attributes," *Technovation* 34, pp. 284–294.

[5] F.A. Maljers. 1992. "Inside Unilever: The Evolving Transnational Company," *Harvard Business Review* 70, no. 5, pp. 46–52.

[6] Rajagopal. 2011. "The Symphony Paradigm: Strategy for Managing Market Competition," *Journal of Transnational Management* 16, no. 3, pp. 181–199.

geographic marketing. Such interactions allow firms not only to understand the customer insights but also to realize the power of cocreation and coevolution of business in the competitive marketplace.[7] A hybrid conversational-communication style drives positive customer-brand relationships and helps firms evaluate the geodemographic association of brands with the consumers. Firms can develop proximity index based on communication, interactivity, cognitive variables, relationship drivers, competitive touchpoints, and business growth. In addition, cocreating customer service and relationship hubs foster marketing, public relations, and communications strategies to develop a positive consumer-business helix and ecosystem.[8] This book argues that until companies understand the contribution of effective communications and relationship management, true growth in business is unlikely.

Market trends and consumer behavior are rapidly changing, and social media is playing a critical role in determining marketing decisions. Volatility of consumer markets can have significant negative effects on market share, profitability, and brand equity of the companies. However, volatility is an embedded attribute of the competitive growth theory. The argument central to the theory of change management is that the companies operating in a competitive business environment consider consumer preferences, innovation, technology, and growth-related investments as dynamic variables. Customer-centric companies, therefore, tend to build simpler products to help consumers choose the right product. Creating interactive platforms and engaging customers and stakeholders in the marketing of products and services help companies in transforming the conventional marketing practices to interactive and proximity-based business model. Successful consumer marketing companies function on "hub and spoke" model in developing relationships through influencer–member exchange (IMX) process to stay need-based and customer-centric

---

[7] B.A. Livingston and T.R. Opie. 2019. "Even at 'Inclusive' Companies, Women of Color Don't Feel Supported," *Harvard Business Review Digital Article* (Cambridge, MA: Harvard Business School Press).

[8] F. Schultz, S. Utz, and A. Göritz. 2011. Is the Medium the Message? Perceptions of and Reactions to Crisis Communication Via Twitter, Blogs, and Traditional Media," *Public Relationship Review* 37, no. 1, pp. 20–27.

in business. The changing media and consumption behaviors of consumers and skepticism toward traditional forms of advertising have prompted the growth of influencer marketing, which is an outgrowth of proximity marketing concept.[9] The critical impact of IMX depends on the interplay of key influencer characteristics and marketing disclosures. The growing changes in the consumer behavior correspond partly with the rise of influencer marketing, defined as a tactic in which companies pay people (influencers), financially or in-kind, to produce social media content on behalf of the brands and influence consumers' preferences and purchase decisions. Consequently, the congruence of influencer attributes with the consumers cognition and reasoning abilities drive higher IMX effects. Consumers expect influencers to share insights on their experience and recommendations about the latest trends to transform the preconceived notion and behavioral stigma.[10]

Customer-centric firms largely support decision making, idea sharing, and emotions in managing business by engaging consumers in the strategy development process. Such companies develop abilities to fight conscious and unconscious biases as they coevolve with people and society.[11] Social interactions often motivate a sustainable and social consumption of products. The interplay of consumers within the social (interpersonal) and digital (remote response) platforms also helps companies to adapt to inclusive business models and stay distinctive in the competitive marketplace. Consumers today are increasingly looking for brands that have a social purpose above functional and competitive benefits. As a result, most companies are taking social stand in highly visible ways. An effective, convergent business strategy creates social and customer values by coevolving the brand in society. The network among society, people, and business

[9] Z. Karagür, J.M. Becker, K. Klein, and A. Edeling. 2022. "How, Why, and When Disclosure Type Matters for Influencer Marketing," *International Journal of Research in Marketing* 39, no. 2, pp. 313–335.

[10] A. Audrezet, G. de Kerviler, and J.G. Moulard. 2020. "Authenticity Under Threat: When Social Media Influencers Need to Go Beyond Self-presentation," *Journal of Business Research* 117, pp. 557–569.

[11] B. Yamkovenko and S. Tavares. 2017. "To Understand Whether Your Company Is Inclusive, Map How Your Employees Interact," *Harvard Business Review Digital Article* (Cambridge, MA: Harvard Business School Press).

stimulates cocreation and collective business designing. This book argues that the convergence of society and business can be better understood by converging crowd perspectives, IMX factors, and continuous learning about the consumer behavior and competitive growth perspectives.[12]

Value is often measured in either economic or social terms. The blended-value proposition emphasizes that true customer value, which is a blend of economic, social, and environmental components, is indivisible. After the success of networking practices of business activities with social media over decades, profit-seeking firms have laid explicit emphasis on the creation of strategic social value. This business philosophy has grown in nonprofit organizations as well. Social values are dynamic and customer-centric companies continuously monitor the perpetual changes in social values, culture, and ethnicity. Consequently, companies adapt to the triadic philosophy of gaining social insights, blending business values in society, and cocreating innovative sociobusiness strategies to drive businesses deep into the social environment. The best practices reveal that these elements boost business performance by enhancing the social values and narrowing the consumer disparities.[13]

Many types of businesses such as retailers use proximity-based marketing and show proximity advertisements to potential consumers who are near their premises. Inside a shopping mall, advertisements indicating maps and discount coupons are a form of localized proximity marketing. Restaurants and fast-food outlets use mobile proximity marketing to show promotions to passers-by and attract them inside. They also show display advertisements about coupons to attract new customers and encourage existing customers to come back and experience repeat buying. Bluetooth beacon technology (BBT) enhances the scope of proximity marketing by fostering customers' reception of relationship marketing programs. By applying proximity BBT, firms can attain more accurate and detailed

---

[12] Rajagopal. 2021. *The Business Design Cube: Converging Markets, Society, and Customer Values to Grow Competitive in Business* (New York, NY: Business Expert Press).

[13] Rajagopal. 2021. *The Business Design Cube: Converging Markets, Society, and Customer Values to Grow Competitive in Business* (New York, NY: Business Expert Press).

customer insights to better deliver the relationship programs to the right person at the right time and at the right location. Consequently, relationships with customers can be developed, maintained, and enhanced more efficiently and effectively than with the use of traditional proximity marketing technologies. Proximity BBT utilizes digital techniques to request permission to acquire data of customers via beacon systems to offer targeted relationship marketing tactics.[14]

The Concept Map

The unique discussion standpoint of this book is the strategy spin of firms around the 3C-factors comprising competition, customer, and consumption ecosystems as illustrated in Figure P1. In the rapidly changing market environment, firms face increasing challenges in focusing on a predetermined business model. Consequently, the firms use the strategy spin approach by changing the strategy orientation across the business touchpoints. Most business-to-consumers and business-to-business firms are engaged in strategic spin aiming at specific growth targets to survive and lead in the competitive markets.[15]

The discussions in the book are connected to the four principal discussion domains comprising relationship marketing, strategy versus tactics, market ecosystem, and information management contextual to the core theme of the book on proximity marketing. The book is divided into five chapters intertwining the concepts and cases across these discussion domains as exhibited in Figure P1. The discussion domain on relationship marketing is central to Chapter 1, which focuses on synchronizing business design through social empowerment, collective intelligence (CI), and social consciousness in the context of social media and CI and

[14] M.Y.C. Lin, T.T. Nguyen, E.Y. Cheng, A.N.H. Le, and J.M.S. Cheng. 2022. "Proximity Marketing and Bluetooth Beacon Technology: A Dynamic Mechanism Leading to Relationship Program Receptiveness," *Journal of Business Research* 141, pp. 151–162.

[15] M.D. Lord, S.W. Mandel, and J.D. Wager. 2002. "Spinning Out a Star," *Harvard Business Review* 80, no. 6, pp. 115–121.

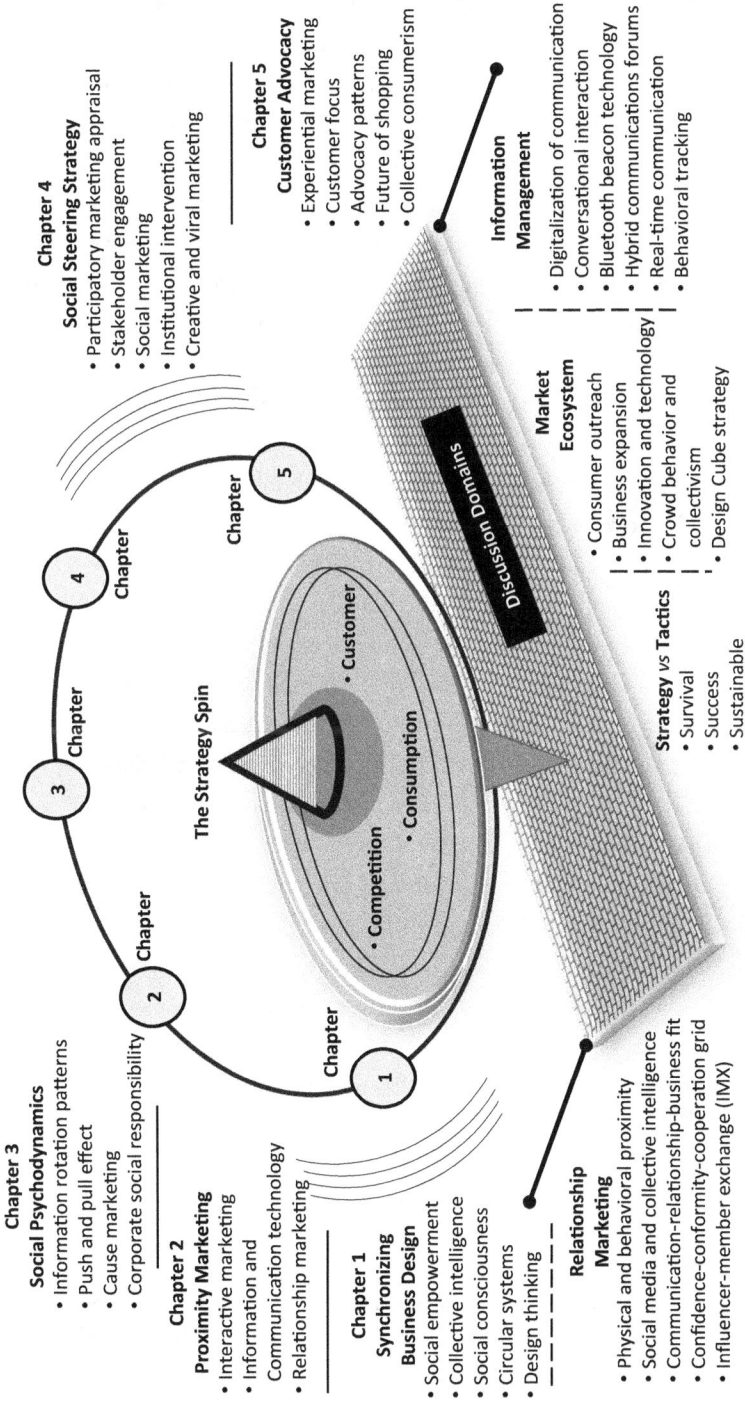

Chapter 3
Social Psychodynamics
- Information rotation patterns
- Push and pull effect
- Cause marketing
- Corporate social responsibility

Chapter 2
Proximity Marketing
- Interactive marketing
- Information and
  Communication technology
- Relationship marketing

Chapter 1
Synchronizing
Business Design
- Social empowerment
- Collective intelligence
- Social consciousness
- Circular systems
- Design thinking

Relationship
Marketing
- Physical and behavioral proximity
- Social media and collective intelligence
- Communication-relationship-business fit
- Confidence-conformity-cooperation grid
- Influencer-member exchange (IMX)

Chapter 4
Social Steering Strategy
- Participatory marketing appraisal
- Stakeholder engagement
- Social marketing
- Institutional intervention
- Creative and viral marketing

Chapter 5
Customer Advocacy
- Experiential marketing
- Customer focus
- Advocacy patterns
- Future of shopping
- Collective consumerism

Information
Management
- Digitalization of communication
- Conversational interaction
- Bluetooth beacon technology
- Hybrid communications forums
- Real-time communication
- Behavioral tracking

Market
Ecosystem
- Consumer outreach
- Business expansion
- Innovation and technology
- Crowd behavior and collectivism
- Design Cube strategy

Strategy vs Tactics
- Survival
- Success
- Sustainable

Discussion Domains

The Strategy Spin
- Customer
- Consumption
- Competition

Chapter 1
Chapter 2
Chapter 3
Chapter 4
Chapter 5

Figure P.1 Discussion paradigm of the book

Source: Author.

communication-relationship business fit.[16] As relationship marketing and proximity marketing are symbiotic, Chapter 2, which focuses on proximity marketing, is woven around physical and behavioral proximity emphasizing the role of interactive marketing with the support of information and communication technology (ICT). The proximity marketing widely depends on social psychodynamics (Chapter 3). This chapter discusses the central issues of relationship marketing encompassing the influencer-member exchange effects to development confidence, conformity with the crowd behavior, and extending cooperation within the consumer community. The information rotation patterns and push–pull effects of proximity marketing constitute the center of discussion in this chapter, which helps readers in reconstructing thematic ties with the relationship marketing. The second discussion domain of the book is based on the arguments and critical discussions in the long-term (strategic) versus short-term (tactical) impact of proximity marketing on the competitiveness and performance of customer-centric businesses.[17] Discussion on the right strategy for survival of both commercial and social brands, critical success factors, and sustainability of the firms and their brands are spread across all chapters in the book. The third discussion domain of market system with focus on consumer outreach, business expansion, and innovation and technology has been integrated in Chapter 2 and Chapter 4, on proximity marketing and social steering strategy, respectively. Chapter 4 discusses participatory marketing appraisal through social marketing and stakeholder engagement. The crowd behavior and collectivism has been discussed in this chapter as a driver of creative and viral marketing. The design cube strategy including design-to-market, design-to-society, and design-to-value, as an innovative approach for the firms to meet the challenges of changing market ecosystem, has been discussed in Chapter 4.

---

[16] S. Gilboa, T. Seger-Guttmann, and O. Mimran. 2019. "The Unique Role of Relationship Marketing in Small Businesses' Customer Experience," *Journal of Retailing and Consumer Services* 51, pp. 152–164.

[17] M. Juntunen, E. Ismagilova, and E.L. Oikarinen. 2019. "B2B Brands on Twitter: Engaging Users With a Varying Combination of Social Media Content Objectives, Strategies, and Tactics," *Industrial Marketing Management* 89, pp. 630–641.

The last discussion domain on information management is central to the conversation and arguments in Chapter 5, which portrays customer advocacy through experiential marketing, collective consumerism, advocacy patterns, and future shopping trends. This discussion model is also aligned with Chapter 1 on synchronizing business design.

Relationship marketing through proximity approach in business benefits the multistake business model and strengthens multistakeholder mechanism in business governance by codesigning the organizational structures, processes, and principles.[18] Successful companies such as Nestle, Wholefoods, and Apple bring business and society back together by creating shared and economic values. In addition, crowdsourcing, crowdfunding, social marketing, and shared economy platforms have been rapidly transforming the production and consumption systems in the developing economies. These platforms connect businesses with economic, social, and environmental factors across geodemographic segments.[19]

This book discusses the philosophy and practices of proximity marketing through theoretical foundations, design arguments, and managerial analysis as illustrated in Figure P1. The concept of proximity marketing has been explained in context to the various ecosystems and the concept of strategy spinning that affect the business orientation, customer acquisition and loyalty, and market competitiveness of firms. Consequently, business-, social-, crowd-, and behavioral ecosystems significantly contribute to the attributes of proximity marketing. Most companies that are currently engaged in building consumer behavior on the triple bottom line principle and aim at earning profit with people, purpose, and sustainability (triple bottom line), while some companies tend to complement the proximity marketing approaches with effective

---

[18] H. Shi. 2021. "The Application of Social Psychology and Collective Internet Governance," *Aggression and Violent Behavior*, (in Press). https://doi.org/10.1016/j.avb.2021.101588.

[19] O. Mont, Y.V. Palgan, K. Bradley, and L. Zvolska. October 1, 2020. "A Decade of the Sharing Economy: Concepts, Users, Business and Governance Perspectives," *Journal of Cleaner Production* 269, (in Press). https://doi.org/10.1016/j.jclepro.2020.122215.

information management, accountability, brand socialization (interactive drive), and transformational initiatives (quadruple bottom line). This book discusses the success factors of the proximity marketing in the context of customer-centric companies, which adopt crowd-based business modeling, cocreation, and coevolution initiatives. The proximity approach has been critically examined in this book with focus on changing patterns of consumer interactivity and psychodynamics. Developing "out-of-the-box" strategies for proximity marketing has also been discussed in the book explaining crowd behavior, market competition, consumer needs, preferences, and associated values.

Crowd behavior often requires streamlining to be able to deliver a predetermined course of action. Such behavior is commonly chaotic, but it enables firms to understand customer performance in general and to develop marketing strategies. Nonetheless, complex crowd behaviors may result from unpredicted interactions among individuals who tend to locally coordinate individual and community issues. However, with a social business goal, a crowd behaves in a self-organized manner and engages in collective dynamics without external control.[20] Most multinational companies such as Nestle, Apple, and IBM have developed their business models with "design-to-society" approach, which helps not only in creating social value to their business but also in gaining customer confidence to sustain in the increasing market competition today. The emerging concepts like profit-with-purpose and coevolution of business designs are discussed in this book as the core themes of inclusive business that are being practiced by most customer-centric multinational companies. Inclusive business approach overrides the conventional wisdom of leader-centric management practices, and is driven by integrative thinking. Proximity approach has many constructive challenges driven by the collective intelligence, to produce more adaptive-reasoning patterns with interdisciplinary dialogue. The new model for business education argues that inclusive business plays a vital role in integrating people in business processes by breaking the managerial stigma of *tough mindedness*

---

[20] M. Moussaid, S. Garnier, G. Theraulaz, and D. Helbing. 2009. "Collective Information Processing and Pattern Formation in Swarms, Flocks, and Crowds," *Topics in Cognitive Science* 1, no. 3, pp. 469–497.

(competitive and profit oriented) to *agile mindedness* to ensure value-centric business management.[21]

This book discusses the socialization of business as a corporate philosophy to understand customers and stakeholders to motivate the cocreation of value-based business performance through interpersonal experience, values, cognitive reasoning, and interactive communication. Reviewing a wide range of literature from empirical research studies to best practices followed by the companies, this book analyzes the emerging theories of communications, social learning, distinctiveness, corporate social responsibility, social learning, and value cocreation. The concepts and models developed in the book are central to the involvement and engagement of people in business with the increase in social-responsive behavior of companies to support coevolution of business with customers and stakeholders. Thematically, the discussion on these perspectives is interpreted as proximity philosophy in business with multilayered marketing strategies across various geodemographic segments. The focus of the discussion on proximity marketing approaches is precisely on using collective intelligence and collective performance through social networks, interactive communication, and crowd consciousness. This book deliberates on the critical success factors of firms, which include diversity and cross-functionality by managing the triple and quadruple bottom lines. It is argued in the book that a timely deployment of streamlined crowd-based marketing strategies in chaotic markets could enhance the effects of social innovation, increase in value spread among consumers, and reduce the growing complexities in the global and regional markets. Collective intelligence creates intrinsic and extrinsic motivation with distinctive effects on prosocial behavior, which helps the firms understand the effects of crowd behavior.[22] This book presents new insights on developing inclusive business models using both aggressive (crowd-driven) and defensive (competitive) marketing strategies in the proximity-driven business

---

[21] R. Martin and M.C. Moldoveanu. 2008. *The Future of the MBA: Designing the Thinker of the Future* (Oxford University Press).

[22] A. Festré and P. Garrouste. 2015. "Theory and Evidence in Psychology and Economics About Motivation Crowding Out: A Possible Convergence?" *Journal of Economic Survey* 29, no. 2, pp. 339–356.

models. The book guides managers on both marketing tactics and strategies using the 5Ts concepts for managing time (first-mover advantage), territory (new market segments), target (potential consumers), thrust (competitive), and tasks (cocreation).

Thematic Discussions

The thematic discussions in this book are divided into three sections comprising interactive business design, business socialization, and future perspectives across five chapters supported by contextual case studies. Chapter 1 discusses the attributes of social empowerment and its impact on proximity-based business modeling among customer-centric companies. The role of social empowerment has been discussed in this chapter in the context of the voice of customers and the liberal community space for sharing consumer experiences, ideas, strategic contributions, and cocreation of need-based products and services. The social empowerment of consumers will help firms understand the communication patterns and consumption behavior across generations such as boomers, generation X, and millennials to restructure their relationship strategies and expand their outreach across geodemographic segments.[23] Their attitudes and behaviors will have profound effects on the economy, the workplace, and social institutions in general. The chapter discusses CI and social consciousness as the drivers of social empowerment, which supports the people-oriented business designs. A CI system allows harvesting of knowledge, experience, and crowd resources through an interactive process, which represents new forms of knowledge acquisition and diffusion.[24] This chapter converges interactive communication and CI for developing synchronized business designs. Explaining the case studies on bioeconomics and design

---

[23] N. Howe and W. Strauss. 2007. "Next 20 Years: How Customer and Workforce Attitudes Will Evolve," *Harvard Business Review* 85, no. 7–8, pp. 41–52.

[24] J. Calof, K.S. Søilen, R. Klavans, B. Abdulkader, and I.E. Moudni. 2022. "Understanding the Structure, Characteristics, and Future of Collective Intelligence Using Local and Global Bibliometric Analyses," *Technological Forecasting and Social Change* 178, (in press). https://doi.org/10.1016/j.techfore.2022.121561.

thinking, this chapter brings together the discussion on bio-economics, design thinking, and circular systems.

Chapter 2 discusses proximity marketing concepts and practices from the point of view of the transformation of conventional wisdom through interactive marketing. The widespread use of digital technologies and online social networks has revolutionized customer-centric marketing practices. Online interactions have overridden the convention personal interface patterns and contributed significantly to the success of proximity marketing. By deploying various digital platforms and ICT tools (e.g., smartphones, social media, mobile apps, and electronic billboards), organizations can develop interactive marketing approaches to enhance customer outreach and narrow-down the proximity of consumer-to-consumer marketing.[25] In view of the advancement of ICT tools, this chapter discusses the frugal and hybrid technology used in managing the relationship marketing by business-to-customers and business-to-business firms. The chapter is woven around the recent research arguments that reveal homophily between influencers and audiences. Such homophily drives customer value cocreation behavior in a proximity marketing process, which leads to the expected brand value and purchase intention that occur through customer value cocreation.[26] The chapter also discusses proximity marketing tools including hybridity, visual effects, and taxonomy of relationship marketing through case studies on interactive marketing and visual marketing experiences.

The ongoing shifts in business trends indicate that most firms have already experienced the effects of deregulation, globalization, technological convergence, and digital revolution, which have transformed the functional efficiency and market competitiveness of firms. The new milestone in managing businesses today has shifted to collective intelligence

---

[25] A.S. Krishen, Y.K. Dwivedi, N. Bindu, and K.K. Satheesh. 2021. "A Broad Overview of Interactive Digital Marketing: A Bibliometric Network Analysis," *Journal of Business Research* 131, pp. 183–195.

[26] Y. Bu, J. Parkinson, and P. Thaichon. 2022. "Influencer Marketing: Homophily, Customer Value Co-Creation Behaviour and Purchase Intention," *Journal of Retailing and Consumer Services* 66, (in press). https://doi.org/10.1016/j.jretconser.2021.102904.

and crowd behavior, which helps firms in cocreation and coevolution processes.[27] Chapter 3 discusses various social dynamics perspectives establishing information diffusion patterns with cyclical and elliptical moves, diffusion and integration of communication, and centripetal and centrifugal strategies of communication, relationship, and social dynamics. With the advancement of ICT, online social networks such as Twitter and Digg have unprecedented quantities of graphic and text data to network users, which are used within the predetermined circle of personal contacts (circular). The information also spreads through snowballing across the social media platforms (elliptical) over time and space. Such communication pattern has encouraged various subways of information diffusion at the niche and local social networks causing both push (brand thrust) and pull (demand stimulation) for products and services.[28] The push–pull factors have been discussed in this chapter in the context of welfare-marketing and marketing strategies at the bottom-of-the-pyramid segment.[29] The role of corporate social responsibility has also been critical to this chapter with focus on consumer outreach, corporate commitment, and customer engagement. The case studies on welfare marketing and cause marketing have been discussed in this chapter to support the concepts and arguments on social psychodynamics affecting marketing strategies of the firm.

Chapter 4 discusses social steering strategy emphasizing various approaches of consumer engagement. The participatory market appraisal (PMA) has been explained in the context of experience sharing and cocreation of marketing strategies by engaging customers. The chapter argues that action research and community problem-solving through interactive communication, experience and ideas sharing, and exploring collective

[27] C.K. Prahalad and V. Ramaswamy. 2000. "Co-Opting Customer Competence," *Harvard Business Review* 78, no. 1, pp. 79–87.

[28] H.T. Tu, T.T. Phan, and K.P. Nguyen. 2022. "Modeling Information Diffusion in Social Networks With Ordinary Linear Differential Equations," *Information Sciences* 593, pp. 614–636.

[29] M. Matear and P.A. Dacin. 2010. "Marketing and Societal Welfare: A Multiple Stakeholder Approach," *Journal of Business Research* 63, no. 11, pp. 1173–1178.

decisions helps firms strengthen consumer outreach, satisfaction, and loyalty. Therefore, the PMA serves as a collective approach to communicate, cocreate, and coevolve customer-centric firms with stakeholders to address PNS factors (problems, needs, and solutions) collectively.[30] Participatory business appraisal as a new concept has been discussed as a continuous learning tool by engaging customers, stake holders, and crowd within the business ecosystem. Participatory appraisals are used as the driver to actions research in resolving social issues and analyzing the cultural, biological, and legal perspectives to promote customer-centric businesses on a social scale.[31] Companies that market sustainable products used to design a participatory appraisal workshop to analyze the situation from a cultural, biological, and legal perspective to social consciousness about green products on a human scale.[32] This chapter also discusses the role of social marketing and public organizations including self-help groups, cooperatives, and crowd partnering in managing the proximity approach to expand consumer outreach and experience. In fact, crowdsourcing has led to the emergence of entirely new business models. Such crowd-based business models (CBBMs) can lead to an important competitive advantage, while simultaneously presenting new challenges to entrepreneurs and executives.[33] The case studies on social marketing and cocreation of marketing practices in this chapter strengthen the discussion on social approach to proximity marketing.

Discussions in this chapter emphasize how lessons can be drawn from the success and failure experiences in doing business with people. The pace at which organizations learn may become the only sustainable

---

[30] R. Chambers. 1994. "The Origins and Practice of Participatory Rural Appraisal," *World Development* 22, no. 7, pp. 953–969.

[31] *For example,* Ibid.

[32] C.S. Lara, A.F. Crispín, and M.C.L. Téllez. 2018. "Participatory Rural Appraisal as an Educational Tool to Empower Sustainable Community Processes," *Journal of Cleaner Production* 172, pp. 4254–4262.

[33] K. Täuscher. 2017. "Leveraging Collective Intelligence: How to Design and Manage Crowd-Based Business Models," *Business Horizons* 60, no. 2, pp. 237–245.

source of competitive advantage over time.[34] Chapter 5 discusses the changing perspectives of consumer advocacy from the point of view of sharing new forms of radical, collaborative, innovative experiences through proximity marketing approaches. The discussion on advocacy patterns includes the consumer focus on anthropomorphism, follower psychology on digital media, out-of-the-box customer advocacy, and creative semantics. Such models in proximity marketing are used to take advantage of structured semantics, reasoning, or decision-making power.[35] This chapter also discusses the future of shopping using technology and collective consumerism. Growing technology-based retailers such as Amazon (VR kiosks), Alibaba (Buy + mobile VR platform), eBay (VR Department Store app), and IKEA (virtual reality kitchen showroom) have been making effort to embed virtual reality into their e-commerce services as a tool to drive relationship marketing and proximity effects. These firms are trying to transform the future of the shopping ecosystem through head-mounted displays, haptic devices, body-tracking sensors, motion-tracked controllers to structure future shopping and smart (omnichannel) retailing ecosystem.[36] This chapter also includes a case study on institutional consumer advocacy.

This book presents innovative concepts, best practices, and case studies on proximity marketing strategy in the emerging markets. Case studies are discussed in relevant chapters to support the discussions on various aspects of proximity marketing. Each chapter is provided with an overview of the discussions and the summary at the end. The visual map of concepts and strategies on inclusive business are supported by the creative figures and appropriate data in each chapter. Such illustrations make this book appealing for readers and offers smooth transition in learning. This book bridges the theory and applications of proximity marketing practices by linking crowd behavior, market competition, and customer

---

[34] P.M. Senge. 1990. "Leader's New Work: Building Learning Organizations," *MIT Sloan Management Review* 32, no. 1, pp. 7–23.

[35] J. Horkoff, N.A. Maiden, and D. Asboth. 2019. "Creative Goal Modeling for Innovative Requirements," *Information and Software Technology* 106, pp. 85–100.

[36] N. Xi and J. Hamari. 2021. "Shopping in Virtual Reality: A Literature Review and Future Agenda," *Journal of Business Research* 134, pp. 37–58.

value in managing multilayered marketing paradigms to achieve long-term business performance. This book specifically discusses the following attributes of the inclusive businesses in building effective business models:

- Linking business with societal modes to reduce whiplashes with the conventional innovation-marketing matrix
- Developing inclusive business into consumer-centric perspectives to strengthen social foundation
- Growing firms as first movers and reaping competitive advantage by developing collective business strategies and build "value-defensive" models
- Understanding cognitive ergonomics of consumers to develop value-led business performance
- Developing collective engagement in business settings

The principal audience of this book are managers, researchers, and students of marketing strategy, marketing research, consumer behavior, and courses on relationship marketing. This book has been developed also to serve as a managerial guide and think tank for the graduate students engaged in studying courses on business strategy and marketing. Besides serving as a reference book to the students, this would also be an inspiring book for managers, market analysts, and business consultants engaged in decision-making process for developing marketing strategy.

The book argues the need for companies to understand about achieving an inner analytic edge to defend value-driven business and augment market share. Though companies draw some competition-based decisions through performance dashboards, the book reviews logical framework analysis and consumer-centered strategies for making sustainable decisions. Customer engagement has emerged as a core concept in developing marketing strategies, though significant research on inclusive business in the context of emotion-decision equilibrium has been limited.[37] The book argues that companies need to consider a broader social perspective to

---

[37] M. Kleinaltenkamp, I.O. Karpen, C. Plewa, E. Jaakkola, and J. Conduit. 2019. "Collective Engagement in Organizational Settings," *Industrial Marketing Management* 80, no. 1, pp. 11–23.

enhance the effectiveness of business models by implementing applied marketing decisions and putting the consumer first in the business management process.

This book will contribute to the existing literature and deliver new concepts to the students and researchers to pursue the subject further. By reading this book, working managers may also realize how to converge best practices with corporate strategies in managing business at the destination markets while students would learn the new dimensions of marketing strategies.

Rajagopal
Mexico City
June 01, 2023

Acknowledgments

Proximity marketing has been a contemporary topic that has triggered as a potential marketing approach to be explored while I was teaching courses on E-commerce Management, and Innovation and Global Competitiveness at Boston University. Proximity marketing has emerged as a promising decision-making domain in the information technology-based strategy platforms of firms. I am thankful to Dr. Tanya Zlateva, Dean, Metropolitan College of Boston University, for giving me opportunity to teach related subjects, which enabled me to apply the research output on sustainability-based business modeling in the classes. Discussion with Dr. Vladimir Zlatev, Associate Professor of Practice at Administrative Sciences Department, Metropolitan College, Boston University, has also benefited the horizon of knowledge on the subject immensely. Discussions with Dr. Irena Vodenska, Department Chair, and Dr. Marcus Goncalves, Associate Chair of the Department, on this topic also enriched the contents of this book.

I would like to acknowledge the support of Dr. Horacio Arredondo, Dean, EGADE Business School, and Dr. Claudia Quintanilla, Director, Marketing and Business Intelligence Department of EGADE Business School, who have always encouraged me to take up new challenges in teaching graduate courses, develop new insights, and contribute to the existing literature prolifically. I thank all my students of graduate and doctoral programs at EGADE Business School for sharing enriching ideas on the subject during the classroom discussions, which helped in building this book on the framework of innovative ideas.

I also acknowledge the outstanding support of Scott Isenberg, Executive Editor of Business Expert Press, who critically examined the proposal, guided the manuscript preparation, and took the publication process forward. I am thankful to various anonymous referees of my previous research works on innovation and technology management, who helped me in looking deeper into the conceptual gaps and improving the quality with their valuable comments. Though it was a solo journey with this publication project from ideation to manuscript preparation, I must acknowledge the encouragement from senior academics to proceed ahead with the project. I express my deep gratitude to my wife Arati Rajagopal, who always reminded me of this task over other deadlines on the agenda. She also deserves kudos for copyediting the manuscript rigorously before submitting it to the publisher.

CHAPTER 1

Synchronizing Business Designs

Overview

This chapter discusses the attributes of social empowerment and its impact on proximity-based business modeling among customer-centric companies. The role of social empowerment has been discussed in this chapter in context of the voice of the customer (VoC) and the liberal community space for sharing consumer experience, ideas, strategic contributions, and cocreation of need-based products and services. The social empowerment of consumers will help firms understand the communication patterns and consumption behavior across generations such as boomers, generation X, and millennials to restructure their relationship strategies and expand their outreach across geodemographic segments. Their attitudes and behaviors will have profound effects on the economy, the workplace, and the social institutions in general. The chapter discusses collective intelligence (CI) and social consciousness as the drivers of social empowerment, which supports the people-oriented business designs. A CI system allows for harvesting of knowledge, experience, and crowd resources through an interactive process, which represents new forms of knowledge acquisition and diffusion. This chapter converges interactive communication and CI for developing synchronized business designs. Explaining the case studies on bioeconomics and design thinking, this chapter brings together the discussions on bioeconomics, design thinking, and circular systems.

Defining Proximity Marketing

Learning from the experience of the successful firms in global and local markets, it has been evident that the philosophy of marketing has been transformed today from *marketing-to-customers*, which reveals a conservative and supply-led corporate behavior, to *marketing-with-customers*, a bottom-up and proximity-driven philosophy. The business psychology behind the notion of marketing-with-customer brings forward the social-proximity approach in marketing by engaging customers emotionally and consciously. Associating consumers in business helps firms to cocreate strategies and to coevolve the business by integrating the crowd, customers, and competition at the nexus of VoCs and value-of-business. Therefore, the proximity marketing philosophy has grown at the grassroots of society as a crowd-way of doing business for firms by converging the following divergent factors:

- Consumer consciousness (including subconscious and nostalgic state of mind)
- Openness for exploring opportunities
- Socialization of business to enhance outreach of consumers
- Driving transformation to lead the business

Proximity marketing can be defined through various perspectives. It can be stated that proximity marketing is a tactic, which drives firms to engross potential consumers by reaching out across geodemographic segments in society through advertising and communication based on user-generated contents, participatory market appraisals (PMAs), and expected solutions delivery to the consumers. Proximity marketing has grown as a contemporary phenomenon in marketing by integrating technologies such as Bluetooth beacons, Wi-Fi, geofencing, near-field communications (NFC), and QR codes. Moving from rural to urban market ecosystem in the 21st century, proximity approaches have been ambidextrously experimented by the firms. Retail outlets and restaurants have emerged as big users of proximity marketing by elevating the sense of proximity within the physical, social, psychological, and neurobehavioral consumer experiences. The principle of proximity states that sharing, analyzing, and predicting the perceived consumer personality and behavior within the social, cultural, and ethnic ambience delivers key resources in making competitive business decisions. Proximity marketing allows firms to target customers at the right place at the right time with social and highly personalized contents. Planning marketing-relationship strategies to attract, acquire, and assimilate consumers based on their proximity to a location allows firms not only to develop business relationships with them but also to coevolve with them in the marketplace. Iconic customer-centric and social companies such as LEGO, IKEA, and Starbucks are successful examples of proximity marketing.

Broadly, proximity can be defined as the feeling that a firm has for consumers through physical, social, and psychological dimensions (e.g., Jones et al. 2008). Contextualizing proximity in competitive purchase decision making implies that consumers who are physically, socially, and psychologically closer to the firm contribute to its success. Consequently, proximity marketing helps firms to coevolve and gain the strength of crowd, consumers, and stakeholders against the radical market competition. *Physical proximity* of firms refers to the geographical nearness of decision makers and consumers who are affected by this act or decision. Consumers' perception on the social proximity of a firm refers broadly to mutual familiarity with the values, norms, customs, and beliefs that influence their engagement with the coevolution in business. Psychological proximity or cognitive nearness with the firm and its business can be described as an affective propinquity or a "high level of engagement" (Mencl and May 2009). *Cognitive proximity* can be built by the firms among consumers through disseminating effective communication, developing dexterity in decisions, and sharing innovative ideas to infuse creativity in firm–society convergence. Such proximity leads to *organizational proximity*, which contextualizes interactive learning where trust-based networks help overcome uncertainty, coordinate transactions, and enable effective knowledge transfer. *Institutional proximity* involves sharing of customer centric and social policies, organizational cultural, working practices and values among the key partners. The proximity marketing thus helps firms in lowering transaction costs and provides a stable basis for interactive learning and coevolution (Villiani et al. 2017).

Consumers can be persuaded to have a socially meaningful relationship with the firm through its socially responsible initiatives. This is because socially responsible practices affect both the consumers' self-actualization and social esteem with the firm, their association with it, and their purchase intention. Socially responsible practices have the potential to affect consumers' purchasing intentions directly wherein strategies of the firm stay congruent with the consumers' beliefs and encourage buying behavior (Sen and Bhattacharya 2001). Based on this rationale, consumers perceive proximity (physical, social, and psychological) with the firm and strengthen the social image of the firm and mutual relationship. This suggests that firms stay motivated to cooperate with the consumers in various geodemographic segments as they can more easily build these commonalities and facilitate knowledge transfer activities and proximity to fortify connectivity (Laursen et al. 2011).

Proximity marketing approaches allow marketers to target a customer at the right place at the right time with highly personalized content. Connecting with customers based on their proximity to a location allows marketers to send relevant content to the customers and transform their consumption practices. The goal of proximity marketing is to enhance the consumer experience by creating a journey within a wider area of business. One of the main benefits of proximity marketing is that it allows businesses to target consumers both personally and socially.

Proximity and Business Ecosystem

In the competitive business environment, large firms operate with open ecosystems to gain competitive leverage by commercializing open-innovation and reverse-innovation products. This strategy helps firms deliver high customer value and inculcate perceptions among customers on collective creativity. Consequently, firms can retain the loyalty and support of ecosystem partners and stakeholders to ensure their continued performance in the marketplace. Continuous learning and exploring ways to catch-up with changes in the industry, drive firms to stay agile with the dynamic business ecosystems. Industrial marketing firms today have moved from relationship-management goals to ecosystems-orchestration process. The business environment is hierarchically arrayed within industry with transitional multimodal business system across large firms. Large firms within industries (such as pharmaceuticals) develop business consortiums and focus on collaborative strategizing and expanding the key partners geographically. The changing business ecosystems today drive greater flexibility in strategic partnership by allowing firms to develop collaborations contextual to the CI, social values, and benefit—spread across the stakeholders (Reeves et al. 2015).

The core- and contextual attributes form the ecosystem of a business, which is a strategic perspective of managing business in a competitive marketplace. The notion of business ecosystem addresses the relative concepts of collaboration and competition, such as customer-centric and market-led strategies of business, in both predetermined and dynamic business systems. Broadly, the extrinsic attributes of a business ecosystem include innovation (social- and market-based), a competition constituent (opportunity mapping, elements of oligopoly and monopsony, and market taxonomy), and social business philosophies of companies (Parente et al. 2018). Traditional firms considered macro elements in the business as exogenous drivers of business ecosystem, and focused on controllable variables such as organizational design, work culture, and marketing mix. Exogenous elements such as competitors, suppliers, stakeholders, and business partners have become endogenous management factors of the business ecosystem. Technology plays a major role in the business ecosystem today, which has evolved from an internally focused factor to customer-facing attributes, leading to agile business development. The bilateral factors in the business ecosystem include government, business partners (manufacturing, logistics, and marketing), financial institutions, and information technology providers. The contemporary marketing philosophy is founded on a polyhedron framework that has a triangular prismatic effect with five faces, six edges, and nine vertices. The philosophical thoughts on modern business can be stretched wide from the geometric structure to the functional propositions in the marketplace, which entails broadly the market, society, and customer values. The variables embedding the faces, edges, and vertices of the prismatic structure of marketing are exhibited in Table 1.1.

The prismatic structure of marketing management has five faces, six edges, and nine vertices that help managers to develop marketing strategies, processes, and make competitive decisions as exhibited in Table 1.1.

Table 1.1 Prismatic structure of marketing management

Faces (5)	Edges (6)	Vertices (9)
• Manufacturers (Global, local, and niche)	• Innovation (Utilitarian and hedonic)	• Organizational culture and behavior
• Suppliers (Regular, contractual, and casual)	• Technology (Cost, time, risk, and value)	• Relationship management (B-to-B, B-to-C, C-to-C, and O-to-O)
• Retailers (Mega, large, medium, and small)	• Society (Proximity and consciousness)	• Interactive marketing (Social media, digital channels, longitudinal, and latitudinal communication)
• Service providers (Direct and indirect)	• Crowd contribution (CI, cocreation, and coevolution)	• Business canvas elements (Core and relational elements to support business operations)
• Consumers (Premier, big-middle, and bottom of the pyramid)	• Industry (Growth, rivalry, automation, and alliances)	• Marketing mix (Conventional, extended, and corporate factors)
	• Government (Public policies, regulation, and legal framework)	• Sustainability and business ecosystems
		• Marketing leadership (Strategy, decision making, and cooperation)
		• Empowerment (Customers and gender) and engagement (Employees, stakeholders, and customers)
		• Geographic, ethnic, and consumer outreach

Source: Author.

The faces of marketing prism constitute manufacturers spread across the global, local, and niche destinations, who are supported by the supplies operating on regular, contractual, and casual terms of reference. Other faces of the marketing prisms include retailers of different sizes (mega, large, medium, and small), direct and indirect service providers, and consumers at the bottom of the pyramid across the geodemographic segments. There are six edges encompassing innovation, technology, society, crowd (public in general), industry, and government that help marketing managers to define governance, openness, action, and learning continuum (GOAL) necessary for business growth in the competitive environment. Innovations supported by crowd impetus through CI, cocreation, and coevolution help firms in seeding new product ideas in the utilitarian and hedonic market segments. Rapidly growing technologies are often attractive to embed innovations, but they need to be scrutinized for relative cost, time, risk, and derived value propositions. Consequently, these edges of marketing prism are sensitive to the problems, needs, and solutions (PNS factors) and resources within the industry and market ecosystems. Innovation, technology, and CI drive the industry to a competitive dome, and induce internal rivalry and competition among the firms to exploit existing opportunities and stay ahead of the leadership race. Nonetheless, society and government also play significant role in marketing management, and good office management practices recommend firms to develop proximity with society and the government. The social proximity of the firm helps in developing social consciousness among consumers on corporate policies, ethics, values, and sustainability. Though the government interventions in marketing are often criticized, public policies on pricing, distribution, advertising, and social media engagements are necessarily to be brought under the categorical public policies to protect the interest of stakeholders and consumers.

There are nine vertices in marketing management as illustrated in Table 1.1, which include organizational culture and behavior of marketing firms, relationship management, interactive marketing, business canvas, marketing-mix sustainability, leadership, empowerment, and customer outreach. The vertices support any straight or angular structure in a construction with defined design. Likewise, the abovementioned vertices streamline the decision making, strategy development, and value creation processes in marketing despite the changing and disruptive influences. Organizational culture and behavior of a marketing firm need to integrate panoramic attributes of consumers, suppliers, manufacturers, and competitors. In a broad contemporary perspective, competition in the marketplace today can be managed through cooperation such as strategic alliances. Managing relationship with key partners and consumers is another important vertex in the prismatic marketing model that encourages relationship marketing to enhance satisfaction, value cocreation, and promoting social business perspective of firms in all segments of business enveloping business-to-business (B-to-B), business-to-consumer (B-to-C), consumer-to-consumer (C-to-C), and online-to-offline (O-to-O). The relationship marketing is further strengthened by the interaction of firms among key partners, stakeholders, and consumers on social media channels. Such interactions may be both longitudinal (with specific clients over long time) and latitudinal (across geodemographic segments). Beside the socialization of business by developing relationships and interactive transversalities across the consumer section, firms tend to strengthen their business foundations by building business canvas[1] and marketing mix[2] block-by-block to gain market leadership. Empowering consumers and engaging them emotionally with the company in marketing activities helps firms in narrowing their social proximity, generating social consciousness, and leveraging the geographic and ethnic outreach of consumers.

Social and Consumer Empowerment

Social empowerment offers both equity and equality across the demographic sections in a society and helps them to exercise equal control over their lifestyle, income resources, and employment. Empowering society holistically drives the members to take important decisions in routine activities and creates equal social and economic opportunities to support their lifestyle and socioeconomic status. Empowering all sections of society equally ensures strong economic growth and social development in a region. On a collective level, social empowerment is implemented through public policies, corporate social responsibilities delivered by the corporations, public sector organizations, and social institutions, which help members of economically marginalized social communities. The

---

[1] Business canvas has universal nine elements consisting of key partners, key resources, key activities, customer relationship, segmentation, distribution channels, value proposition, cost structure, and revenue stream.

[2] The advanced marketing mix has 11 core elements known as 11Ps comprising product, price, place, promotion, packaging, pace, people, promotion, psychodynamics, posture, and proliferation (Rajagopal 2019).

social empowerment is aimed at improving the social and economic stature of marginalized communities including gender-based classes to improve their returns on assets, good health, education, social belonging, self-esteem, self-confidence, and develop economic opportunity. Holistically, social empowerment is developed across the four principal dimensions comprising psychological, organizational, economic, and cultural among the members of the community.

Improving social quality in the context of values and lifestyle, communication, decision making, and 3Es comprising equity, equality, experience within the community entails many challenges. Often communities are built orthogonally and grow independently over time. Such communities with rigid values do not accept external influence and adapt to new environment. Such behavioral independence in the community is often challenging to introduce any alterations in the societal attributes, as understanding and influencing the social conventions, acquiring, and testing new attributes, or modifying the existing practices within the community is rigid and time consuming. Therefore, it is necessary to meticulously embed social empowerment in the community and specify its distinctiveness in relation to other theories and practices of empowerment. Social empowerment should be considered in the context of existing social and economic conditions and establishing distinction in relation to the social quality experience. The social empowerment requires the social institutions, corporations, and public governance to develop social proximity and linear communication flow, and to improve the capabilities and competencies among the communities to reach at predefined social-quality standards. Accordingly, empowerment can showcase its benefits and play the role of a catalyst to improve the social quality, consumption, and values and lifestyle.

However, often it has been a subject of debate that the social empowerment of consumers has helped both manufacturers and retailers to transform consumption trends and buying behavior. The network companies such as Mary Kay Cosmetics (United States), Avon Cosmetics (United States), and Hindustan Unilever Limited (HUL), India, have gained significant advantage of socially empowering women in both marketing and consumption. The social empowerment of women also sets the fashion trends, conscious consumption, and economic benefits.

Social empowerment of women under the very important performer (VIP) program of Mary Kay Cosmetics and Shakti (strength in Hindi language) program of HUL in India has driven the socioeconomic impact holistically across business, consumer behavior, and stakeholders' economy among women. The HUL has experimented the concept of social empowerment of women in rural areas who were deprived of several social and economic advantages, while the Mary Kay cosmetics has driven women in their urban and semiurban neighborhoods. Nonetheless, there remains the question of how to objectively evaluate social and economic benefits of social empowerment from the perspectives of both consumers and the company.

Social empowerment benefits can theoretically be linked to the implementation of marketing of products and services. In the sustainability sector, various studies on health, energy, and communication have highlighted that large-scale social marketing infrastructure for renewable energy products like solar photovoltaic panel for home lighting, appliances, and to some extent machine functions, have made significant dent in delivering the social and economic benefits to the stakeholders (Zang et al. 2021). Previous studies have shown that the social empowerment of women toward using the nonconventional energy for domestic use has significantly increased the use of solar cookers in the developing countries, which has consequently improved the social and economic status of women. Social empowerment builds cognitive reasoning, capabilities to develop strategy, and appropriate decision making among the consumers and stakeholders. It is crucial to the idea of coping with changing corporate strategies and managing behavioral change proneness and resistance of consumers and stakeholders (Gruss et al. 2020). Social empowerment benefits consumers' lives, values, and lifestyle by creating new consumption opportunities and setting community participation and self-esteem goals. Local knowledge and shopping facilities in various geodemographic segments contribute to community participation and developing sociopersonal behavior. CI empowers the consumers of both genders in improving their quality of life through transforming their consumption behavior by analyzing the social proximity. Such proximity effect infuses new social consumption attributes and alters the existing consumption behavior with collective mandate and social fairness. Social skills on relationship building, and empowerment, may contribute to improved collaboration in establishing new consumption trends and social learning through proximity effects. Such social dynamics and empowerment help both consumers and companies understand the community power in socially conscious consumption through productive relationships to provide and coordinate with consumers and stakeholders (Craig et al. 2020).

The crowd behavior toward consumer firms, their business offerings, and social proximity is often vague and unfocused, which makes it difficult for the firms to align with the crowd cognition. Consequently, convergence of crowd behavior and CI (open communications across the social domains) with the customer-centric firms is often challenging. However, some firms engaged in the marketing of innovative consumer products, such as IKEA and LEGO, have successfully converged their corporate strategies with the CI to stay competitive and democratic (ideally for the consumers and of the consumers). Such engrossment of these companies with the consumers to cocreate products for future markets empowers them with 7E factors comprising equity, equality, experience, ecosystem (existing and transitionary), enhancement of internal and external (IE) values, emotional intelligence, and engagement with the firm. These factors further escalate the leader-member exchange (LMX), social consciousness, and social proximity, which may benefit the firms by enabling them to stay close to the consumers within the social ecosystem. Broadly, empowerment has social and digital dimensions in the contemporary philosophy of business socialization as illustrated in Figure 1.1.

Knowledge sharing, social learning, and delivering social outcomes are challenging propositions for the firms as they move toward digital empowerment as exhibited in Figure 1.1. The assimilation of these factors incredibly drives design-thinking phenomenon in consumer-centric firms, which tend to make digital workspace for consumers and stakeholders. Convergence of digital empowerment, design thinking, and proximity to society and business need to be laid on the quadratic P-factors comprising proximity, privacy, permissions, and performance. The proximity of firms within society enables people to get together, converse, and prioritize the common PNS factors to guide firms to

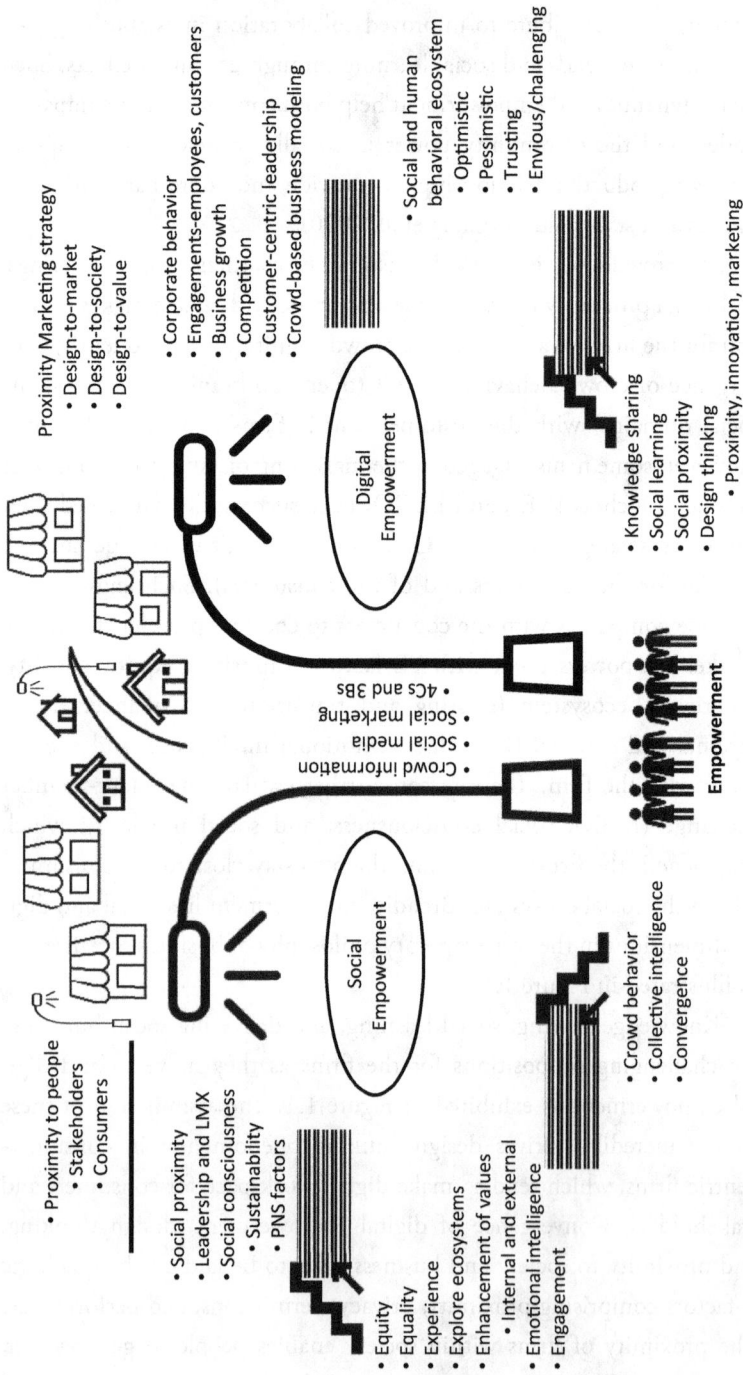

Figure 1.1 Social empowerment and social proximity

Source: Author.

acculturate business and marketing strategies accordingly. While making the space for people or crowd in a firm, privacy of the information must be protected by the firms, social institutions, or through public policies. The social communication channels must have controlled access to the customers and stakeholders to maintain ethical conversations and engagement with the firm. The basic social purpose of the social space needs to develop business relations through open conversations expressing experience, emotions, and emancipation of thoughts. The social contribution to the firm's performance can be supported by narrowing the proximity to people, maintaining privacy of information, and drawing legitimate permissions to build the marketing strategies and business performance (Fayard and Weeks 2011). The convergence of 7Es and 4Ps can help in reconstructing the corporate philosophy with focus on consumers and encourage consumers and stakeholders' engagement through the crowd-based business model. Such transformation in businesses will induce customer-centric leadership to gain competitive leverage. Digital empowerment of consumers also helps them in transitions through various human behavioral ecosystem, from challenging to optimistic, and trusting by overcoming the latent pessimism about the firms on the consumer welfare and well-being concerns.

Like HUL, there are other international streamlined companies operating in the consumer products segments that play the significant role of a global commercial organization. These companies have also shown commitments toward social empowerment. The Coca-Cola Company in developing markets has focused its corporate social responsibility (CSR) toward augmenting the knowledge and skills of business in digital marketing through a strategic approach to social and economic contribution. The company's initiatives are complimentary to the public policies within the triadic model that aligns government, civil society, and the private sector. The CSR activities can be focused on empowerment of women and youth in local marketing, leveraging social consciousness in managing water depletion, replenishment, encouraging community distribution, and developing sustainable logistics model. In addition, cocreating social proximity of firms helps in carrying out multilocal operations through diverse human traits to encourage inclusivity and diversity (Banks 2016). CSR is extended to 2Ws activities comprising well-being and women's empowerment. In a model, the company offers women the access to business skills training courses, financial services, and connections with peers or mentors by providing a business starter kit that include three cases of product—a table, a cooler, and an umbrella.

In managing socially sustainable business projects, stakeholder- and gender-empowerment programs help firms in delivering social products and services effectively and creating consistent value. In addition, systems thinking in a firm engaged in developing sustainable business plans and its implementation helps firms in making appropriate decision making. One of the major challenges in the conventional social and cultural environment is the empowerment of entrepreneurs that builds confidence among the innovators to inculcate proinnovation cognitive drive. Entrepreneurs need to scrutinize enormous personal and professional information of the interested people to induct into the innovation project and constitute appropriate teams. Besides driving the innovation project through the challenges of managing the resources efficiently, handling operational risk, marketability, and cost and time overrun, entrepreneurs often face market failures and piling-up of sunk cost due to radical and experimental innovation approach. Such endeavors cause risk rollouts throughout the project leading to abort the innovation untimely, which develops serious cognitive dissonances among entrepreneurs (Rajagopal 2016).

Women's self-help groups in India provide an interesting and concrete example of an intervention that is well aligned with theoretical ideas about development as a process of capability expansion. These groups contribute to the policy priorities of gender empowerment laid in the global sustainability development goals. The JEEVikA (livelihood) program in Bihar, India finds that economically and socially marginalized groups have been benefited from self-help group (SHG) membership through a reduction in reliance on high-cost sources of borrowing. These SHGs have helped to increase the participation of women in household decision making and delivered positive impacts on human development in rural areas. Similarly, another SHG in Andhra Pradesh, a southern state in India, has shown the impact on enhancing social capital as the organization has motivated program members on higher savings to move freely within their village and interact within their caste. Protein and energy intake, and consumption of nutritional supplements, also increased among members of the group as income or asset changes. These groups establish sustainability in human development and rural wealth generation (Anand et al. 2019). Governing sustainability projects with adequate public policies, and social empowerment, have emerged as conscious efforts within the societal and corporate business environment. Social empowerment has been effective in developing countries through transformative leadership and increasing awareness about the sustainability benefits among stakeholders. In addition, the engagement of business companies in implementing sustainability-led business models in the B-to-C and B-to-B market segments has motivated social governance at the local level. Sustainability programs in rural farm- and nonfarm sectors have contributed significantly in the process of social governance. The public policies administered by the social institutions help in the implementation of social sustainability projects and educating stakeholders about the circular economy concepts.

Digital Empowerment

Enormous growth in information technology has shifted the social practice of face-to-face to digital discussion platforms. Such a shift has widened the outreach of customers and increased the inflow of participants' information. Consequently, social media has become a major tool for crowdsourcing and managing data related to CI. The digital platforms for sharing personal opinions, new ideas, and experiences have transformed the conventional wisdom of people to stick to the brick-and-mortar forums, organize community meetings, and share experiences. Yet, community cultural centers serve in different sectors such as social health, natural medicinal forums, handicrafts, and handloom cooperative center as the places of human relations in developing countries. Social networks are also supported by the self-help groups working on specific social and economic themes such as women empowerment, women entrepreneurship, sustainability, and many more. Similarly, social rights activists, business leaders, and political groups also promote communication hubs that attract participants to share their experience and new ideas related to the development of society and economy. Social relations widely rely on information technology infrastructure irrespective of its sophistication.

The major concern in digitalizing emotions and social relationships is to ensure effective knowledge management through diffusion of dialogues across the social genre. Social empowerment depends on the active digital connectivity in which people exchange their perceptions and values on brands, benefits, and benevolence (3Bs) to express their compassion to the companies within the existing social ecology. Convergence of business and social ecology drive expectations of consumers and stakeholders to strengthen their association and social fit with both insiders and outsiders of their social regime. Such sociological bonding with business allows sharing and mobilizing knowledge in identifying opportunities of social well-being, and reconstructing effective and efficient relationship channels to integrate changing business philosophies (Gupta and Govindarajan 2000).

The web-based relationship infrastructure has been enormously supported by the stakeholders and supporters online for exchange of views for a business or a social cause. Consequently, CI has become a principal knowledge repository, fostering economic consumer empowerment and a democratic transformation of the business sector in small and large enterprises. Though there are complexities in managing digital ethics in exchanging opinions on the social media platforms, there is a need to set ethical norms via social and voluntary approaches to manage the social information dynamics on digital platforms than enforcing formal institutional mechanisms. The proximity of social institutions to business and innovation not only helps in building collective behavior of consumers but also encourages utilitarian and low-cost innovations through start-up enterprises. The proximity of social interactive groups inculcates consciousness on consumption and sustainability through social engagement, empowerment, and public participation embodying crowdsourced and crowdfunded entrepreneurial and corporate activities. Consequently, proximity marketing plays a vital role in promoting consumer consciousness, innovation, and social marketing prospects with low cost, and encourages effective operations in the niche market (Sedalo et al. 2022). The combination of proximity marketing, socialization of business, and hybridity has significantly encouraged the prospects of social marketing to promote a democratic philosophy in marketing strategies of large multinational companies. Such shift in the B-to-C, C-to-C, and O-to-O marketing strategies have driven new relationships between consumers, markets, and companies. The social elements such as LMX and information management through CI help customer-centric companies in developing proximity marketing model not only on focusing in achieving customer outreach through empowerment of vulnerable segments such as women and low-resource entrepreneurs but also on generating value by socializing the business. The social capital generation can be linked to social networks, and enhancing customer outreach, while triggering crowd behavior in support of brands and corporate images. Effective social governance of marketing communication, and shared narratives, targeting social factors help in attracting crowd.

The free flow of information is essential to well-functioning democracies and consumer marketplaces since both politicians and marketers need a communication system that has long outreach. It is not always simple—there are privacy issues, government regulations, and lack of access for many people. However, many see the democratization of information as offering possibilities for new forms of citizen engagement and empowerment that will give the people a greater voice in government and markets (Quelch and Joch 2007). The basic claim is that consumer education needs to become *empowering or* emancipatory, and that this can be reached through emphasizing the futures aspect and skills concerning *everyday futures work.* This is not enough in a rapidly changing world in which consumers face completely new challenges (Jarva 2011). Consumer empowerment is a psychological construct related to the individual's perception of the extent to which he or she can control the distribution and use of his or her personally identifying information. It has been argued to have an impact on consumers' privacy concerns and trust in e-commerce. However, very little is known about the difference in male and female perceptions of this control. This investigation is focused on examining how perceptions concerning consumer empowerment and privacy concerns differ between the genders, and how consumer empowerment results in perceptions of trust and decrease in privacy concerns (Midha 2012).

The role of marketing strategies in fostering controlled consumer empowerment is reflected in the development of information-based, consumer-centric marketing strategies that seek to enable, control, monitor, and promote proximity of firms within the society. In designing such strategies, consumers' familiarity with the use of information and communication technologies (ICTs) is both strengthened and widened, emphasizing the uncontrolled nature of the consumer empowerment process. There is a need to regain control over the marketing process, that is, to either manage the technological empowerment of consumers, or to devise new strategies cognizant of the possibility that such technological empowerment cannot be managed. The valuation of consumer loyalty in this environment rises significantly (Pires et al. 2006). The social domain intends to promote sustainability-led businesses and drive bottom-up (local) economy. The public domain drives social innovation through CI (crowdsourcing) for ideation and contextual information pooling, and crowdfunding to cocreate and coevolve crowd-based business models.

Social empowerment of consumers has been adopted by many companies as a tool to build trust on the companies and their market ecosystem. Consumer-centric companies such as LEGO (Denmark), IKEA (Sweden), Mary Kay Cosmetics (United States), and AMUL (India) have gained prominence in business by socially empowering the consumers and engaging them in the cocreation process. The social empowerment of consumers and their emotional stakes in designing new products and marketing is largely founded on the mutual trust between the consumers and the company. In this context, trust as a driver of social empowerment can be defined as the willingness to be open and adaptable to business policy and exhibit cooperative behavior through mutual belief in a consistent and predictable manner (Gefen 2000). Value perceptions among customers are induced by social, economic, and relational factors. The social learning theory explains this phenomenon as positive reinforcement, and it occurs when a behavior (response) is followed by a favorable stimulus (commonly seen as pleasant) that increases the frequency of that behavior. In the conceptual foundations of social learning theory, respondent conditioning and observational learning are the empirically supported approaches to understand the normative human development and the etiology of psychosocial problems. The social learning process is widely influenced by the manifold growth of social media, digital networks, and interpersonal communications. Information technology has dramatically changed the social communication inflow by the customers sharing their experiences, values, new product ideas, and complaints about companies and products. Online customer reviews extend word-of-mouth from new acquaintances and transform information from personal to public channels on social media platforms where interactions among experienced customers occur (Pfeffer et al. 2014).

Collective Intelligence

Proximity, creativity, and CI in marketing are linearly aligned with the contemporary marketing strategy as integrated by multinational customer-centric companies like many mentioned in the pretext. Consumer durable and electronics companies from Southeast Asia such as Casio, Samsung, and LG have expanded their social outreach to narrow the proximity of consumer with companies and encourage consumer engagement in cocreation though collective design thinking. Narrowing the corporate proximity to consumers drives wider outreach, social interactivity, and scope to build homophily among the consumers with common interest. Such marketing approach also helps companies to develop crowd-based business models to gain competitive advantage. Most companies pay attention toward stakeholder engagement to manage innovation in entrepreneurial ventures. The open innovation based on crowdsourcing and crowdfunding concept appears complementary to the prospective collaborative efforts of micro-, small-, and medium enterprises with their primary and secondary stakeholders. The stakeholder engagement helps companies in cost and risk control, and in streamlining the sharing of knowledge and other resources for innovation management. Stakeholder engagement is implicitly understood as an umbrella concept for communication, collaboration, mutual understanding, and partnership between the firm and the collaborators. Effective communication and stakeholder participation contribute to the critical success factors in crowd-based business models, and such practice widens the scope of collective or collaborative decision making. The practice of stakeholder engagement in business modeling and decision processes inculcates stakeholder value and confidence. Stakeholder engagement bridges communication gap with the business, facilitates systems planning, and thereby improves business and investor alignments (Niemi and Pekkola 2017).

Stakeholders' engagement provides them the opportunities to explore strategic benefits for third parties and streamline the advantage of economies of scope. In addition, stakeholder confidence is boosted by continuous growth of the firm, utilizing cross-selling opportunities across geodemographic segments, and increasingly involving users and the crowd. These strategies place a strong emphasis on stakeholder commitment. Google has coevolved over the years as a crowd-based company. The founders of the company realized that appearing on search results lists holds tremendous value for stakeholders with a willingness to pay, as stakeholders (firms and investors) and other players incur high satisfaction in being found on the Internet. Toward both revenue and cost dimensions, the crowd-based business model strongly emphasizes stakeholder involvement (Schröder et al. 2015). Often, some stakeholders, who have been previously related to the firm in various roles, play a motivating role in business expansion and performance by serving as referrals. The advertisers, as stakeholders, enjoy traffic from Google's search engine even before the introduction of AdWords, and discretely benefit from positive externalities of the Google offer. A sophistication in the crowd-based business model involves these shareholders and starts a formal relationship with them in coevolving the business (Kesting and Günzel-Jensen 2015).

CI has emerged as a dynamic tool in the business ecosystem today, which is supported by the stakeholders. They support companies in cocreation and coevolution process with stakeholders through social interaction, social innovations, and social governance. The ecosystem of crow-based businesses linked with the sustainability goals drives public–private entrepreneurship (both upstream and downstream collaborations) to meet the sustainable development goals through social- and frugal innovations. Upstream collaboration refers to strategic alliances with national or international firms to have regional or global focus of business, while downstream collaborations are associated with social business and community governance. Taxonomy of leadership and employee engagement largely drive the corporate governance practices as central to the business ecosystem (Rajagopal 2021). Crowd-based business models emerge out of the CI generated through crowdsourcing. As crowdsourcing evolves, new research finds a pitfall the companies should be alert to: Consumer voting on the ideas submitted on open innovation platforms is often skewed by social bias, or people's tendency to like and vote for ideas whose progenitors have liked and voted for their own. CI led business models to rely more on consumer preference and social criteria while evaluating the ideas that are generated through open innovation. Successful crowdsourcing ventures require more than an online platform and some kind of brand connection. Without an understanding of participant motivations and behaviors, casual attempts to leverage the wisdom of the crowd may backfire and lead to unintended results. Prominent examples of crowdsourcing failures are myriad. Consider General Motors, which provided users with web tools to make their own ads for the Chevrolet Tahoe, resulting in several viral videos that lampooned the company's products and the American automotive industry's gas guzzlers more generally. In the fast-moving consumer goods industry, Mountain Dew successfully crowdsourced part of its product development through the Dewmocracy contest series, but a similar project asking fans to name the brand's new apple-flavored drink brought on a slew of ironic suggestions, including Diabeetus (Fedorenko et al. 2017).

The CI as a marketing tool drives collective judgment from a group of people who tend to outperform a competitive and SMART marketing approach. The CI supports companies to make SMART decisions comprising the attributes of strategic, measurable, accessible, responsive, and timeliness. CI addresses the PNS factor, which includes problems, needs, and solutions to cocreate innovative products and through collective problem-solving approaches. The CI typically addresses the optimal design to develop new products and diffuse information through communication networks to wider consumer outreach. The key networks reach out to maximum number of members in engaging problem-solving exercises and communicating outcomes with society and companies. Social media and other information channels such as e-mails, social institutions, and blogs enhance informational efficiency in outreaching social and business ends. The "wisdom of the crowd" shows the overwhelming response to social calls in various information genre for optimal proximity impact in marketing. The key network property that governs the wisdom of the crowd is network centralization (Centola 2022). The CI has become synonymous with collective judgment, which helps in the statistical aggregation of independent opinions of the crowd, active and passive information-sharing among peers, experience dissemination, and solution-sharing to support decision making or innovation research teams. The CI thus outperforms a company-centered or computer-aided decision with social and cognitive reasoning (Page 2007).

Crowd behavior is often observed critical to the consumer touch points driven by core marketing-mix elements (Rajagopal 2019) comprising 11 P-factors as discussed in the following:

Product: Comparative attributes, quality, shelf life, life cycle, competitive advantages, innovation, technology, and perceived use value.

Price: Affordable price, price competitiveness, and value for money.

Place: Availability of product, 360° distribution, hybridity, delivery, and convenience.

Promotion: Comparative benefits, sales, and relationship advantages.

Packaging: Socially conscious consumers will motivate sustainable packaging and low-cost ethnic packaging for high-value products.

Pace: Driving first-mover advantage through the social media, proximity networks like micro blogs, and crowd events.

People: Interactions of social leaders with corporate managers to develop value-based relationship among the consumers and stakeholders. Derive the LMX effects at the macro level to enhance outreach, impact, and performance of the products, brands, and services. The LMX is widely intrigued by the corporate image, which is driven by crowd behavior.

Performance: The success or failure of products and services in the B-to-C and B-to-B segments are judged by the crowd and social norms are drafted for doing business in the future.

Psychodynamics: This unique proposition of crowd behavior empowers consumers, stakeholders, and any member of

society to share his emotions, experiences, engagements, and epistemologies with others. Psychodynamics is fundamentally a C-to-C, which generates
pull (consumer-to-company demand) and push
(company-to-consumer thrust through promotions)
effects. Psychodynamics is a consequence of conventional word-of-mouth, digital interactions, or a
hybrid proximity in the marketplace or business.

Posture: Crowd behavior and CI is helpful in building corporate image. Social media has played significant
role in building the social face of HUL, ITC-
Agribusiness Division, and AMUL a cooperative giant of India. Social media has significantly
emphasized HUL on its move to empower rural
women in the *Shakti* (Power) and *Amma* (Mother)
programs in India, which provided economic independence to rural women through marketing of
HUL brands. Similarly, ITC-agribusiness division
of India has been supported by the social media
for its farmer's communication program *e-choupal*
(e-community meet) aimed at generating awareness on improved agricultural practices, marketing,
and sustainability approaches.

Proliferations: Diversifications of business, markets, and processes
of local companies are also significantly induced by
the CI and crowd behavior.

However, industry attractiveness describes competition among traditional pipeline brands, which succeeds by optimizing the activities in their
value chains. In addition, crowdsourcing and CI have helped companies
and their brand to streamline customer perceptions, brand value, and competitiveness. Uber (transport service), Alibaba (e-commerce), and Airbnb
(urban housing), are growing in the market by improving the consumer
chain and delivering satisfaction through active customer engagement and
CI (Van Alstyne et al. 2016). Substitute products in the market affect the
industry potential adversely and pose a threat to customer preferences.

Proximity and Social Consciousness

Social conscience, which converges a person's intuitive values with a *mass moral-compass* toward the society in general, can be described as the collective value. While rational, sociological, and philosophical arguments often justify that conscience is primarily emotional, the secondary feelings are associated with community action and values. These emotions help to motivate social choices and behavior, playing an important role in the maintenance and transformation of social norms. These norms are the sum of collective values and priorities of the society. In view of the global pressure on environmental protection and role of companies on managing social responsibility, corporate sustainability is often considered as a top strategic priority. Companies, however, struggle to link the social responsibility projects with the profitability goals and often fail to gain the stakeholder value. Accordingly, corporate sustainability complements the traditional triple bottom approach through social consciousness and motivation to achieve relevant and timely competitive and societal impact (Schneider 2015).

Social proximity is increasingly narrowing with the advancement of information technology, user-friendly digital communication platforms, and the rising number of communication hours spent by the users on mobile applications. The social media-driven relationship has helped people to restructure their virtual communities by region, themes, and personal preferences to enhance the effectiveness of communication and reduce the geodemographic proximity. Such efforts of delimiting boundaries of the digital relationship and debating on the thematic threads have not only streamlined the crowd behavior but also aligned customer-centric companies of food, fashion, and family products with consumer preferences. Social proximity has been central to creating social consciousness on sustainable consumption, gender, and psychographic ethics in business, and corporate policies on creating social value. These are intangible factors where trust plays a key role in building cognitive ergonomics among the consumers. In addition, consumer knowledge and social consciousness build the foundations of socially acceptable consumer behavior. As the management of green products is based on intangible factors, trust plays a central role in building cognitive ergonomics among the consumers. In addition, consumer knowledge and social consciousness build the foundation of green consumer behavior (Rajagopal 2020).

Learning communities are developed by consumer-centric companies to transfer knowledge on social consumption causes such as healthy foods, green consumption, organic farm products and the like. Such learning communities are designed primarily to increase consumer attitude toward learning new consumption patterns, and building convergence with social, ethnic, and personal values. Companies monitor consumer needs, perceptions, and expectations through the learning communities and identify marketing strategies, which contributes to augmenting the consumer involvement in learning new consumption experiences and the perceived satisfaction. Online consumer learning communities do attain positive outcomes; however, consumer education programs need to be developed specific to the requirements of geodemographic segments (Andrade and Cohen 2007). Consumer engagement in companies not only builds high-perceived values among consumers but also helps in developing social consumption behavior. The positive psychodynamics among consumers through social media and interpersonal relations helps in developing probrand perceptions, attitude, and behavior. Popular brands try to develop positive perceptions among consumers along the path to purchase, while utility brands influence consumer experience at every touchpoint. Whole Foods in the United States is an example of perceived value-based retailing on organic and sustainable products, which tends to generate consumer consciousness, experience, and organic consumption attitude. Consumers, with the support of growing information technology, view that purchase of organic brands are conventional, while the digital brands are utility brands.

Sustainability concerns, proenvironment knowledge, and the social dynamics of markets drive the consumption behavior of green products among consumers. As the management of green products is based on intangible factors, trust plays a central role in building cognitive ergonomics among consumers. In addition, consumer knowledge and social consciousness build the foundation of green consumer behavior. Some previous studies reveal that the global sustainability drive has influenced consumers to change their behavior and purchase decisions through the consumption of ecofriendly alternatives (Paco and Rapose 2009). The green consumption behavior has emerged over time in food consumption and transport sustainability, and toward renewable energy usage. Public policies and social consciousness also contributed significantly to transforming the consumption behavior at macro level. Therefore, many consumers are interested in modifying their consumption behavior with less impact on natural resources, particularly fossil fuels (Chen 2016), as the social dynamics is also contributing to the development of green energy. Consumers in the energy market today are committed with environmental protection through green electricity (Strupeit and Palm 2016)

Behavioral process is supported by the consumer's perceived value emerging out of the economic benefits and risk analysis in using technology-based sustainability products and services. The behavioral process stage leads to the defensive behavior stage by critical evaluation of needs, awareness, and their fit into the values and lifestyle. The stage following defensive behavior stage drives consumers to justify their perceptions and attitude toward green decisions and optimize output. Most people at this stage seek social validation and reward for their decision to stay with the sustainable products and tend to lead environmental advocacy and green leadership at niche and regional levels of society. However, as social consciousness grows, self-actualization on sustainability commitments increases. Further, the political ideologies, government support, and stakeholder engagement contribute to the definitive green behavior of people on sustainable products and services. Over the definitive state of behavior, most stakeholders enjoy the benefits of sustainable products and services and tend to push green goals as a social movement and stay as referrals to diffuse lessons and vision on the green consumerism in the society.

Proximity marketing strategy is an agile approach to marketing that involves engaging customers in key business activities such as innovation, distribution, services, and product promotions as illustrated in Figure 1.2.

Customer engagement tends to drive creativity and CI to benefit the firm's decisions on manufacturing, process improvement, and marketing. The proximity marketing strategy can be developed ambidextrously for upstream and downstream markets with both brick-and-mortar and digital interface. Most customer-centric firms such as Unilever, Apple, and General Electric have also developed hybrid marketing interfaces

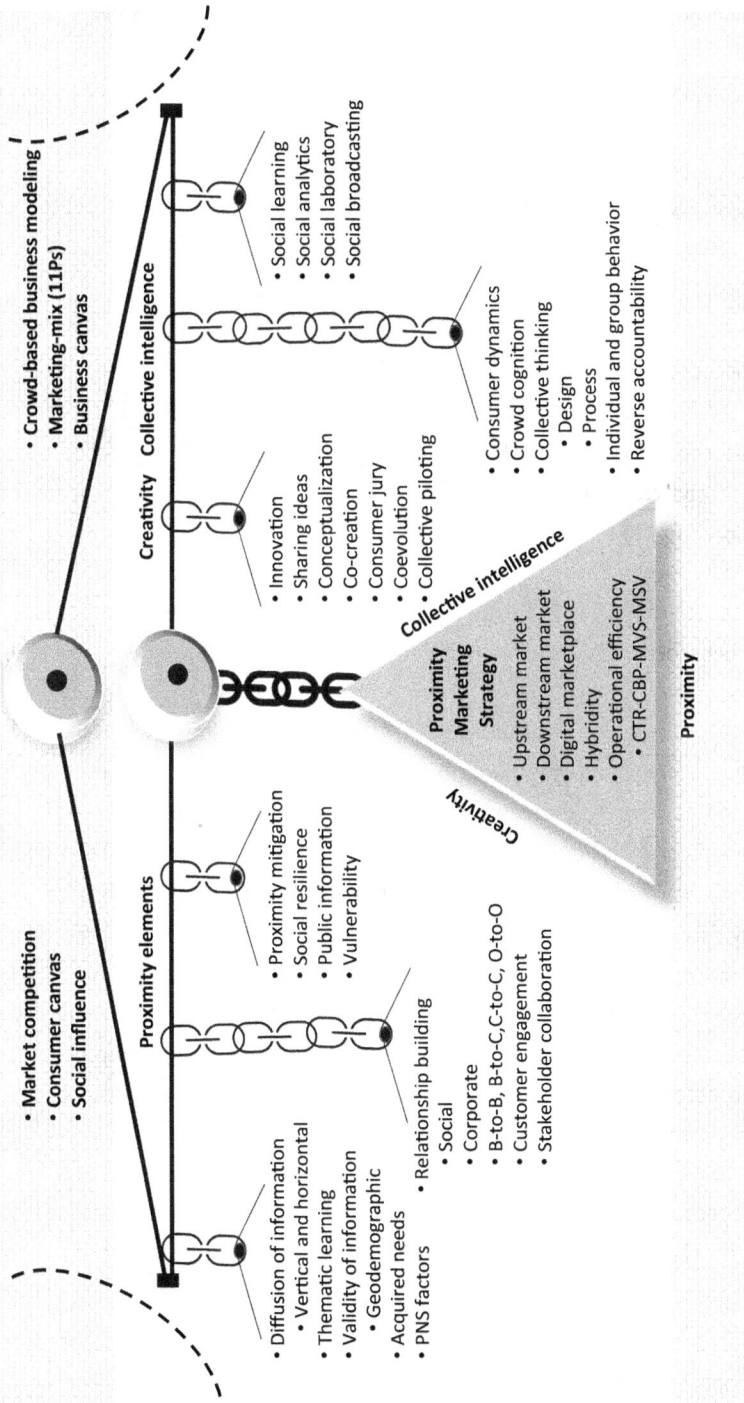

Figure 1.2 Ecosystem of proximity marketing strategy

Source: Author.

to drive tangible and intangible experiences of consumers. However, operational efficiency in proximity marketing depends on some critical matrices as follows:

- Cost factor in relationship building and business continuity, estimated time to develop social proximity, and expand the outreach of consumers and stakeholders (Cost, Time, and Risk [CTR])
- Measuring the cost-benefit ratio and its impact on market performance and business growth of the company (Cost, Benefit, and Performance [CBP])
- Defining minimum viable segments (MVS) to nurture customer relationship effectively and deliver the desired satisfaction to the consumers within the defined MVS
- Managing the linear path of the manufacturing, supplies, and value chain (MSV) in business by engaging consumers and stakeholders in decision-making processes

Vertical and horizontal diffusion of information to facilitate thematic learning across geodemographic segments help consumers to critically examine and validate the source and contents of the information. Empowering consumers to validate information offers one of the best ways to exercise peer control over CI. Information management at the public repository, Wikipedia can be cited as one of the most suitable examples of information input, processing, control, and delivering the output. Accordingly, firms can streamline the flow of CI, and learn about the PNS factors and acquired needs of the consumers to develop appropriate marketing strategies. However, as firms tend to invest resources in acquiring new customers by narrowing down the proximity gap and launching relationship programs to boost the consumer outreach campaign, there is a possibility of chaos with the predefined segments. Therefore, firms need to tactically reduce proximity mitigation and social resilience to work collectively with zero bias. Such care would also help firms in reducing the vulnerability of unfiltered information flow on the firms, products, and market competition. The CI in society increases with the proximity enhancement of the firms, which helps in the cocreation of innovative products, processes, and services. Sharing of ideas on social media helps firms not only in conceptualizing new products and services but also in the cocreation and coevolution of innovative products for competitive gains. The ideas generated by the crowd and through collective cognition are evaluated by the consumer jury, a multidisciplinary team comprising consumers, product engineers, suppliers, marketing, sales, and administrative executives, and legal experts. Consumer empowerment provides opportunity to the company to collectively pilot test and launch the cocreated products or services. Changing consumer dynamics, cognition, and collective thinking drive continuous social learning and idea broadcasting through interpersonal and digital channels.

Consumer perceptions are often agile, which need to be endorsed by peers, friends, and family to support decision making and to put them into practice over the long term. Such cognitive process creates consumption attitude among consumers. Perceptions linked to emotions are commonly impulsive and temporary, which do not make a dent on cognitive process continuity and help in decision making. The perceptions should be measurable. Consumers generally measure their perceived values in reference to the desired satisfaction in terms of value for money derived through the convergence of quality and price. The higher perceived value of consumers not only justifies the quality of the perceptual process among consumers but also determines the social leadership by way of how many follow a right perception of a consumer as referral (Rajagopal 2019).

There are several approaches to determine social environmental consciousness. However, they are united by their common methodological position that embeds the individual- and social consciousness toward sustainability in multiple social sectors (agriculture and allied sectors, natural resource management, public health, housing, education, and nonfarm industries). There is a wide range of perspectives concerning social sustainability that needs to be supported by the preferences of environmental consciousness. With the increasing social consciousness, global markets have entered into the new generation management involving stakeholders in developing customer-centric business strategies and growing sustainable in the competitive marketplace. Consumers form perceptions on the viable solutions to the predetermined needs (recognized as problems), which match with their self-congruence and could offer sustainable value (satisfaction). Social media is an attractive medium where consumers with changing mindsets interact with peers demonstrating their perceptual rationale and validate their feelings and emotions. Their objective in engaging in social media is to learn about recent trends, new development of knowledge, or certain skill sets for further improvement in making buying decisions (Mathur et al. 2016). Most social-centric companies develop new products as "design-to-value" by involving consumers in the cocreation process. Consumer and stakeholder engagements in new product development help companies manage seasonality of products effectively in the marketplace and develop sustainable consumer attitude and consumption behavior. Therefore, it is observed that like social needs, consumer behavior also turns value oriented over time. The consumer value chain often supports sustainability and social consciousness.

Companies focusing on marketing of social- or learned values-based products and services, need to understand the social culture, ethnicity, and consumption pattern before getting started with the customer-centric business. Boehringer Ingelheim (BI), a German-based multinational pharmaceutical company in Mexico, has been engaged in developing its business in convergence with the increasing social consciousness on services-driven product marketing. BI is discretely operating the patients service centers (in Spanish *Centro de Atencion a los Pacientes*), which offer free diagnostic services (only for referred patients) leading to support clinical diagnosis of the patients. The diagnostic services of BI at the abovementioned centers include the data analysis of arterial pressure ambulatory monitors, cardiovascular monitors, and respirators. Such services of BI are indirectly linked with the marketing of pharmaceutical products of the company through prescriptions. Linking social services with the products marketing, thus, creates the social value of BI pharmaceutical brands (Rajagopal 2021).

A social media activist may have a mix of experience with product designing, marketing, software applications, and the extended reach of communication. Companies should analyze customer experience centered on social interactions to develop community-linked marketing approaches. Such customer connectivity helps the managers stay on social media platforms such as Facebook page, and work with the social media account management and social advertising and social media campaign management, which are the typical customer-centric marketing tasks for a company. As social networks are growing fast and gaining psychodynamics, there emerges the need for a new executive-level social marketing strategist, who can fully embrace the focus on social marketing. Social consciousness and business are growing simultaneously among the customers and stakeholders because of the ease of use of technology and transformation of communication systems from conventional wisdom to digital networks. CSR has become the tool to generate social consciousness and value streams to support social marketing perspectives of business. Public policies and the media have become proficient to stimulate the companies to take initiatives in developing social markets and inculcating the social consequences in the future business modeling to grow their business with the social outlooks. Consequently, the social face of business has emerged as an inescapable priority for the customer-centric companies to gain competitive leverage. Some successful B-to-C companies such as Amazon discovered Whole Foods as a social business place to generate social values and drive business growth faster. Similarly, Toyota and Volvo have found design-to-society approaches in business more as a source of innovation and competitive advantage than as a path of smooth transition of technology-oriented business in society. Companies, while developing social imperatives in business, need to identify the social consequences of their actions and discover opportunities to benefit themselves and society by strengthening the competitive benefits. The design-to-society business modeling has, therefore, emerged as a collective thinking mindset for strategic growth of business through the social value stream (Porter and Kramer 2011).

Bioeconomy and Crowd Cognition

Bioeconomy is a progressive branch of social science, which integrates the disciplines of economics and biology to support sustainability theories, which explain macroeconomic and social effects within the existing biological ecosystem. Bioeconomy embeds the transformational concepts converging business and society, which are required to coevolve amidst the dynamic social and business ecosystems. Some of these systems of social business designs including sustainable agriculture, sustainable fishing, forestry and aquaculture, and food- and feed manufacturing are added bio-based products and bioenergy. Bioeconomy has emerged as a topic for crowd cognition, CI, and social marketing. Companies engaged in bioeconomic business operations need to drive social consciousness among consumers by developing the triadic business strategy converging design-to-market, design-to-society, and design-to-value. The bioeconomic product includes bioplastics, biodegradable clothing (organic textile), and plant fiber-based packaging material besides other products with eco-design. Green consumption is more a social phenomenon than a personality trait based on self-reference decisions. Consumer attitudes, subjective norms, and perceived behavioral control influence purchase intention toward social and sustainable products. The changing trend of social innovation, and products and services provided by social enterprises are diverse and the consumers behavior is shifting gradually toward green consumerism (Defourny and Nyssens 2017).

Bioeconomy is a dynamic and complex process in social transformation, which is supported by the long-term policy perspectives of the government in both developed and developing economies. Countries can define their bioeconomic plans based on national requirements and the existing capabilities and competencies. Broadly, production through utilization and conservation of biological resources using technology and innovation to contribute to the sustainable economy can be explained as the attributes of bioeconomy. One of the major challenges for the firms working with bioeconomy is to promote social inclusion (e.g., family farming, youth and women, and indigenous peoples) and the reduction of territorial development gaps within markets and economies. The bioeconomy integrates local (niche), regional, and global policies; public and private actions; institutional silos; and economic sectors to general productive markets within the social proximity. This includes initiatives for the industrialization of agriculture and marketing of raw and processed products of sustainable farming through proximity marketing approaches to the communities. The addition of value to biomass at source, and the promotion of Industry 4.0 in commercializing agriculture based on biological resources constitutes a continuous challenge among the developing economies.

Bioeconomic modeling in marketing provides a framework to evaluate the trade-offs between ecological and economic objectives common in B-to-Cs segments. Bioeconomic models for consumer products need multiple-criteria strategy for decision-making (MSDM) approach to gain marketing competitiveness by understanding the PNS factors of the consumers at the grassroots. MSDM is well-suited to the broad range of consumer products that are often blended with the concerns of society, market, and value generation. Therefore, the MSDM strategy is built with triadic focus comprising design-to-market, design-to-society, and design-to-value (Purwanto et al. 2023). Biotechnology has been a critical driver in the ability to transform biological resources for enhanced economic wealth and societal benefit, which leads to bioeconomic performance in a sector and a geographic region. Contextually, bioeconomics and sustainability are closely linked and driven by social consciousness and crowd behavior. Thus, business proximity to society, consumers, and stakeholders helps companies adapt to the linear path of marketing integrating the abovementioned triadic elements. Bioeconomics is therefore a social marketing subject, as bioenergy, and chemical and industrial biotech processes need social proximity to enable higher value extraction from the primary (agriculture) sector, which supports bioeconomy through biofuels, bioproducts, advanced food, and fiber production (Guo and Song 2019). Social sustainability is manifested in corporate culture, organizational behavior, and functional practices of the companies. Collaborative and longitudinal approaches over a phased time-span work better to create and measure the impact of sustainable business models on environment, society, economy, and other key stakeholders. Successful businesses in manufacturing and service sectors tend to understand the challenges and opportunities linked to business transition toward sustainability in a society today. They create considerable awareness on the environment and green consumption practices in society (Rajagopal 2020). The ambidextrous perspectives of proximity to society and its impact on social consciousness, bioeconomics, sustainability, and crowd business concepts are exhibited in Figure 1.3.

Proximity of business to society with people-oriented attributes, accessibility, and acculturation of firms with social practices, and ethnicity can meet both the social and market challenges as illustrated in Figure 1.3. Proximity marketing encourages people's participation and experimentation of cocreated innovations. The social information exchange is consistent and continuous in proximity marketing, which

Proximity Marketing Strategy

Constant ● Open ● Projective ● Customer-centric ● Co-creation ● Digitization Systematic ● Value-based ● Competitive

Self-esteem
Self-actualization
Vision and goals
Intellectual base
Value propositions
Lifestyle and proximity
Hybrid communities
Peer management

Strategy
Cost, time, and risk
Strength and opportunity
Behavioral threats
Polarization
Defection
Randomness
Strategy and tactics
Decision making

Attributes

Accessibility

Acculturation

Proximity of Business to Society

People's participation
Ethics and communication
Exploring PNS factors
Crowd business concepts
Cocreating value
Building relationship system
Experimentation
Refining design and delivery process

Market Challenges

Social Challenges

Social Information Exchange

Continuous ● Discrete ● Futuristic ● Critical Validating ● Constructive ● Alternative Systematic ● Utilitarian ● Analytical

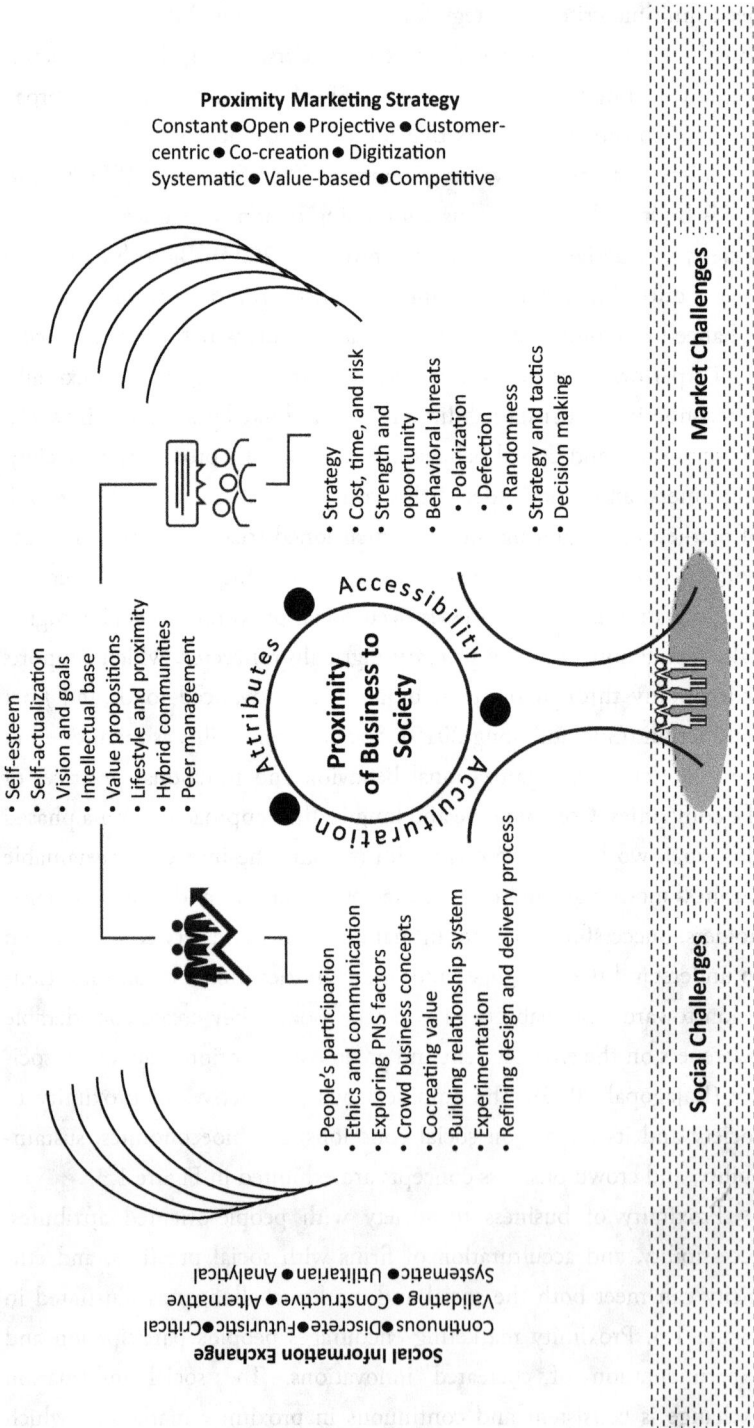

Figure 1.3 Proximity of business to society: ambidextrous perspectives

Source: Author.

offers a systematic, analytical, utility-based information exchange. Proximity of business to society augments corporate visions and goals, intellectual base, and value proposition among consumers and stakeholders in the society. Consequently, as firms become closer to the people and society, the self-actualization, self-esteem, and lifestyle among the consumers and stakeholders significantly increase. Thus, proximity marketing strategy is a constant, open, customer-centric, systematic, and value-based approach, which gains competitive advantages through projective and digitization to transform conventional processes. Customers, stakeholders, and the crowd contribute to this process indirectly through cocreation and channelizing communication through social media (Bedggood et al. 2023).

Disruptive forces, low-cost technology products, and social marketing strategies drive consumption behavior and rapid shifts in the consumer experiences on the use of green products. Consumerism, therefore, is now shifting from emotional phenomena to materialistic attributes in making consumption decisions. In this context, companies need a fact-based analysis of the consumer behavior to monitor their perceptions and consumption experience. Consumers develop attitude and behavior in due course of time. The theory of behavior can be analyzed in the context of global markets. In addition to the socioeconomic indicators, attributes corresponding to the changes in consumption patterns have occurred due to the increase in convenience shopping, focus on wellness, and green consumption. In demographic context, rapid shifts in the consumer behavior have also become noticeable, as the growth among aging populations in developed markets is outpacing the growth in the number of younger consumers in emerging markets. However, elderly consumers are inclined toward learning the new consumption patterns of the millennials in the emerging markets (Rajagopal 2019).

The growing social awareness, peer motivation, and the experimentation about green products and services ranging from renewable energy to organic food-products consumption help in generating proactive green behavior among consumers. In addition, public policy and stakeholder knowledge on green consumerism also play dynamic role in inculcating proactive behavior for green products and services. The interest of people in investing in, and their conformity to, the adaptability of sustainable energy, water conversation, green products and services, and health and housing projects establishes lean behavior. This behavioral process is supported by the consumers' perceived value emerging out of the economic benefits and risk analysis in using the technology-based sustainability product and services. The stage of behavioral process leads to the defensive behavioral stage by critical evaluation of needs, awareness, and their fit into the values and lifestyle. The following stage of defensive behavior drives consumers to justify their perceptions and attitude toward green decisions and optimize output. Most people at this stage seek social validation and reward for their decision to stay with sustainable products and tend to lead environmental advocacy and green leadership at niche and regional levels of society. However, as social consciousness grows, self-actualization on sustainability commitments increases. Further, the political ideologies, government support, and stakeholder engagement contribute to the definitive green behavior of people on sustainable products and services. Over the definitive state of behavior, most stakeholders enjoy the benefits of sustainable products and services, tend to push green goals as a social movement, and stay as referrals to diffuse lessons and vision on the green consumerism in the society.

Marketing of green products has become complex due to the mixed perceptions of consumers derived from the experiences shared through personal, social, ethnic, and corporate platforms. Therefore, green marketing has not reached the anticipated heights in society. The consumer experience on sustainable products consistently shows that their preference to choose a green product over a conventional one, which is less friendly to the environment, rarely triggers the rationale in the minds of consumers for various reasons build on 4Cs comprising cost to customer (tangible and intangible cost), communication (clarity and conceivable), convenience (availability, delivery, and services), and change (resistance versus adaptation). Consequently, when consumers are directed through public policies to make trade-offs between product attributes or helping the environment, the transformation in adapting to sustainability often fails. The success of green products is also hit by the negative perceptions of consumers related to 4Cs in combination with the 4As, which include awareness, attributes, affordability, and adaptability. In this context, some consumers assume that such products are of lower quality or don't really deliver on their environmental promises. Companies, therefore, do not forget to consider that consumers are unlikely to compromise on conventional products and the change in view of the psychosocial and economic factors comprising convenience, availability, price, quality, and performance (Ginsberg and Bloom 2004).

Innovation in consumer products and services has proved to be the strongest motivational tool, which induces the 4E's effect to drive motivation comprising explorative, experiential, expectative, and emotional cognition among consumers. The social media, digitalization of business, attractive purchase offers, and rapidly changing fashion trends have become the major motivational sources for the consumers toward perceiving new consumption and value paradigms. The gaps in the transfer of brand knowledge between consumers and media often distract the consumer learning process. Companies engage consumers in knowledge cocreation and collaborative knowledge diffusion processes to support an interpretive model of the consumer knowledge. The knowledge cocreation process encourages diffusion of customer-generated contents on social media and helps in strengthening the community learning design. Consumers learn about products, services, and new consumption patterns through community resources. The community learning process prompts coshopping and coviewing of brands in the marketplace, which stimulates consumers to also review the referrals and conform to community decisions. Hence, most referral programs of consumer products companies focus on diffusing brand awareness among the family or community as a source of knowledge hub of consumers (Rajagopal 2019).

Circular Systems and Design Thinking

In the evolving industrial era, society, corporations, and consumers are living in a linear economy. The *single-use* lifestyle has set the industrial manufacturing and marketing around the philosophy as *take, make, and dispose* products across all sectors. This refers to a unidirectional model of production as the linear economy is driving mass production and mass consumption. Therefore, the socioeconomic system has become unsustainable in most developing regions, and the shift toward circular economy is becoming inevitable. Consequently, customers develop consumption priorities through self-reference and analyzing the CI about the effects of products and services developed under the circular economy (CE) business model. Customers evaluate the rationale of purchase of single-use and unnecessary products against prolonging the lifetime of products through maintenance and repair activities. CE business model consumption philosophy requires allowing products to recirculate and provides the scope of sharing, leasing, and buying second-hand or recycled products as compared to the new ones (Maitre-Ekern and Dalhammar 2019). However, changing the consumption patterns is a complex process as it is widely determined by the consumption value chain and competitive value matrix with the socioeconomic and cultural paradigms.

Circular economy revolves around 4C factors comprising cost, cyclicality, competition, and consumption. Several business opportunities and challenges of initiating and managing circular models have been experimented at various levels of industries. Such opportunities are visible as remanufacturing and asset reuse with focus on developing second-generation products with acceptable use values, at lower cost, for the consumers of relatively lower strata. Accordingly, companies engaged in practicing CE tend to develop optimal pricing strategies, brand extensions, and taxonomy of geodemographic segmentation for consumers to match the second-generation products with their self-image congruence. In the process, cannibalization issues, feedstock challenges, consumer acceptance, and reverse supply chain design appears to be the head-on challenges for the companies. Marketing designer products made from granulated plastic waste in the premium consumer segment has an embedded issue of perceived values because they are recycled products. If such cognitive stigma of consumers can be replaced by the knowledge on sustainability and conscious consumption, products with CE philosophy can be positioned in the upstream markets. However, challenges in CE are largely viewed in making decisions on resources and product cyclicality as how often to remanufacture by infusing high rate of innovation and short usage cycles (Wagner 2017). The radical concepts of circular economy emphasize that it is restorative process by design, using and reusing natural capital as efficiently as possible, and exploring value until the end of the life cycle of finished products.

Design thinking can be a critical facilitator of new technologies, but it is also a technology in its own right—a social technology that encourages more productive innovation conversations that are strategically valuable for dynamic capability building. By overcoming social and psychological barriers in innovation processes, design thinking accelerates progress on critical imperatives: Allowing innovators at all levels to sense new opportunities; seize them by overcoming cognitive biases and aligning stakeholders; and transform and reconfigure resources. It accomplishes this through a set of well-recognized practices. In fact, recognizing and responding to human irrationality underlies many popular management approaches including design thinking, agile software development, lean start-up, and choice architecture. A shared premise of these approaches is that while attempting to predict or control human conduct is hazardous, behavior can be anticipated and shaped to the mutual advantage of humans, their organizations, and society.

Technology development to meet social challenges in developing economies is largely based on the collective design thinking process, which has six principal domains comprising inspiration, stakeholders' involvement, alignment, cocreation, articulation to facilitate technology operations, and social visualization toward sustainability. The social challenges broadly include technologies to support low-cost renewable energy, green housing, farming operations, and public health management. The social connectivity and CI-driven technology development support innovations to be used at community commons to meet social challenges. The involvement of technology developers with society is an important consideration to understand the problems, needs, and probable solutions for the stakeholders within the given demographic attributes. The stakeholder preferences on technology-based solutions help in designing and development of affordable technologies at the grassroots. The involvement of stakeholders, therefore, strengthens the process of design thinking through user insights. Community involvement, technology cocreation, and user insights foster the social acceptance of technology through perceived use value and ease-of-use perceptions of stakeholders. The user insights in technology transfer to the stakeholder inspire all categories of users including lead users, early adapters, early majority, and late majority except laggards. However, the technological attributes determine the cost of technology and its life cycle, which affect the social entrepreneurship and stakeholder engagement. Commonly, social technologies address the triple bottom line embedding people (stakeholders), planet (sustainability), and profit (social payoff). The governance of social technology can be well-managed by the stakeholders with adequate knowledge and experience. Therefore, adequate knowledge and skills should be imparted to the technology governance teams. Transfer of social technologies requires need-based user alignment and articulation to manage its applications, which helps diffusion and adaptation of technology. Cocreation helps design thinking to develop social technologies through consortiums supported by the government and public–private partnership programs. Converging the divergent factors as discussed earlier, the quadruple domains of involvement, inspiration, alignment, and cocreation help in developing technologies contextual to ecological engineering and socioeconomic development. The major concern of challenge-based research is to manage the uninterrupted technology transition and generation effects by ensuring continuous improvement. The prototype development and experimentation widely support the process of social visualization of technology, which not only delivers experience but also stimulates social actions through continuous learning. The Four A's comprising awareness (PNS factors of stakeholders), attributes (preferred solutions), affordability (cost of technology) and adaptability (technology acceptance) remain central to the development of social technology.

Cocreation helps design thinking to develop social technologies through consortiums supported by the government and public–private partnership programs. Converging the divergent factors as discussed earlier, the quadruple domains of involvement, inspiration, alignment, and cocreation help in developing technologies contextual to ecological engineering and socioeconomic development. The major concern of challenge-based research is to manage the uninterrupted technology transition and generation effects by ensuring continuous improvement. The prototype development and experimentation widely support the process of social visualization of technology, which not only delivers experience but also stimulates social actions through continuous learning. The Four A's described previously remain central to the development of social technology.

Case Studies

Bioagriculture in Developing Economies: India and Nigeria

Bioagriculture has emerged as a sophisticated practice toward sustainable farming with the support of government programs and corporate partnership to promote bioeconomic growth in the country. The bioagriculture concept penetrated society with the proximity approach of social marketing, which evolved through social consciousness and CI over the years. Placing of one or more genes from a common soil bacterium, *Bacillus thuringiensis*, Bt cotton has been genetically modified, which encode the plants to produce insecticidal proteins. The genes that have been inserted into cotton produce toxins that are limited in activity almost exclusively to caterpillar pests (Lepidoptera). Consequently, genetically transformed plants with the aforementioned technology produce one or more toxins as they grow, which develop immunity on pests and control the infestation genetically. Current Bt cotton technologies greatly reduce the need to spray for caterpillar pests.[3] Approval for the commercial release of Bt cotton hybrid varieties as resistant to cotton bollworm was given by the government in the early 21st century.

Bt cotton is the main stay of bioagriculture segment in India, which accounts for 92 percent share of the total bioagriculture economic value of U.S. $10.48 billion in India. Major consumer of this variety of cotton is the textile industry, which contributes significantly to the economic development of the Bt cotton segment. During the period 2020 and 2021, the high cotton prices have put pressure on the value chain, though farmers received better price for their crop. The minimum support price, a price guarantee determined by the government per a bale of cotton of 170 kg was around $128 in 2020, and around $177 in 2021. Nearly 53 percent of the total cotton production of India has been dominated in the central zone. Gujarat, the state in the western region of India, was the highest cotton producer with 9 million bales of cotton in 2021. Maharashtra Hybrid Seeds Company (Mahyco) introduces first the Bt cotton seeds of Monsanto, an American farm seeds company, in the 1980s. Mahyco is a farmer-centric company and invested substantial

---

[3] For details on Bt Cotton variety, see UT Crop News https://utcrops.com/cotton/insects-and-mites/biological-control/bt-cotton/.

resources on agricultural extension services in farmers training and laboratory research. The company's research focuses on developing insect resistance as a value-added trait in crops such as rice, brinjal, and okra. The products contain one or more genes from *Bacillus thuringiensis*—that have proven efficacy in the management of specific target insect pests. India's first insect-resistant transgenic product Bollgard cotton was commercialized in 2002, followed by a two-gene product Bollgard II in 2006. Mahyco Monsanto Biotech (MMB), India, a joint venture with India's Mahyco, licenses a gene that produces its own pesticide to several local seed companies in lieu of royalties and an up-front payment (Das 2016).

Mahyco has stepped out of India to cater to the needs of the cotton growers in other developing economies. In 2019, the primary objective of Mahyco demonstrated the value of the hybrid technology to Nigerian farmers in their own fields and distributed more than 2,000 samples to selected farmers to let them understand the crop and trained the farmers on appropriate product use with the right agronomy to optimize the yield in their fields. The company trained the farmers through proximity camps on pollination of the male and female flowers to get the hybrid seeds. This has developed social consciousness and helped farmers to learn seed development process. The proximity program to transform the cotton-growing practices have been further taken over by the National Biotechnology Development Agency of Nigeria to develop and deploy biotechnology in partnership with national and international stakeholders and for the benefit of mankind, both directly as food and indirectly as raw material.

ITC Agribusiness India

The agribusiness division of ITC is one of the largest exporters of agricultural commodities and has opted the *e-choupal* business model.[4] *E-Choupal* is conceived as a more efficient communication center and supply chain that delivers value to customers on a sustainable basis. This

---

[4] Digital forum of farmers to discuss farming and agribusiness related topics. For details on *e-Choupal* program of ITC, see www.itcportal.com/businesses/agri-business/e-choupal.aspx.

model has been specially designed to meet the challenges of marginal and small farmers in marketing their produce. The involvement of middlemen and intermediaries, and the weak market infrastructure in the agriculture sector have deprived farmers from marketing their produce at better prices. This *e-choupal* program has empowered farmers, raised rural income, and developed the rural ecosystem. This program also aimed at redesigning the procurement practices of soy, tobacco, shrimp, wheat, and other cropping material required by the company. The model has created a highly profitable distribution and product-design channel for the enterprise. ITC procures major food grains directly from farmers, which results in eliminating middlemen and saves cost in warehousing and delays. This practice has also led to consistency and predictability in the supply chain. The use of informational technology has been promoted in *e-choupal*; and as an inclusive business experiment, the company has invested in the setting-up of broadband digital networks and logistics even in remote areas to enable farmers to receive updated information on pricing and procurement logistics. This has brought transparency, increased access to information, and catalyzed rural transformation while enabling efficiencies and low-cost distribution of food grains that make the system profitable and sustainable. Farmers are provided with critical information and relevant knowledge on farm productivity, prices, and markets through the *e-choupal* digital infrastructure. In addition, farmers are also provided access to quality inputs to augment productivity. The company has set up an integrated rural service, which provides multiple services under single window delivery system. Sustainable nonfarm livelihood opportunities for over 40,000 rural women through microenterprises with financial support also have been provided by the company as a part of *e-choupal*. Inclusive business cultures emphasize agility, open-mindedness, and collective actions to cocreate and innovate services to enhance the stakeholder values. The power of community and culture should be aligned with inclusive business strategy for each stakeholder-oriented business project. However, the efficacy of employees and stakeholders' engagement provides sustainable business environment by reducing the impact of cost, time, and risk factors (Cheng and Groysberg 2021).

The inclusive business model of *e-choupal* economically empowers the marginal and small farmers who have low risk-taking ability, low investment, low productivity, weak market orientation, low value addition, and low income. Such economic conditions make agribusiness an uncompetitive enterprise to small farmers. Such a market-led business model can enhance the competitiveness of marginal and small farmers, and trigger a virtuous cycle of higher productivity, higher incomes, enlarged capacity for farmer risk management, larger investments, and higher quality and productivity. The inclusive business model of *e-choupal* serves as an information pool, logistics management, lowering risk, and bridging financing gaps. Real-time information and customized knowledge provided by *e-choupal* enhance the ability of farmers to take decisions and align their farm output with market demand. The aggregation of the demand for farm inputs from individual farmers gives them access to high-quality inputs from established and reputable manufacturers at fair prices. As a direct marketing channel, the program is virtually linked to the regulated agricultural marketing system for price discovery and eliminating wasteful intermediation and multiple handling. Consequently, this program helps in significantly reducing transaction costs.

Summary

Proximity marketing approaches allow marketers to target a customer at the right place at the right time with highly personalized content. Connecting with customers based on their proximity to a location allows marketers to send relevant contents to the customers and transform their consumption practices. This chapter argues that proximity marketing approaches enhance the consumer experience by creating a journey within a wider area of business. One of the main benefits of proximity marketing is that it allows businesses to target consumers both personally and socially. The social proximity of the firm helps in developing social consciousness among consumers on corporate policies, ethics, values, and sustainability. Consequently, firms can retain the loyalty and support of ecosystem partners and stakeholders to ensure their continued performance in the marketplace. The philosophical thoughts on modern business can be stretched wide from the geometric structure to the functional propositions in the marketplace, which broadly entails the market, society, and customer values. Companies should analyze customer experience centered on social interactions to develop community-linked marketing approaches.

Before discussing the corporate philosophy on proximity marketing, this chapter presents a telescopic view on the modern marketing attributes. The prismatic structure of marketing management has five faces, six edges, and nine vertices that help managers to develop marketing strategies, processes, and make competitive decisions. Design thinking can be a critical facilitator to connect proximity marketing with new technologies. Social technology that encourages more productive innovation conversations need to be strategically adopted by the firms. The core argument raised in this chapter is for the firms to develop dynamic capability to build social and customer relations for implementing proximity marketing strategies successfully. The crowd behavior toward consumer firms, their business offerings, and social proximity is often vague and unfocused, which makes it difficult for the firms to align with the crowd cognition. One of the major challenges in the conventional social and cultural environment is the empowerment of entrepreneurs that builds confidence among the innovators to inculcate proinnovation cognitive drive. CI has emerged as a dynamic tool in the business ecosystem today, which is supported by the stakeholders. Social proximity, therefore, has a major challenge to continuously reduce the distance between a firm, and use the information technology, user-friendly digital communication platforms, and the rising number of communication hours spent by the users on mobile applications.

References

Anand, P., S. Saxena, R. Gonzalez, and H.H. Dang. 2019. "Can Women's Self-Help Groups Contribute to Sustainable Development? Evidence of Capability Changes From Northern India." *Policy Research Working Paper #9011.* Washington, DC: World Bank Group.

Andrade, E.B. and J.B. Cohen. 2007. "On the Consumption of Negative Feelings." *Journal of Consumer Research* 34, no.3, pp. 283–300.

Banks, H. 2016. "The Business of Peace: Coca-Cola's Contribution to Stability, Growth, and Optimism." *Business Horizons* 59, no. 5, pp. 455–461.

Bedggood, R., R. Russell-Bennett, R. McAndrew, C. Glavas, and U. Dulleck. 2023. "Challenging the Social-Power Paradigm: Moving Beyond Consumer

Empowerment to an Energy Ecosystem of Shared Value." *Energy Policy* 173 (in press). https://doi.org/10.1016/j.enpol.2022.113405.

Centola, D. 2022. "The Network Science of Collective Intelligence." *Trends in Cognitive Sciences* 26, no. 11, pp. 923–941.

Chen, M.F. 2016. "Extending the Theory of Planned Behavior Model to Explain People's Energy Savings and Carbon Reduction Behavioral Intentions to Mitigate Climate Change in Taiwanemoral Obligation Matters." *Journal of Cleaner Production* 112, pp. 1746–1753.

Cheng, Y.-J. and B. Groysberg. 2021. *Research: What Inclusive Companies Have in Common.* Cambridge, MA: Harvard Business School Press.

Craig, S.L., A.D. Eaton, M. Belitzky, L.E. Kates, G. Dimitropoulos, and J. Tobin. 2020. "Empowering the Team: A Social Work Model of Interprofessional Collaboration in Hospitals." *Journal of Interprofessional Education & Practice* 19 (in press). https://doi.org/10.1016/j.xjep.2020.100327.

Das, K.N. 2016. "India Antitrust Body Suspects Monsanto JV Abused Dominant Position. US Legal News, February 17." www.reuters.com/article/india-monsanto/india-antitrust-body-suspects-monsanto-jv-abused-dominant-position-idUSL2N15W1I0 (accessed March 30, 2023).

Defourny, J. and M. Nyssens. 2017. "Fundamentals for an International Typology of Social Enterprise Models." *Voluntas: International Journal of Voluntary and Nonprofit Organizations* 28, no. 6, pp. 2469–2497.

Fayard, A.L. and J. Weeks. 2011. "Who Moved My Cube?" *Harvard Business Review* 89, no. 7–8, pp. 102–110.

Fedorenko, I., P. Berthon, and T. Rabinovich. 2017. "Crowded Identity: Managing Crowdsourcing Initiatives to Maximize Value for Participants Through Identity Creation." *Business Horizons* 60, no. 2, pp. 155–165.

Gefen, D. 2000. "E-Commerce: The Role of Familiarity and Trust." *Omega* 28, no. 6, pp. 725–737.

Ginsberg, J.M. and P.N. Bloom. 2004. "Choosing the Right Green Marketing Strategy." *MIT Sloan Management Review* 46, no. 1, pp. 79–84.

Gruss, R., A. Abrahams, Y. Song, D. Berry, and S.M. Al-Daihani. 2020. "Community Building as an Effective User Engagement Strategy: A Case Study in Academic Libraries." *Journal of Association of Information Science and Technology* 71, no. 2, pp. 208–220.

Guo, M. and W. Song. 2019. "The Growing US Bioeconomy: Drivers, Development and Constraints." *New Biotechnol* 49, pp. 48–57.

Gupta, A. and V. Govindarajan. 2000. "Knowledge Management's Social Dimension: Lessons From Nucor Steel." *MIT Sloan Management Review* 42, no. 1, pp. 71–81.

Jarva, V. 2011. "Consumer Education and Everyday Futures Work." *Futures* 43, no. 1, pp. 99–111

Jones, M.Y., M.T. Spence, and C. Vallester. 2008. "Creating Emotions Via B to C Websites." *Business Horizons* 51, no. 5, pp. 419–428.

Kesting, P. and F. Günzel-Jensen. 2015. "SMEs and New Ventures Need Business Model Sophistication." *Business Horizons* 58, no. 3, pp. 285–293.

Laursen, K., M. Francesca, and A. Prencipe. 2011. "Regions Matter: How Localized Social Capital Affects Innovation and External Knowledge Acquisition." *Organization Science* 23, pp. 177–193.

Maitre-Ekern, E. and C. Dalhammar. 2019. "Towards a Hierarchy of Consumption Behavior in the Circular Economy." *Maastricht Journal of European and Comparative Law* 26, no. 3, pp. 394–420.

Mathur, P., H.H. Chun, and D. Maheswaran. 2016. "Consumer Mindsets and Self-Enhancement: Signaling Versus Learning." *Journal of Consumer Psychology* 26, no. 1, pp. 142–152.

Mencl, J. and D.R. May. 2009. "The Effects of Proximity and Empathy on Ethical Decision-Making: An Exploratory Investigation." *Journal of Business Ethics* 85, no. 2, pp. 201–226.

Midha, V. 2012. "Impact of Consumer Empowerment on Online Trust: An Examination Across Genders." *Decision Support Systems* 54, no. 1, pp. 198–205.

Niemi, E. and S. Pekkola. 2017. "Using Enterprise Architecture Artefacts in an Organisation." *Enterprise Information Systems* 11, no. 2, pp. 313–338.

Paco, A. and M. Rapose. 2009. "Green Segmentation: An Application to the Portuguese Consumer Market." *Intelligence and Planning* 27, no. 3, pp. 364–379.

Page, S.E. 2007. *The Difference: How the Power of Diversity Creates Better Groups, Firms, Schools, and Societies.* Princeton, New Jersey, NJ: Princeton University Press.

Parente, R., A. ElTarabishy, M. Vesci, and A. Botti. 2018. "The Epistemology of Humane Entrepreneurship: Theory and Proposal for Future Research Agenda." *Journal of Small Business Management* 56, pp. 30–52.

Pfeffer, J., T. Zorbach, and K.M. Carley. 2014. "Understanding Online Firestorms: Negative Word-of-Mouth Dynamics in Social Media Networks." *Journal of Marketing Communications* 20, no. 1–2, pp. 117–128.

Pires, G.D., J. Stanton, and P. Rita. 2006. "The Internet, Consumer Empowerment and Marketing Strategies." *European Journal of Marketing* 40, no. 9–10, pp. 936–949.

Porter, M.E. and M.R. Kramer. 2011. "Creating Shared Value." *Harvard Business Review* 89, no. 1–2, pp. 62–77.

Purwanto, E.C., A.W. Franklin, and R.M. Ses. 2023. "Multiple Goal Bioeconomic Programming to Address Conflicting Management Objectives in Indonesian Small Pelagic Fisheries." *Marine Policy* 150 (in press). https://doi.org/10.1016/j.marpol.2023.105519.

Quelch, J.A. and K.A. Jocz. 2007. *Information: Knowledge Is Power—Leveraging Information in the Consumer and Political Marketplaces.* Boston, MA: Harvard Business School.

Rajagopal. 2016. *Sustainable Growth in Global Markets: Strategic Choices and Managerial Implications.* Basingstoke, UK: Palgrave Macmillan.

Rajagopal. 2019. *Contemporary Marketing Strategy: Analyzing Consumer Behavior to Drive Managerial Decision Making.* New York, NY: Palgrave Macmillan.

Rajagopal. 2020. "Barriers and Benefits Towards Sustainability Driven Business Models." In *Encyclopedia of Renewable and Sustainable Materials*, eds. S. Hashmi and I.A. Choudhury, vol. 5, 318–327. New York, NY: Elsevier.

Rajagopal. 2021. "*The Business Design Cube: Converging Markets, Society, and Customer Values to Grow Competitive in Business.*" New York, NY: Business Expert Press.

Reeves, M., K. Haanaes, and J. Sinha. 2015. "Navigating the Dozens of Different Strategy Options." *Harvard Business Review* 93, no. 6, pp. 1–17.

Schneider, C. 2015. "Social Participation of Children and Youth With Disabilities in Canada, France and Germany." *International Journal of Inclusive Education* 19, no. 10, pp. 1068–1079.

Schröder, A., B. Falk, and R. Schmitt. 2015. "Evaluation of Cost Structures of Additive Manufacturing Processes Using a New Business Model." *Procedia CIRP* 30, pp. 311–316.

Sedalo, G., H. Boateng, J.P. Kosiba. 2022. "Exploring Social Media Affordance in Relationship Marketing Practices in SMEs." *Digital Business* 2, no. 1, (in press).

Sen, S. and C.B. Bhattacharya. 2001. "Does Doing Good Always Lead to Doing Better? Consumer Reactions to Corporate Social Responsibility." *Journal of Marketing Research* 38, no. 2, pp. 225–243.

Strupeit, L. and A. Palm. 2016. "Overcoming Barriers to Renewable Energy Diffusion: Business Models for Customer-Sited Solar Photovoltaics in Japan, Germany, and the United States." *Journal of Cleaner Production* 123, pp. 124–136.

Van Alstyne, M.W., G. Parker, and S.P. Choudary. 2016. "Pipelines, Platforms, and the New Rules of Strategy." *Harvard Business Review* 94, no. 4, pp. 54–62.

Villani, E., E. Rasmussen, and R. Grimaldi. 2017. "How Intermediary Organizations Facilitate University–Industry Technology Transfer: A Proximity Approach." *Technological Forecasting and Social Change* 114, pp. 86–102.

Wagner, T.P. 2017. "Reducing Single-Use Plastic Shopping Bags in the USA." *Waste Management* 70, no. 1, pp. 3–12.

Zang, D., F. Li, and A.A. Chandio. 2021. "Factors of Energy Poverty: Evidence From Tibet, China." *Sustainability* 13, no. 17, pp. 1–20.

CHAPTER 2

Proximity Marketing

Overview

This chapter discusses proximity marketing concepts and practices from the point of view of the transformation of conventional wisdom through interactive marketing. The widespread use of digital technologies and online social networks has revolutionized customer-centric marketing practices. The online interactions have overridden the conventional personal-interface patterns and significantly contributed to the success of proximity marketing. By deploying various digital platforms and ICT tools (e.g., smartphones, social media, mobile apps, and electronic billboards), organizations can develop interactive marketing approaches to enhance customer outreach and narrow down the proximity of C-to-C marketing.[1] In view of the advancement of ICT tools, this chapter discusses the frugal and hybrid technology used in managing the relationship marketing by B-to-C and B-to-B firms. The chapter is woven around the recent research arguments that reveal homophily between influencers and audiences. Such homophily drives customer value and cocreation behavior in a proximity marketing process, which leads to the expected brand value and purchase intention that occur through customer value cocreation.[2] This chapter also discusses proximity marketing tools including hybridity, visual effects, and taxonomy of relationship marketing through case studies on interactive marketing and visual marketing experiences.

---

[1] A.S. Krishen, Y.K. Dwivedi, N. Bindu, and K. Satheesh Kumar. 2021. "A Broad Overview of Interactive Digital Marketing: A Bibliometric Network Analysis," *Journal of Business Research* 131, pp. 183–195.

[2] Y. Bu, J. Parkinson, and P. Thaichon. 2022. "Influencer Marketing: Homophily, Customer Value Co-creation Behaviour and Purchase Intention," *Journal of Retailing and Consumer Services* 66, (in press). https://doi.org/10.1016/j.jretconser.2021.102904.

Interactive Marketing and Proximity

Interactive marketing has always been beneficial to the firms, as the collaborative and cocreated marketing strategies help in developing proximity and outreach to the consumers. The proximity between firms and consumers and stakeholders inculcates a sense of engagement and trust in the long run, which strengthens the partnership of firms with consumers. Interactive marketing has been proved to be a good tool for firms to operate in niches. In case, the niches are too small to be served, the firms become profitably viable as marketing efficiency improves. Communications can reach small or diffused targets with increasing precision, and feedback on marketing through interactive platforms among the target consumers and stakeholders. In interactive communication, all communities exchange their attention, interest, desire, and action distinctly with the specific interest groups. Each person has an individual vision of insightful communication being watched by all. The critical mass for the group floats on analyzing perceptions and driving opinions on the communication platform. Thus, the critical mass of consumers is socially constructed by individuals based on their communication with others in their system. Interactive communication is based on six attributes including emotions, relative advantage, compatibility, complexity, trial ability, and observability that affect its rate of diffusion and adaptability (Rogers 1995). Such interactive communication supports interactive marketing management in the field of complex services and can help the creation of a specific service delivery system.

The possibilities of cocreation and coevolution of marketing strategies, process innovation, and new product development are built around the consumers and stakeholders through interactive tools, which help in increasing substantially of the firms. The chronological evolution of interactive marketing can be observed in the changing directions of the journey from broadcasting marketing (radio, catalog, and physical mails) to electronic interactive marketing (television and telemarketing) and virtual marketing (seamless, smart television and smart mobile phones, social media, and online marketing). The course of interactive marketing is changing continuously with the advancement of ICT. The global penetration of digital technologies and online diverse spread of social networks, blogs, and video platforms have revolutionized the engagement of firms with consumers (Berezan et al. 2018). Interactive marketing today empowers consumers to raise voices both for and against the firm's innovation, manufacturing, distribution, and marketing policies. The interactive marketing on digital platforms has given an enormous rise to e-commerce supported by visual and functional technologies such as artificial intelligence (AI), augmented reality, and virtual reality (VR). Such advancements in technology have contributed to the conceptualization of Metaverse as a virtual space for business. Some firms are also engaged in establishing connectivity between online and offline to facilitate tangible shopping on Metaverse.

By deploying various digital platforms, and ICT tools (e.g., smartphones, social media, mobile apps, and electronic billboards), marketing firms tend to compete in establishing customer-centric, relational, and interactive marketing techniques to lead the market. Coevolving with consumers and stakeholders on innovative and data-driven marketing through smart devices leverage digital advertising to enhance consumer outreach and acquisition. Consequently, digital marketing has emerged as a better informed, empowered, and connected approach for the firms to network consumers in doing business (Krishen et al. 2021). Digital interactive marketing experience contributes to CI to support crowd-based decisions in the emerging customer-centric companies. Online interactions have expanded the customer outreach and refined the value perceptions and cocreation perspectives in managing disruptions in business and competitive leverage for growing firms. The growth of interactions and dialogues between the firm, community, and the consumer through online social networks such as MySpace.com and Facebook.com are just the prominent examples of these conversational platforms. Such interactions and dialogue exchanges help firms in penetrating business into society by understanding the customer values and social needs to deliver the most appropriate solution. Firms embrace and listen to customer-community dialogues to understand their views and suggestions to improve the business strategies (Rajagopal 2021).

Most customer-centric companies such as Unilever, Mary Kay, Kellogg's, Nestlé, and IKEA have customized their websites and installed digital device interfaces to learn customer views, needs, and proposed solutions. Most firms are opening the opportunities for consumers to interact across multiple channels to stay customer-centric, crowd-focused, and competitive in the marketplace. The Internet, remote communication devices, large consumer databases, and advances in mobile information technology have introduced new forms of direct-to-consumer marketing approaches. However, as companies seek more outreach and customer accountability from their advertising, they rely on customer-generated contents and interactive means to develop customer-friendly communications. Consequently, crowd-driven companies are investing rapidly in interactive marketing platforms. It is evident from crowdsourcing and crowdfunding practices in business that demand for interactive marketing is continuous, seamless, and sustainable (Shankar and Malthouse 2007). There is a new computer-based experimental platform called *dialogue marketing*, which is, to date, the highest step on an evolutionary ladder that ascends from database marketing to relationship marketing to one-to-one marketing. The major advantages of dialogue marketing over conventional communication approaches are that it is completely interactive, and it runs on multicommunication channels. This platform continuously tracks every nuance of the customer's interaction with the business. Thus, dialogue marketing responds to each transition in that relationship now the customer requires attention (Kalyanam and Zweben 2005). The elements of the interactive marketing grid are illustrated in Figure 2.1.

Proximity- and communication mix has spread across several elements within the broad six domains as illustrated in Figure 2.1. The domains comprising communication mix, meta social behavior, relationship inflators, relationship drivers, social attributes, and public policies for setting the information dissemination norms play a significant role in connecting 3Cs that include corporate, consumer, and crowd participation. The 3Cs information management practices are widely founded on the interactive communication mosaic, which has six information quadrants each focusing on the following strategies:

- Assimilation of information
- Efficiency in disseminating information
- Managing surprises in communication (unthinkable)

Public Policies
- Right to information
- Ethical contents
- Gender sensitivity
- Honesty and realistic
- Accountability

Meta Social Behavior
- Human element
- Machine learning
- Crowd behavior
- Collective intelligence
- Sociopsychological factors
- Emotions
- Experience
- Empathy
- Ecstasy

Relationship Drivers
- Creators
- Inflators
- Deflators
- Aggregators
- Defenders
- Disruptors
- Eudaimonia

Social Attributes
- Social expectation
- Social resilience
- Social engagement

Relationship Inflators
- Affinity
- Referrals
- Sociocognitive
- Self-esteem
- Self-actualization
- Information aesthetics
- Exclusivity
- Shared relationship

Interactive Marketing Proximity and Communication-mix

Crowd

Consumer

Corporate

Assimilation	Efficiency	Unthinkable
Acquired	Situational	Generic

Interactive Communication Mosaic

Communication Mix
- Transparency
- Cocreation
- User-generated contents
- Verbal and nonverbal elements
- Digital diffusion
- Visualization
- Crowd communication
- Corporate Communication
- Psychodynamics (C-to-C)

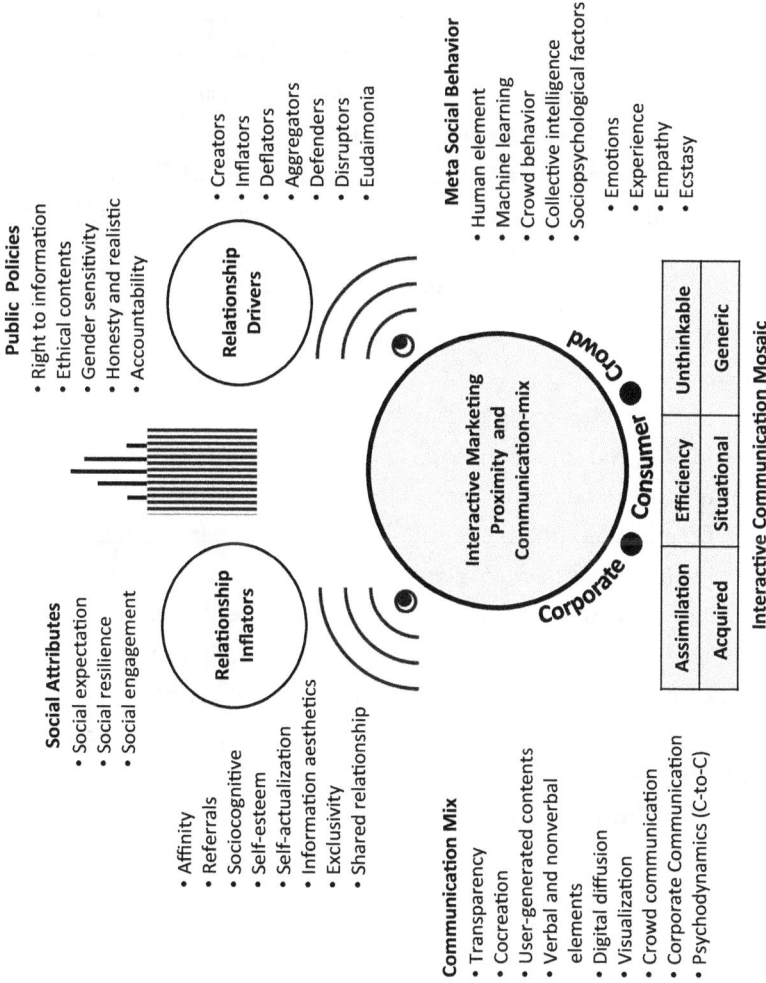

Figure 2.1 Interactive marketing grid

Source: Author.

- Validating acquired information
- Structuring situational information
- Diffusing generic user-based contents to build proximity between consumers and firms

The communication mix suggests that interactive communication can be effective if it is cocreated through user-generated contents, including both verbal and nonverbal contents, to optimize the visual emotions. However, transparency in communication is a noncompromising attribute in both physical and digital diffusion of communication. The previously discussed approaches can generate high psychodynamics (C-to-C interactions) in crowd-based and corporate communication. Effective communication increases the proximity of firms with consumers and other business partners to stay abreast of corporate policies, consumer needs, and market competition. Interactive communication and marketing strategies help in developing metasocial behavior, which converges crowd behavior, CI, and corporate values to openness. The sociopsychological factors of 4Es comprising emotions, experience, empathy, and ecstasy significantly affect the metasocial behavior. However, machine learning and robotic information management with AI also encourages interactive marketing and social proximity. Figure 2.1 exhibits many relationship inflators that can support the relationship drivers to maximize the outreach of consumers and implement proximity strategies effectively. The relationship inflators can be of personal and public nature. Affinity, self-esteem, self-actualization, perceived information aesthetics, exclusivity, and shared relationship constitute the personal relationship inflators, while sociocognitive learning and referrals constitute the public inflators in strengthening customer-centric relationship of firms. Inflators are among many relationship drivers, while other pro-relationship and proximity drivers include creators, who serve proximity builders for business innovation as practices in the cocreational firms such as LEGO and IKEA. Relationship aggregators not only bring people together but also segment relationships by gender, age, consumption preferences, region, and socioeconomic strata, so that firms can invest in proximity marketing strategy with high precision. However, firms must eliminate disruptors and deflators from the proximity market space to reduce the social resilience to crowd interactions and crowd-based business models of firms. Sometimes, crowd dynamics act negative to the social proximity of firms and stay critical to the strategies of the firm. Such situations have been observed with high social involvement of agrochemicals and agricultural seed producing and marketing firms. Therefore, it is necessary for the local governments to implement public policies by emphasizing the posting of ethical contents, respecting gender sensitivity, observing honesty, claiming accountability, and staying realistic with public–private partnership programs and crowd communications. However, under the public policy, the right to information must be established, so that consumers can legitimately demand for information from the firm or its business partners.

Hybrid governance model is an emerging phenomenon in the corporate world. In this model, a large number of representations from various groups (stakeholders, customers, technology experts, government, financial institutions, and social platforms) occupy the middle ground in the state-owned, public-sector enterprises, and fully privatized companies operating in emerging markets. As sizable government stakes in leading industries in the form of ownership, management, subsidies, or other preferential forms are common in the public-private programs. Such shifts are both market-driven and regulatory, and they lead to hybrid governance with a blend of human resources, technology, and regulatory framework. Hybrid governance helps firms in multistakeholder management, crowdfunded business projects, and publicly financed corporations that compete in the local and global marketplaces (Khanna 2012). The hybrid governance also encourages public–private partnership in businesses, and induces crowd cognition and collective controls (commons), which operate with strategic goals and operational plans.

Customer-centric firms practice interactive marketing using various customer-convenience tools such as direct mail, catalog retailing, telemarketing, social media channels, digital advertising and marketing, and mobile marketing. Firms operating congruent to the ICT adapt to network technology to encourage crowd participation, and CI to stimulate psychodynamics among consumers to review, react, and reaffirm the brands on the social media. A positive psychodynamics helps companies to lower the brand promotion costs and enhance the customer outreach across geodemographic segments. Firms gain the attention of consumers through new, green, digital, and consumer-friendly technologies. Interactions beyond boundaries through social media drive consumers to express their views, needs, probable risks, and the preferred solutions (Gere et al. 2022). A pooled repository of such knowledge forms CI, which can be used by the firms effectively to develop customer-centric marketing strategies. Therefore, putting the people together to create CI through psychodynamics is central to proximity marketing.

Machine Power and Proximity

AI in marketing has a new space to grow in the customer-centric firms. AI has gone beyond robotics structures for the customers as it is now emerging as a tool for decision making among consumer-oriented firms. Coding multiple ICTs have been central to the value creation, and have provided efficient services for enhancing consumers' experiences. AI is now able to manage the data analysis and deliver managerial decisions to the tourism firms. However, the human element is not totally replaced with machines in managing firms. AI is integrated with ICTs to be omnipresent in all stages of a tourist's journey, and supports the ecstasy of customers (Buhalis et al. 2019). Early in this century, social robots played a pivotal role in serving the social institutions and tourism industry to disseminate information and converse with humans. Broadly, Alexa and Siri are also accommodated as social robots with AI to interact with humans. The Chat-GPT has the new AI revolution in the public domain to develop interactive relationship and mutual dependency to learn and widen the information silos. AI robots serve as co-workers and analysts for decision making in large multibrand and international customer-centric firms. AI has yet to support tourism and hospitality industry robots with trust, anticipation, and emotions. Happiness, arousal and merriment have a significant impact on robot sentiment polarity, while anticipation and surprise do not significantly affect the AI logarithms. Therefore, one major challenge is to anthropomorphize robots for tourism and hospitality industry (Jörling et al. 2019).

Coevolving with consumers and stakeholders, firms can identify appropriate technologies, carry out innovations, and prepare for effective technology transfer through training programs on face-to-face and digital platforms. Such integrated efforts leverage social and industrial consciousness for developing new products in the fields of renewable energy and sustainability, and meeting the social challenges such as poverty alleviation, housing, and community health. The technological revolution has driven the digital transformation, as firms are engaged in cocreating value in industrial markets. Among the many forms of technology development, digital technologies have encouraged AI, which has the strongest pervasive impact (Molina and Rajagopal 2023). Corporate giants such as Amazon and FedEx have already been experimenting with sending delivery robots to doorsteps. Now Piaggio, the Italian company that makes the Vespa scooter, is offering a stylish alternative (brand name GITA) of utilitarian machines, which could carry a weight up to 50 pounds and stroll along with the shoppers within the market space. There are two attractions associated with this AI robot to drive proximity: social attraction to the product and opening hedonic conversation for a utilitarian product. The AI is being actively used in public parks to regulate resource use and reinforce the basic civil laws in public places. Robot dog, a machine with AI and cameras, is used for surveillance and maintaining social distancing during the Covid-19 pandemic (2020–2022) in Singapore. In a real-life situation, using AI to train dogs and train low-cost robots to perform tasks previously achievable by machines is 10 times more expensive (Hsu 2022).

ICT and AI make a strong contribution to adventure shopping. American retailers that excel at adventure shopping manifestation fetch the highest sales per square foot in leisure and sport seams. Customers seem to happily wait in the long queues and chaos to experience the adventure shopping, which can be defined as stores where the merchandise is ever-changing and unpredictable, the prices are usually acceptable, and the goods are of high quality. Macy's for apparel and housewares, TJ Maxx in varied merchandise, and Costco for innovative products along with utilitarian items can be the good examples of adventure shopping in the United States. It is all about spotting surprises, taking a trial, and sharing experiences on digital media within known and unknown communities. Such customer interactions lead to generate 360° proximity and relationship.

Eudaimonism in proximity relationships is an attractive attribute of tourists to gain a sense of self-achievement, ultimately leading to health and well-being. The ICT and AI complement to the tourist knowledge, help in narrowing down the unveiled biases, and encourage eudaimonic behavior in adventure tourism. Adventure shopping enhances eudaimonic emotions, which is marginally different from perceived happiness or hedonic pleasure (George et al. 2021). However, when proximity products and services are commoditized, their benefits would enormously serve the customer-centric firms. AI-based robots, unlike machines with predefined functions, could revolutionize the retail industry by offering interactive solutions. Cutting-edge technologies significantly affect the social and industrial development in transitional economies. The prominent technological edges that drive challenge-based research include AI, augmented reality, VR, wearable technology, robotics, and big data analytics. The growing environmental concerns, public policies, and scientific communities describe the efforts that utilize ecosystem processes to boost challenge-based research in engineering and technology to address societal challenges. The challenge-based research outputs have significantly contributed to the development of the consumer sector economy.

The technological revolution has driven the digital transformation, as firms are engaged in co-creating value to improve the markets in the services sector by adding the power of AI to acquire new customers. Among the many forms of technology development, digital technologies have encouraged AI, which has the strongest pervasive impact. By mobilizing resources and capitalizing on the growing AI revolution, firms in the tourism and hospitality industry can converge this sector with the mainstream technology revolution at Industry 4.0. However, knowledge and skills, service design process, and cocreation of business models in core services industry must be congruent with the embedded PNS factors in the society (Leone et al. 2021). Social relations widely rely on information technology infrastructure irrespective of its sophistication. The major concern in digitalizing emotions and social relationships is to ensure effective knowledge management through diffusion of dialogues across the social genres. Social empowerment depends on the active digital connectivity in which people exchange their perceptions and values on brands, benefits, and benevolence (3Bs) to express their compassion to the companies within the existing social ecology. Convergence of business and social ecology drives the expectations of consumers and stakeholders to strengthen their association and social fit with both insiders and outsiders of their social regime. Such sociological bonding with business allows sharing and mobilizing of knowledge to identify the opportunities of social well-being and reconstructing effective and efficient relationship channels to integrate the changing business philosophies (Gupta and Govindarajan 2000).

Relationship and Hybridity

The social brands today have higher potential to both create and shift consumer behavior by stimulating consumers toward experimentation and value creation, aligning with the corporate goals and strategies, and judging the performance of products and services through CI and perceived values. In addition, partnering with social institutions and creating a crowd movement to validate the corporate strategies on creating value among consumers and markets also play a significant role in determining the consumer behavior today (Sidibe 2020). This approach has allowed Unilever's sustainable living brands, such as Dove, to help over 35 million young people around the world with self-esteem education since 2005; and Lifebuoy, which has reached over a billion consumers with its handwashing campaigns, educating social preventive health care measures and created immense consumer value. Similarly, Ben and Jerry's food products, which are followed by the campaigns for social justice and climate change, and Unilever's social strategy of empowering rural women through the *Shakti program* have created enormous customer value and sustainable behavior.

The acquired and shared culture among consumers drives awareness about the new trends, which in turn arouses new consumer preferences. For example, consumer preferences for 3D games, VR products, and trendy consumer electronics influence consumers in the emerging markets as the *millennial effect*. The experience sharing over the digital platforms further influences the consumer behavior over a long time. Patterns of consumerism are changing in the society, as there are shifts in the consumer demography in the markets. The explosion of mass consumer segment, urbanization, and increase in the size of the population of aging consumers have contributed significantly to the shifts in consumer preferences and the overall consumption behavior. Direct-to-customer marketing strategies, convenience shopping, and social media-driven marketing approaches of companies have increased social and cultural influence on developing consumer behavior. However, disruption in technology and attraction toward local consumption also contribute in driving the consumer behavior dynamic across geodemographic segments.

Visual attraction of products, emotions, self-congruence and perceived experience, knowledge and beliefs, and psychosocial insights about the products, drive the perceptions of consumers, which later helps in developing attitude and behavior in future. The consumer philosophy today is woven around the practice of *touch, feel, and pick* of products and services, wherein the perceptual process among consumers is observed in four stages beginning with sensitive feeling, attention, review, and cognitive affirmation. Consumer perception is backed also by ACCA factors comprising awareness, comprehension, conviction, and action. Social media channels are the effective propagators of consumer experiences, which help in community interactions and enhances the social networks. Engagement of firms in reaching out to the remote consumer communities, and discovering the latent PNS factors can be the right tool to cocreate proximity-based marketing strategies. Consumers develop purchase decisions from perceived value and crowd-based motivation. However, conscious choice also helps in determining behavioral dynamics among consumers. The buying behavior is often jolted by the chaotic crowd comments, incomplete information, and ambiguous customer advocacy on social media. Customer intuitions, crowd-based brainstorming, collective opinions, and selected preferences that are learnt in customer communities affect consumer behavior. However, intuitive judgments remain powerful moderators and often override the collective decisions induced on social media. They are heavily influenced by the cognitive dynamics of the individuals, a phenomenon known as cognitive processing fluency, which conforms the *just feels right* notion of the individuals at the given time (Lafley and Martin 2017).

The proximity marketing strategy considers various dimensions of proximity among the key partners including consumers, suppliers, retailers, and manufacturing firms. Proximity is measured through geographical, cognitive, organizational, institutional, social, and personal connectivity. These proximity dimensions significantly influence managerial decisions, and affect the success of collaborative approaches with key partners in business including consumers. It is challenging for the firms to distinguish the thin line between the proximity (customer interactions within niche) and distance (geographic distance and outreach of the firm) while making collaborative decisions. Depending on the PNS factors, CI, and social consciousness about the products and services, firms need different partners at varying distances to collaborate and cocreate products and services. For example, Nestlé in India has introduced varied options of its baby food brands Cerelac and Nestum by understanding the problems, needs, and expected solution for mothers across the multicultural communities. The company has modified its offerings of mono-grain, milk-base baby food in both brands. The company learned the single cereal and milk-base requirements by enhancing the proximity to consumers by geographic regions in India, which enabled the company to target specific cereals in preferred regions such as Nestum Rice (southern market), Nestum Wheat (central and northern market), and Nestum Corn in the parts of the western markets of the country.

Therefore, geographical proximity is an essential approach for the firms to explore PNS factors and possibilities to cocreate innovative products. Firms can gain access to new consumer segments and markets through geographically distant partners; however, to develop new products, customer-centric firms usually resort to partners with close geographical proximity. In fashion products, diet products, and natural prophylactic-medicines segments, open marketing strategy trends have emerged, in which firms develop marketing strategies in collaboration with the consumers and stakeholders. Firms such as LEGO (creative games), IKEA (home decor), Walmart (low-cost consumption basics), and CVS store (nonprescription drugs) largely rely on the cocreation and trials to develop new products and open marketing strategies. Several open innovation firms adapt to the proximity marketing approach to understand the consumer and market ecosystems, PNS factors, and typical barriers associated with the open innovation and open strategy process (Ooms and Piepenbrink 2021).

Consumer perceptions are often agile and need to be endorsed by peers, friends, and family to support decision making and to put them into practice over the long term. Such cognitive process creates consumption attitude among consumers. Perceptions linked to emotions are commonly impulsive and temporary, which do not make a dent on cognitive process continuity and help firms in decision making. Consumers form perceptions on the viable solutions to the predetermined needs (recognized as problems), which match with their self-congruence and could offer sustainable value (satisfaction). Consumers review their perceptions formed on products, services, brands, or business companies in reference to the public opinions and their own observations. Accordingly, consumers justify their perceptions and develop purchase intention. Upon developing the right perceptions, consumers try to refine their needs, and find means and ends to acquire the product. Consumption of products establishes the perceived value among consumers and validates their buying decision. Perceptions initially formed by the consumers are often subject to change in view of the reviews, referrals, and self-reflections. Perceptual mapping is a useful exercise for customer-centric companies to understand various underlying cognitive dimensions that affect the decision-making process. Perceptual maps have been proved to be a useful tool for marketers in understanding product design, product differentiation, product positioning, and product preferences among consumers. Commonly, perceptual maps are constructed by asymmetric observations, perceived values, and self-reference criteria to determine the product optimization and value-led marketing strategies. Consumers exhibit many perceptual dimensions corresponding to a product or brand in the market (Chaturvedi and Carroll 1998).

Social proximity can be achieved through both interpersonal word-of-mouth and sharing of experience on digital platforms. However, it is a big challenge to the firms to inculcate social values by converging the perceived values and corporate policies that benefit customers and stake holders. The low-cost, high-quality cardiac specialty hospital Narayan Health (NH) in Bangalore, India, has risen to international order by expanding its proximity to patients, cocreating services by understanding the PNS factors, and encouraging interactions of the patients, peers, and family across communities. NH had been successfully delivering affordable high-quality tertiary care to the patients of various socioeconomic segments in India including the bottom-of-the-pyramid segment at relatively low cost as compared to the existing private hospitals. The proximity marketing approach has been driven by both the communities and the NH by providing community education, encouraging participatory appraisals, and communicating on digital networks. The proximity approach has not only stimulated the inflow of patients but also portrayed the need for expansion of NH network locally and internationally. To encourage the adoption of the NH affordable care delivery model worldwide, the NH company has been exploring the opportunity to establish a hospital in the western hemisphere. The backstage agenda of NH might have been to demonstrate the NH model to the United States to strengthen the health care system at the grassroots. The Cayman Islands Government supported this project as a medical tourism hub to promote the triadic goals of enhancing proximity, promoting health tourism, and social cause marketing during the period 2008 to 2009. The Health City Cayman Islands (HCCI), a 2,000-bed conglomeration of multiple superspecialty hospitals within a single campus located on the Grand Cayman Island, was planned by the NH. The first phase of HCCI, a 104-bed hospital focused on cardiac care and orthopedics, was developed jointly by NH and Ascension, the largest nonprofit hospital system in the United States (Khanna and Gupta 2014). This project was all about the people, communication, knowledge- and experience sharing, and widening the outreach through proximity marketing approaches in the health care industry.

Diffusion of knowledge through social media, and developing effective relationships are the most popular ways to cocreate consumer behavior. Some consumers not only want to acquire knowledge through crowd sources but also want to be *confident friends* with a brand, while others might look for a *passionate fling* and would welcome a closer bond. Companies following crowd-based business models search for kick-start signals from multiple sources to understand the consumer perceptions in the context to various relationship portfolios. Accordingly, firms cocreate consumer perceptions and build a strategic mix of connections to gain competitive advantage, augment customer value, and inculcate strategic relationships with customers. In the growing perspective of dynamic market competition, it has been evidenced by customer-centric companies such as HUL, Samsung, and PepsiCo that relationship-driven consumer behavior is sustainable and more profitable than other market-oriented strategies, as these companies tend to cocreate and coevolve with consumers (Avery et al. 2014). Creating digital communities for social knowledge transfer also serves as public referral, and helps companies in the acquisition of new consumers and retention of the existing consumers (Geisler 2007). Learning communities are developed by consumer-centric companies to transfer knowledge on social consumption causes such as healthy foods, green consumption, organic farm products, and the like. Such learning communities are designed primarily to increase consumer attitude toward learning new consumption patterns, and building convergence with social, ethnic, and personal values. Companies monitor consumer needs, perceptions, and expectations through the learning communities, and identify marketing strategies, which contribute to augment the consumer involvement in learning new consumption experiences and augmenting perceived satisfaction. Digital consumer learning communities do attain positive outcomes; however, consumer education programs need to be developed specific to the requirements of the geodemographic segments (Andrade 2007). The digital marketing strategies with hybrid self-experience stations attract more consumers to experience the products online, develop and share experience, and measure the perceived use value (satisfaction) of the products. Such web exposures for the product and services are accessible to many consumers today, which drives them to develop perceptions and attitude for the products and services of their choice. The breakthrough ideas emerging from brainstorming at the crowd platforms are focused on new and amateur innovation concepts, social perspectives, radical and nonconventional ideas, and hybrid combinations to gain potential leverage in the competitive markets (Bouquet et al. 2018). The relationship and proximity marketing mosaic are exhibited in Figure 2.2.

In managing people–firm relations through hybridity and proximity, a quintuple model with critical elements comprising relationship culture, ICTs, interactive marketing, perceptual elements, and quality

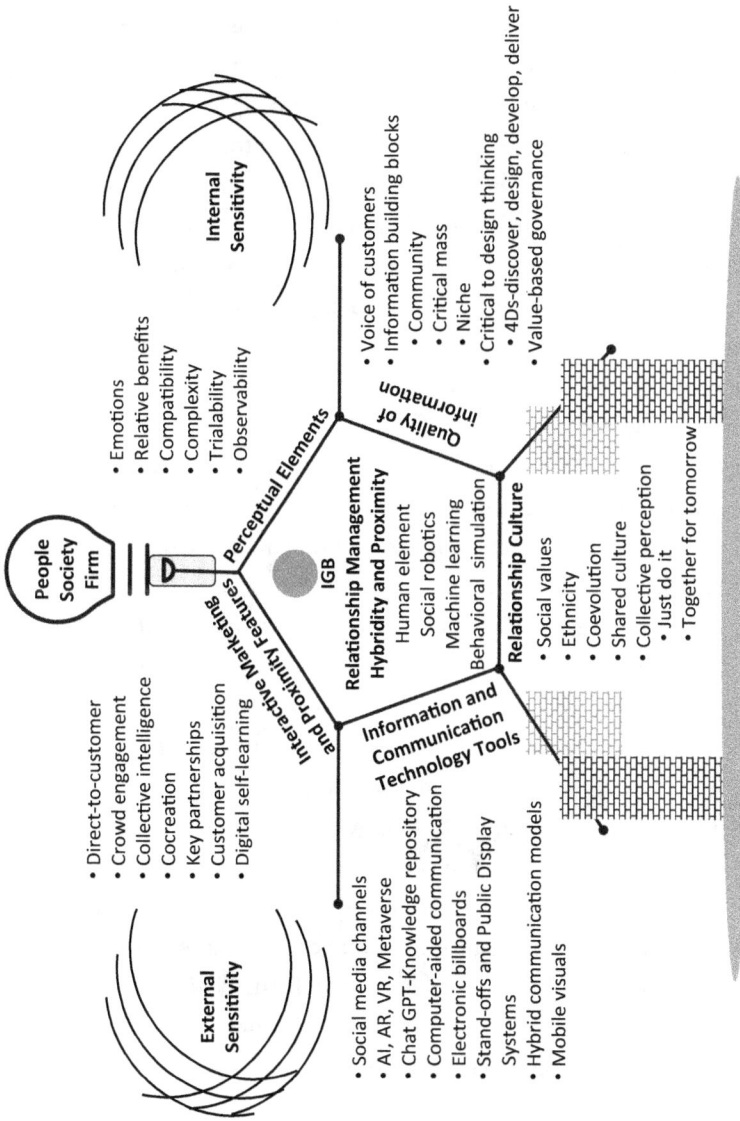

Figure 2.2 Mosaic of relationship and proximity marketing

Source: Author.

of information, plays a critical role in developing people-oriented marketing strategies. As exhibited in Figure 2.2, relationship management is central to human development, though with the advancement of ICT, machine learning and behavioral simulation applications are integrated in the process. Social robots play a significant role not only in disseminating communication but also in building and bridging the proximity of target people. A social robot is an AI system that is designed to interact with humans and other machines. Social robots are contributing significantly in catering to the people in health care, education, and diffusion of information in public places such as tourist attractions, parks, and transit stations. Proximity marketing is to drive people through 3E factors consisting of empowering, encouraging, and engaging, which help firms in driving the collective perceptions like *just do it* (Nike) and *together for tomorrow* (Samsung), which are beyond the brand tags. Shared culture and ethnicity can be coevolved by the firms with people and create sustainable social values. The individual and group behavior is developed within the relationship culture, and can be restructured if faded over time due to change in perceptual and social values through reinforcing proximity approaches.

ICT tools have redesigned and redeployed interactive communications on digital platforms through social media channels. Advancement of ICT has been diversified to AI, augmented reality, VR, and metaverse as the new branches of interactive technology to drive business to social proximity. AI has high social contributions to information dissemination, which is evident after the evolution of Chat-GPT as a hub of computer-aided communication beside various hybrid communication models. Electronic billboards, stand-offs and public display systems, and mobile visual systems have made consistent impact on generative local proximity. The principal features of interactive and proximity marketing include wider outreach strategies such as direct-to-customer, crowd engagement, and CI to accelerate customer acquisition, cocreation, and developing key partnerships with customers and stakeholders to enhance social value as illustrated in Figure 2.2. At the same time, firms need to keep track of consumer perceptions such as emotions, relative benefits, compatibility with consumption, social consciousness, and economic, personal and social observability, and trialability. These factors are sensitive to the proximity marketing strategies. Firms must consider the voice of customers to improve the user-generated contents and perceptions. Accordingly, firms can cocreate information building blocks for community, critical mass, and niche consumers. Successful consumer-centric firms such as AMUL (India), LEGO (Denmark), IKEA (Sweden), and Grameen Bank (Bangladesh) have used these blocks to strategically expand their market outreach and proximity to customers in the long run. Maintaining the social quality of information can streamline and improve design thinking and value-based governance of business. The social proximity can be used by the firms as a collective tool to discover PNS factors, design innovative solutions, develop products, services, and cocreate marketing strategies, and deliver them effectively to the target consumers.

The digital marketing strategies with hybrid self-experience stations attract more consumers to experience the products online, develop and share experience, and measure the perceived use value (satisfaction) of the products. Such web exposure for the product and services are accessible to many consumers today, which drives them to develop perceptions and attitude for the products and services of their choice (Potter and Naidoo 2009). AI and CI enhance and complement each other and together serve as a hybrid concept. Both require training in personal development and high performance. The hybrid CI process coordinates with Industry 4.0 management processes and encourages firms of various sizes and industries to learn together. Many proximity-based ideas have benefited creative companies such as LEGO, Samsung, and Sony (gaming division products) by reaching out to the crowd and communities. The dynamic attributes of crowdsourcing of these companies have ranged from localization to globalization, and disruption to hybridization. However, while implementing society-linked business models, companies tend to develop community hubs for customers and stakeholders to interact on face-to-face, digital, or hybrid communication models. The interactions of customers on these platforms help companies document the VoCs to support strategy designs. Wisdom of crowd is a broad-spectrum cognitive pool, which contributes to the CI with liberal thinking. Hybrid knowledge (a blend of conventional and technology-oriented knowledge) and group behavior have emerged as the principal source for firms to learn the perceptions of customers and stakeholders at large. The wisdom of crowd is motivated by the firms by creating a free space for thinking together on a predetermined topic. The digital networks and the enhanced scope of interpersonal meetings among peers have helped CI grow manifold over the years. The brainstorming in the crowd-cognition process categorically exhibits individual and group behaviors.

People in the marketing-mix constitute front-liners in markets, who manage the sales of products and services. Selling is an art largely associated with the behavioral skills of the sale personnel of a sales organization. In a competitive marketplace, selling is performed using scientific methods of product presentation, advertising, and various approaches drawn to take the customer into confidence. Performance in the marketing mix is considered as a hybrid element. This element is evolved through various factors comprising all basic elements of marketing mix, innovation and continuous improvement, organizational culture, employee engagement, and consumer involvement, which helps in cocreating products to enhance consumer value. The grapevine effect has emerged as an outgrowth of psychodynamics, which has evolved as CI, and is a critical element in creating tangible interactions among consumers in a competitive marketplace. The grapevine effect is contributed by the social media through word-of-mouth that stretches throughout the market, irrespective of the various measures taken by the firms to build their brand and competitive posture. Grapevine develops psychodynamics among consumers by sharing various consumer experiences (Rajagopal 2013).

The community creation model functions more as social governance than a corporate venture in managing renewable business projects across the downstream market comprising rural household and farm and nonfarm sectors. The governance mechanism for managing green energy projects in the rural areas lies between the hierarchy-based (closed) mechanism and the market-based (open) systems. Social behavior is built by attaining social needs through stakeholder governance and effective social governance. Business transformation in consumer-centric companies evolve over the years in reference to values-based governance. The necessity of creating hybrid business models infuses with local cultures and practices in global markets, leveraging strategic partnerships by encouraging cocreation with consumers (Gupta and Shapiro 2014). Accordingly, the impact of C-to-C communications is magnified manifold in the marketplace through their participation on social media.

Social media is a hybrid element of the promotion mix because, in a traditional sense, it enables companies to interact with their customers, while in a nontraditional sense, it enables customers to interact directly among their peers. Firms use digital platforms significantly to boost their business, post marketing messages through page views, and advertise on the Internet channels to enhance their outreach in a short time. Such push strategies on social media serve as an advertising tool that could share net-surfer behavior. However, it is difficult for the companies to precisely target the communications to a specific audience, as this kind of marketing strategy is too broad to effectively target connectors, referrals, and salespeople. Most crowd-based firms tend to develop long-term digital relationships using value-driven promotional strategies that emphasize cocreation and grow in user experiences and user-generated contents. To this end, electronic word-of-mouth communication appears to be a trendy, convenient, and cost-effective solution (Whitla 2009).

Visual Effects and Proximity

The mainstream retailing industry has transformed from traditional shopping practices to multichannel retailing by developing the retail business through e-commerce platforms. Such transformation in retailing technology has increased the global market outreach and online penetration of potential customers with increased visual satisfaction and ease-of-use of technology. The visualization features have allowed retailers to demonstrate the 3D store effect by allowing multiple presentations supported by visual technologies to provide sensory perceptions (Zha et al. 2022). The virtual merchandising blended with the virtual store ergonomics, product dimensions, and sensory experience tend to instantly substitute the need for physical inspection such as fitness trials, touching, and appearance satisfaction. Effective merchandise display helps shoppers to coordinate a cross-product mix and develop purchase intentions. Visual merchandising stimulates self-image congruence, ontological reasoning, and neurobehavioral outcomes leading to perceptual stimuli and satisfaction reinforcing the feeling of *seeing is experiencing*. The positive attitude toward seeing, believing, and experiencing leads to a decision-making phenomenon within the perceptual triangle of elements comprising knowing, experiencing, and being. The virtual merchandising through clear arraying of product portfolios and simultaneous display of contextual products have given wide options to the consumers, which has supported buying decisions and enabled the business model innovation among the digital retail competitors (Mostaghel et al. 2022). One of the major impacts of digital technologies has been toward 3V factors comprising value creation, value delivery, and value capture. AI and VR have supported the consumer learning process on product design, attributes, and values, which have helped consumers to make appropriate buying decisions quickly. In addition to AI and VR, the chatbots and robot-driven responses have enhanced the consumer experience online and supported consumer perceptions on *seeing is experiencing*.

The fusion of conventional communication, brick-and-mortar shopping behavior, and community interactions with technology-led virtual shopping experiences have encouraged consumers to attain a holistic experience of virtual merchandising and an integrated buying experience. Virtual communications supported by enhanced products information, real-time prices, customization advise, order and delivery tracking, and information on purchased transactions have supported consumer perceptions and purchase intentions on various retail technology platforms (Riegger et al. 2021). Fashion apparel is effectively promoted on social media mainly targeting Twitter, Facebook, Instagram, and Tik Tok through emoticons, social speech tags, and unigrams and bigrams linguistic tags. The virtual display mannequins with anthropomorphic dimensions presenting the human-like musculoskeletal morphology attract consumers to explore the array of products on virtual retail sites to make instant purchase decisions. In addition, embedded videos of models anchoring vogue products on virtual retailing websites stimulate appearance similarity, physical congruence, and social consciousness among consumers to inculcate purchase intentions (Song and Kim 2020). The visual effects on proximity to customers and factors influencing the relationship marketing strategy are illustrated in Figure 2.3.

Visual proximity and customer centricity are largely influenced by information outreach, information appeal, and the potential to nurture both face-to-face and virtual relationships as exhibited in Figure 2.3. Customer-centric companies can be engaged in providing information

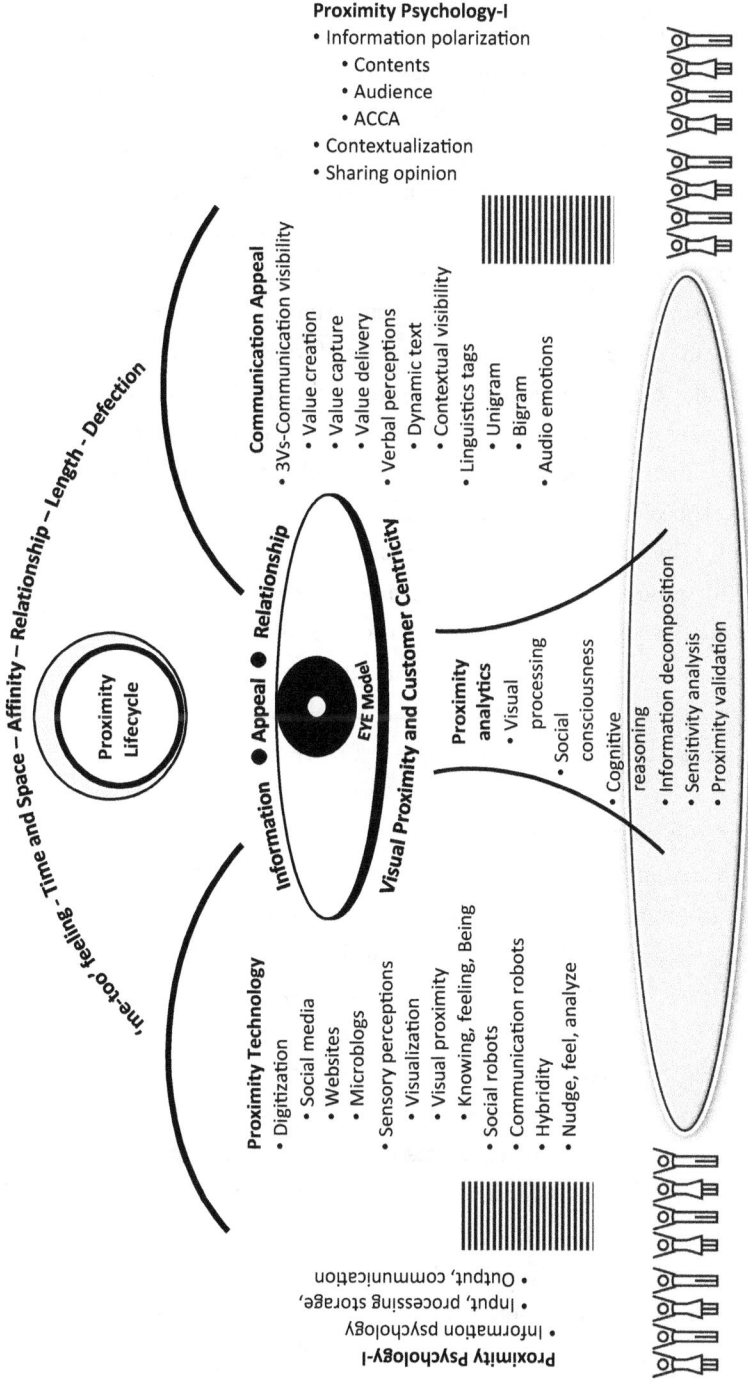

Figure 2.3 Visual proximity and customer centricity

Source: Author.

literacy by accelerating vertical (within a specific market) and horizontal (across geodemographic segments in new destinations) to enhance social proximity. By stimulating the consumers to share their prolonged experience on social platforms and analyzing their cognitive feelings, firms can architect EYE model of proximity marketing, which comprises empowerment, yearning, and emotions. Empowering consumers to lead and manage interactive information forums on products, competition, corporate policies, and PNS factors contributes to the expansion of customer proximity, outreach, and value perceptions (POV). Localized forums can culminate in a regional and global forum. LEGO forums and handicrafts forums in India follow such communication hierarchy, where local artisans interact with the institutional forum to refine their design thinking concepts and processes. Such upward movement drives POV and offers opportunity to them to put forth their point of view as well. The proximity metrics can be analyzed by the firms by measuring the input- and output time of processing visual communications, information decomposition effects (number of views and extent of information entropy), and information effectiveness to proximity. Cognitive reasoning at the individual and social level helps firms in analyzing social consciousness and sensitivity in consolidating perceptions of people on categorical interactions across social domains, interest groups, and information leads. Proximity technology has transformed physical interactions to digital platforms, which attracts sensory perceptions through visualization, visual proximity, and inculcating the sense of knowing, feeling, and being. Hybridity in information systems and social robotics have significantly contributed to indoctrinating the wisdom of nudge, feel, and analyze the crowd information or CI, which is pivotal in building proximity among people, society, and firm.

In managing proximity-based strategies, firms need to consider the proximity life cycle, which has six stages in response to the communication of brands of a firm. These stages of life cycle consist of me-too feeling (attraction to join the brand community), time and space (brand evolution and platform), affinity (peer response and point of view), relationship (consistency in interactions and proximity to the community), length (desired time frame to stay with the community), and defection (quitting the digital space, polarization, and migrating to other communities). The proximity life cycle significantly affects the proximity marketing strategy of the firms. Therefore, firms need to meticulously develop the communication visibility appeal and drive proximity campaigns focusing on 3V factors, which embed the challenges of value creation, value capture, and value delivery. Verbal and nonverbal perceptions can enhance the communication appeal using the dynamic text and augmenting the contextual visibility with the text, word cloud, semantics, and images. As language plays a critical role in generating communication appeal, linguistic tags such as unigram (I, We, You, They, Us) and bigram (I love, You win, Run ahead) tend to consolidate consumer perception and bring them to a proximity. The language tags, therefore, have wide geodemographic effects in both corporate and crowd communications to build proximity. In convergence of communication and cognition, the psychology of information input, processing, storage, output, and verbal or nonverbal communication performs a significant role. In addition, the quality of contents, attributes of target audience, and ACCA factors determine the interest of the target audience to polarize with the proximity drive of the firms.

The phenomenon of *seeing is experiencing* is founded on the maxims of visual perceptions, which leads to cognitive reasoning and developing perceptions on the visual objects. The visual data is analyzed within internal neural space, forms perceptual images, and drives cognitive reasoning through perceptual motions. The theories of visual perceptions argue that visual objects are perceived through neural networks and cognitive brain imaging to develop contextual semantics and decision making by the subjects. Visual perceptions are often sensitive to judgments, as inadequate construction of visual scenarios generate a gap between cognitive actualization and deception. Visual perceptions are affected by the quality of construction of visual scenario, cognitive inhibition, speed of visuals, and the combination of verbal (dynamic text) and nonverbal (contextual image, color, music, graphics, and appearance of anchors) elements. The scientific development on the theory of visual perceptions has indicated several neural space dynamisms in mapping visual perceptions through visual pathways, optic tract, and topographical images (Jerath et al. 2018) within visual space. The visual perceptions are stimulated by motion and dynamics, and oscillatory activities. These factors drive the brain activity for visual processing, decomposing information, and analyzing the effects of visual consciousness.

The social theory of appearance states that the virtual appearance of fashion objects influences purchase intentions and conformity in association with the social identity model, which integrates self-image congruence and individual value perceptions to justify the appearance-based consumption decision. The switching of virtual images of fashion apparel to self-image congruence-based physical appearance helps individuals to make judgment on the 4A factors comprising appearance, adorability, anthropomorphism, and anxiety marginalization. Accordingly, virtual merchandising develops congruence with the body image. The fashion apparel being displayed on various social media channels such as Facebook, Twitter, and Instagram are exhibited through the innovative devices such as VR glasses to enhance the body image and bridge the gap between VR and physical appearance.

The cognitive reasoning and decision-making process can be explained by emphasizing the Heider's Balance Theory (Heider 1958), which supports individual and group problem-solving by describing experimental behavior among consumers. The visual merchandizing showcased by fashion apparel firms stimulates psychosocial perceptions within the framework of PNS factors that lead the expected performance of apparel, body image, and social validation. The balance theory proposes that consumers prefer an equilibrium between need-based decisions (consistent and coherent) and cognitive reasoning influenced by beliefs and attitudes. Heider's theory proposed different elements of human cognition supported by individual and social reasoning. Accordingly, the structural properties of virtual merchandising, social networks, and individual and group behavior tend to balance the positive and negative sentimental relations such as like versus dislike, approve versus disapprove, familiar versus unfamiliar buying decisions of consumers.

The content analysis of the study suggests that virtual shopping with a wide array of visual merchandising enhances the visual perceptions of consumers to critically examine their choices and narrow their preferred buying decisions. Visual perceptions stimulate the sensory inputs to the brain to evaluate their experiences to derive purchase decisions. The result of the study supports the theory of visual perceptions bridging the intangible (visual merchandising) and tangible (shopping behavior) platforms within the virtual shopping ecosystem. The high interactivity images enhance ownership and product valuations during online shopping using mobile devices. This experience enhances the scope of the theory of visual perceptions. The study reveals that personal beliefs about online shopping builds the interdependence between physical attractiveness and choice of merchandise on virtual channels to drive satisfactory and romantic relationship among consumers. Such consumption behavior supports the theory of reasoning and the theory of appearance and reality.

E-commerce platforms displaying fashion apparel can be successful with user-friendly technology by optimizing the information at a single click. Virtual retailers of fashion products need to understand the shoppers' perspective for personalizing 3D store atmospherics (Ha et al. 2007). Though consumers enjoy browsing products, they might withdraw interest if navigation becomes complex and nonsuggestive to explore identical or similar products. Firms engaged in the marketing of fashion apparel through virtual platforms need to ensure display of varieties and arraying products to facilitate easy search with no time limits for making buying decisions. Hurrying consumers to make buying decisions and timebound canceling of shopping carts not only cause dissatisfaction but also build distrust toward the brand. Product attractiveness should be the primary concern for the retailers to build their virtual stores, which also matters to consumers in navigating the products. The navigational support can be enhanced by displaying suggestive products with visual endorsements (videos) to develop awareness, comprehension, conviction, and action among consumers engaged in virtual shopping. The anthropomorphic emotions can be developed by the retailers through celebrity endorsements, consumer-oriented videos, and social voices. Virtual retailers should consider modularization of displaying, arraying, and recommending contextual products by similar design, color, size, fashion trends, seasonality, and perceived use values. The anthropomorphic emotions contribute to self-actualization and self-esteem, which helps the consumers in nonconflictive decision making. Virtual retailers should also develop online simulators based on anthropometric data of consumers to drive visual stimulus and help them in experiencing the body image congruence with apparels. Online fashion apparel retailing firms should also be engaged in developing user-generated contents through communications on social media encouraging experiential videos, slogans, and reviews. In addition, retailing firms also need to conduct data-text mining to learn the consumer experiences posted on discrete platforms such as microblogs (Rajagopal and Rajagopal 2023).

Case Studies

Interactive Marketing: Heineken USA

Heineken, a Dutch brewing company, used an interactive video as a marketing tool for a part of a HR campaign in 2016 to showcase the work culture in the company, visualizing it as an employee-friendly environment. The video illustrated the fun company culture with focus on freedom to work in a destressing corporate work culture.[3] The video shows recruiters checking the personality of candidates and introducing them to the corporate work culture of the firm. In the video, the employer asks 12 questions, the answers to which let candidates decide whether they are a good fit for Heineken. The interactive marketing campaign has gone viral, and the company has seen an increase in the number of applicants by three times. The engagement statistics have shown that this interactive campaign had crowd appeal and 67 percent of the users took all the tests and spent nearly seven minutes watching the video. This marketing campaign not only focused on the recruitment needs and corporate ambience but also promoted proximity of crowd to the company.

In addition, Heineken launched a global campaign featuring a bottle opener that instantly shuts down all work appliances as the bottle of Heineken is opened. The video titled "The Closer" addresses a growing work–life imbalance in the busy corporate work culture and inspires them to stop overworking.[4] Dramatizing the campaign through the video appeal, the film delivers the solutions to the always-on work culture. Heineken brand emphasizes that this proximity video based on the crowd sentiments and hidden PNS factors, "The Closer" bottle opener empowers employees through this media to have a work–life balance.

---

[3] For details, see Heineken video on YouTube www.youtube.com/watch?v=0QoGzV72wR8.

[4] For details, see Heineken video on YouTube www.youtube.com/watch?v=cP3JRx4p9BQ&t=7s.

This campaign explores the PNS factors to outreach customers and reaffirm the proximity of the company to the people. The video begins with an office employee stuck in a meeting, unable to meet his friend who is at a party. Leveraging this opportunity to introduce both its Heineken bottles using the bottle opener, the employee then finds that with the opening of the bottle all work appliances begin shutting down and the office becomes totally dark. As the video progresses, it showcases the same happening at different places where employees are working including in a world summit, news broadcast room, and even a bar. Consequently, the video ends with the employees being able to take a break from their work and enjoy themselves while holding Heineken bottles.

Heineken promotes proximity marketing and manages changing relationships with the customers and stakeholders through the carefully crafted social media campaigns such as #ShareTheSofa and #ChampionThe-Match. These initiatives support the marketing efforts by enhancing the proximity to people and delivering online interactions through boosting brand awareness and positioning the brand among the target customers. The company's popular social media platform is Facebook, which has over 20 million Likes and the company has optimized the Facebook page with a geotargeting approach. Heineken serves content-specific communication to their Facebook fans, which are aggregated by the general Likes tend to exhibit impressive result. In 2012, Brazil Fan page launched a famous real-time campaign called *One Like One Balloon*, which turned out to be incredibly successful in producing spectacular fan engagement and following. The idea behind such proximity marketing campaign was to answer to every new Page Like by blowing up a green balloon and placing it in the Brazilian Heineken's office space. The office space got full in just one (symbolically) day and this initiative had driven enormous user-generated contents in addition to more than 1 million new Fans in a short time.

Hindustan Unilever Limited in Developing Countries: India and Ethiopia

HUL, a multinational consumer product, has exhibited corporate excellence by developing an inclusive business model not only to create social value but also to market its products at the bottom-of-the-pyramid market segment. Implementing the inclusive business model, the company has focused on empowering rural women economically and create social value by providing opportunities to improve their social value and quality of life. The inclusive business activities and initiatives of the company are aligned with their business operations and practices. Out of various projects of HUL, *Project Shakti*[5] has been able to deliver and create a positive impact on the people at the bottom of the pyramid, which provided substantial economic empowerment to the women stakeholders. *Project Shakti* enables rural women in villages across India to nurture an entrepreneurial mindset and become financially independent. Their role enables them to sell HUL products to the small retail outlets in their immediate village as well as directly to the households within the community. This project was launched in 2001, with an objective to empower underprivileged rural women by training them in health and hygiene and allowing them to undertake income-generation activities such as distribution and retailing of HUL consumer brands.

The women, known as *Vanis* (communicators) have been engaged in selling soap, shampoo, and other personal care products of HUL through social forums such as schools and village gatherings. *Project Shakti* entrepreneurs, who are commonly known as *Shakti Ammas* (empowered women in local dialect and ethnic expressions), reach out to over 4 million households across 1,65,000 villages spread over different states in India. These households form a new market for HUL where its products are sold, generating revenue for the company, while simultaneously improving the per capita income. This model expanded the outreach of products of the company and employment opportunities to the rural women. HUL also promotes skill development by providing training in sales practices, financial knowledge, and bookkeeping to help them become microentrepreneurs. The company had increased the number of *Shakti* entrepreneurs to 75,000 in 2015 in which women entrepreneurs were complemented by 48,000 *Shaktimaans* (empowered men in local dialect and ethnic expressions), who are typically the husbands or brothers of

---

[5] For details on the Shakti experiment of Hindustan Unilever Limited toward adapting to the diversity and inclusivity in business, see www.unilever.com/news/news-search/2019/becoming-a-micro-entrepreneur-in-rural-colombia/ (accessed March 12, 2022).

the women entrepreneurs. *Shaktimaans* sell HUL's products on bicycles in surrounding villages, covering a larger area than *Shakti Ammas* used to cover on foot. At the end of 2020, we have nearly 1,36,000 Shakti entrepreneurs spread across 18 states. *Project Shakti* has helped generate income by selling our products and has created a great impact on the livelihoods of women. This project has been designed, developed, and delivered by Unilever as a strategy to enhance social proximity of the company by empowering women.

After the success of *Shakti* program in India, Unilever Ethiopia has launched the *Shakti* initiative, creating as a last-mile distribution channel in rural Ethiopia to explore substantial latent market opportunities. This program aims to address the promise of achieving greater diversity, equity, and inclusion in its business strategy of the company. Accordingly, the program rollout has proved highly challenging. To facilitate the initiative, Unilever Ethiopia's search for a partner had led to Kidame Mart, a local social enterprise and with the funding from Unilever, the Kidame Mart recruited economically vulnerable women in rural Ethiopia as *Shakti* entrepreneurs and provided them a basket of Unilever goods with a few noncompeting items from other companies to sell locally (London 2022). The rural salesmen extended their support to both men and women entrepreneurs by going beyond their traditional roles of capturing demand, driving awareness on handwashing, and maintaining proper hygiene. Experiencing the *Project Shakti Model*, similar programs have been launched by the company across Sri Lanka, Pakistan, Egypt, and Columbia. And so, the journey of *Project Shakti* continues beyond 2021.

Summary

Interactive marketing and proximity have become symbiotic with the advancement of information technology. Social media and interactive marketing have been proved to be a good tool for firms to implement proximity approaches, enhance local operations by opening niches, and widen their social outreach. In interactive communication, all communities exchange their attention, interest, desire, and action distinctly with the specific interest groups. Thus, the critical mass of consumers is socially constructed by individuals, based on their communication with others in their system. This chapter argues that interactive marketing today empowers consumers to raise voices both for and against the firm's innovation, manufacturing, distribution, and marketing policies. Most customer-centric companies such as Unilever, Starbucks, Mary Kay Cosmetics, Kellogg's, Nestlé, and IKEA have customized their websites and installed digital device interfaces to learn customer views, needs, and proposed solutions. Customer-centric firms practice interactive marketing using various customer-convenience tools such as direct mail, catalog retailing, telemarketing, social media channels, digital advertising and marketing, and mobile marketing. Cutting-edge technologies significantly affect the social and industrial development in transitional economies. AI in marketing has a new space to grow in the customer-centric firms. AI has gone beyond robotics structures for the customers, as it is now emerging as a tool for decision making among consumer-oriented firms. The chapter argues that the prominent technological edges that drive challenge-based research include AI, augmented reality, VR, wearable technology, robotics, and big data analytics.

Direct-to-customer marketing strategies, convenience shopping, and social media-driven marketing approaches of companies have increased social and cultural influence on developing consumer behavior. These approaches enhance the social proximity of firms, which can be measured through geographical, cognitive, organizational, institutional, social, and personal connectivity. These proximity measures significantly influence managerial decisions and affect the success of collaborative approaches with key partners in business including consumers. Therefore, geographical proximity is an essential approach for the firms to explore PNS factors and possibilities to cocreate innovative products. Social proximity can be achieved through both interpersonal word-of-mouth and sharing of experience on digital platforms. The chapter reveals that the fusion of conventional communication, brick-and-mortar shopping behavior, and community interactions with technology-led shopping experiences have encouraged consumers to attain a holistic buying experience of consumers. One of the new concepts on visual proximity has been discussed in this chapter by illustrating the EYE model. Firms can architect EYE model of proximity marketing, which comprises empowerment, yearning, and emotions. This model can help firms in motivating consumers to share their prolonged experience on social platforms and analyze their cognitive feelings. It is therefore advised that firms need to meticulously develop the communication visibility appeal and drive proximity campaigns focusing on 3V factors, which embed the challenges of value creation, value capture, and value delivery.

References

Andrade, M.S. 2007. "Learning Communities: Examining Positive Outcomes." *Journal of College Student Retention: Research, Theory and Practice* 9, no. 1, pp. 1–20.

Avery, J., S. Fournier, and J. Wittenbraker. 2014. "Unlock the Mysteries of Your Customer Relationships." *Harvard Business Review* 92, no. 7, pp. 72–81.

Berezan, O., A.S. Krishen, S. Agarwal, and P. Kachroo. 2018. "The Pursuit of Virtual Happiness: Exploring the Social Media Experience Across Generations." *Journal of Business Research* 89, pp. 455–461.

Bouquet, C., J.L. Barsoux, and M. Wade. 2018. "Bring Your Breakthrough Ideas to Life." *Harvard Business School Digital Article.* Cambridge: Harvard Business School Press.

Buhalis, D., T. Harwood, V. Bogicevic, G. Viglia, S. Beldona, and C. Hofacker. 2019. "Technological Disruptions in Services: Lessons From Tourism and Hospitality." *Journal of Service Management* 30, no. 4, pp. 484–506.

Chaturvedi, A. and J.D. Carroll. 1998. "A Perceptual Mapping Procedure for Analysis of Proximity Data to Determine Common and Unique Product-market Structures." *European Journal of Operational Research* 111, no. 2, pp. 268–284.

Geisler, E. 2007. "The Metrics of Knowledge: Mechanisms for Preserving the Value of Managerial Knowledge." *Business Horizons* 50, no. 6, pp. 467–477.

George, A.J., E. Rajkumar, R. John, R. Lakshmi, and M. Wajid. 2021. "Mindfulness-Based Eudaimonic Enhancement for Well-Being of Individuals With Alcohol-Dependence: A Pilot Randomized Controlled Study." *The Open Psychology Journal* 14, no. 1, pp. 167–178.

Gere, A., A. Harizi, N. Bellissimo, H. Moskowitz, and Z. Kókai. 2022. "Consumer-Driven- and Consumer-Perceptible Food Innovation." In *Innovation Strategies in the Food Industry*, ed. C.M. Galanakis, 97–120. 2nd ed. Cambridge, MA: Academic Press.

Gupta, A. and V. Govindarajan. 2000. "Knowledge Management's Social Dimension: Lessons From Nucor Steel." *MIT Sloan Management Review* 42, no. 1, pp. 71–81.

Gupta, S. and D. Shapiro. 2014. "Building and Transforming an Emerging Market Global Enterprise: Lessons From the Infosys Journey." *Business Horizons* 57, no. 2, pp. 169–179.

Ha, Y., W.A. Kwon, and S.J. Lennon. 2007. "Online Visual Merchandising (VMD) of Apparel Shopping Experience in an Online Store." *Journal of Interactive Marketing* 25, pp. 159–168.

Heider, F. 1958. *The Psychology of Interpersonal Relations*. New York, NY: Wiley.

Hsu, J. 2022. "Using AI to Train Robot Dogs Makes Them Cheaper." *New Scientist* 256, no. 3411, p. 14.

Jerath, R., S.M. Cearley, V.A. Barnes, and M. Jensen. 2018. "Micro-Calibration of Space and Motion by Photoreceptors Synchronized in Parallel With Cortical Oscillations: A Unified Theory of Visual Perception." *Medical Hypotheses* 110, pp. 71–75.

Jörling, M., R. Böhm, and S. Paluch. 2019. "Service Robots: Drivers Perceived Responsibility for Service Outcomes." *Journal of Service Research* 22, no. 4, pp. 404–420.

Kalyanam, K. and M. Zweben. 2005. "Perfect Message at the Perfect Moment." *Harvard Business Review* 83, no. 11, pp. 112–120.

Khanna, P. 2012. *The Rise of Hybrid Governance*. New York, NY: McKinsey & Company.

Khanna, T. and B. Gupta. 2014. *Health City Cayman Island*. Cambridge, MA: Harvard Business School Publications.

Krishen, A.S., Y.K. Dwivedi, N. Bindu, and K.K. Satheesh. 2021. "A Broad Overview of Interactive Digital Marketing: A Bibliometric Network Analysis." *Journal of Business Research* 131, pp. 183–195.

Lafley, A.G. and R. Martin. 2017. *Customer Loyalty Is Overrated*. Cambridge: Harvard Business School Press.

Leone, D., F. Schiavone, F.P. Appio, and B. Chiao. 2021. "How Does Artificial Intelligence Enable and Enhance Value Co-Creation in Industrial Markets? An Exploratory Case Study in the Healthcare Ecosystem." *Journal of Business Research* 129, pp. 849–859.

London, T. 2022. *Unilever Ethiopia's Shakti Initiative: Building a Rural Sales Channel*. Cambridge, MA: Harvard Business School Press.

Molina, A. and Rajagopal 2023. *Challenge-Based Learning, Research, and Innovation: Leveraging Industry, Government, and Society*. A Palgrave Macmillan Imprint. Cham, Switzerland: Springer.

Mostaghel, R., P. Oghazi, V. Parida, and V. Sohrabpour. 2022. "Digitalization Driven Retail Business Model Innovation: Evaluation of Past and Avenues for Future Research Trends." *Journal of Business Research* 146, pp.134–145.

Ooms, W. and R. Piepenbrink. 2021. "Open Innovation for Wicked Problems: Using Proximity to Overcome Barriers." *California Management Review* 63, no. 2, pp. 62–100.

Potter, C. and G. Naidoo. 2009. "Evaluating Large-Scale Interactive Radio Programs." *Distance Education* 30, no. 1, pp. 117–141.

Rajagopal and A. Rajagopal. 2023. "'Seeing Is Experiencing': Impact of Showcasing Fashion Merchandises on Digital Platforms." *Qualitative Market Research.* Vol. ahead-of-print No. ahead-of-print. https://doi.org/10.1108/QMR-05-2022-0080.

Rajagopal. 2013. *Managing Social Media and Consumerism: The Grapevine Effect in Competitive Markets.* Basingstoke, UK: Palgrave Macmillan.

Rajagopal. 2021. *Crowd-Based Business Models—Using Collective Intelligence for Market Competitiveness.* New York, NY: Palgrave Macmillan.

Riegger, A.S., J.F. Klein, K. Merfeld, and S. Henkel. 2021. "Technology-Enabled Personalization in Retail Stores: Understanding Drivers and Barriers." *Journal of Business Research* 123, pp. 140–155.

Rogers, E.M. 1995. *Diffusion of Innovations.* New York, NY: Free Press.

Shankar, V. and E.C. Malthouse. 2007. "The Growth of Interactions and Dialogues in Interactive Marketing." *Journal of Interactive Marketing* 21, no. 2, pp. 2–4.

Sidibe, M. 2020. "Marketing Meets Mission." *Harvard Business Review Digital Article.* Cambridge: Harvard Business School Press.

Song, S.Y. and Y.K. Kim. 2020. "Factors Influencing Consumers' Intention to Adopt Fashion Robot Advisors: Psychological Network Analysis." *Clothing and Textiles Research Journal* 40, no. 1, pp. 3–18.

Whitla, P. 2009. "Crowdsourcing and Its Application in Marketing Activities." *Contemporary Management Research* 5, no. 1, pp. 15–28.

Zha, D., P. Foroudi, T.C. Melewar, and Z. Jin. 2022. "Experiencing the Sense of the Brand: The Mining, Processing and Application of Brand Data Through Sensory Brand Experiences." *Qualitative Market Research* 25, no. 2, pp. 205–232.

CHAPTER 3

Social Psychodynamics

Overview

This chapter discusses various perspectives on social dynamics establishing information-diffusion patterns with cyclical and elliptical moves; diffusion and integration of communication; and centripetal and centrifugal strategies of communication, relationship, and social dynamics. With the advancement of information and communication technology (ICT), online social networks such as Twitter and Digg have provided unprecedented quantities of graphic and text data to network users, which are used within the predetermined circle of personal contacts (circular). The information also spreads through snowballing across the social media platforms (elliptical) over time and space. Such communication patterns have promoted various subways of information diffusion at the niche and local social networks causing both push (brand thrust) and pull (demand stimulation) for products and services. The push–pull factors have been discussed in this chapter in the context of welfare-marketing and marketing strategies at the bottom of the pyramid segment. This chapter also discusses the spiral effects of social proximity of firms by illustrating the attributes of centripetal and centrifugal proximity. This discussion is followed by the categorical analysis of various stages involved in the planning and implementation of proximity strategies. The role of corporate social responsibility with focus on consumer outreach, corporate commitment, and customer engagement has also been critical to this chapter. The case studies on welfare marketing and cause marketing have been discussed in this chapter to support the concepts and arguments on social psychodynamics affecting marketing strategies of the firm.

Proximity Patterns

Diffusion is a process in society that flows bidirectionally, circularly, or within the communities in a single or double loop and in an elliptical way with wider outreach and closer proximity. In the process of social diffusion, information is spread geodemographically across destinations through social interactions. The social proximity and information flow encompass hybrid techniques including conventional evolution of information path through physical interface and simultaneously moving through the digital platforms engaging social media and ethnographic broadcast. Proximity circles have a lot of locus points on a social platform. They are equidistant from all geodemographic segments comprising social clusters, neighborhoods, socioeconomic levels, gender, age, preferences, social consciousness, social media, and consumption. The equidistance can be measured from one point at its center to infinite number of points. The elliptical proximity is largely based on two axes: firms with the controlled manufacturing, marketing, and services operations govern the long axis, while the society, stakeholders, and consumers govern the short axis, which is equally important to construct the social proximity. Mathematically and managerially, proximity can be explained as the core output of social psychodynamics, which converges society, crowd, and firms in proximity-based decision making in employing marketing strategies effectively.

The rising digital information acquisition and dissemination system have laid increasing importance on building intellectual assets contributed by the consumers, crowd, and competition in the market (3C factors). These assets have encouraged firms to improve social proximity, outreach to consumers, and value creation (POV) underlying their businesses. Knowledge management in the social domain is a sociopsychological approach to motivate consumers, stakeholders, and key partners in business to consolidate their points of view on the products and services of the firms and refocus partnership vision in business. Customer-centric firms operating in health care, food marketing, fashion, consumer electronics, and services are leaning toward knowledge-based proximity marketing strategies through information management systems on social and interactive media. The knowledge-based proximity marketing model in a circular system is built around 6A factors as follows:

- Awareness (sharing experience, point-of-views, and research outputs)
- Attributes (taxonomy of knowledge consisting of learned, acquired, and interrelated domains)

- Appraisal (consumers and stakeholders evaluate proximity program of the firm and their roles)
- Acquaintance (motivating informal association with brands, firm, and market ecosystem)
- Acquisition (firm expands proximity and outreach to the consumers and society)
- Alignment (firm develops alignment strategies with acquired consumers, drives collective intelligence, motivates cocreation of brands, and coevolves with consumers and crowd)

As a conscious practice of consumer acquisition, proximity, and expanding outreach to consumers in a market, firms tend to strengthen their public ties through social media channels, information repositories like Chat GPT, and Internet search engines. However, there are two different knowledge management strategies in practice. In some firms that manage products of common needs, knowledge is carefully codified and stored in databases to be accessed and used by the consumers, stakeholders, and key partners in business; whereas some firms provide highly customized solutions, and knowledge is disseminated through interpersonal exchanges. In either of these two practices of knowledge management, firms must use knowledge, adaptability, and proximity to support the competitive strategy. Emphasizing the wrong proximity strategy might adversely affect the business of the firm and give leverage to the competitors (Hansen et al. 1999).

Information diffusion and proximity cycle have five social actors comprising lead catalysts, early adopters, early majority, late majority, and footdraggers. The lead catalysts acquire information and rediffuse them within the neighborhood to analyze and make decisions with confidence. The catalysts constitute the core of the information diffusers and attract early adopters who intend to join the core and raise confidence within the neighborhood on the information disseminated. Such forward move of crowd, consumers, and collaborators helps the firms enhance their proximity in society and expand their outreach to the consumers. Lead catalysts and early adopters of corporate and crowd communication significantly influence the population in early and late majority except the footdraggers who are indifferent to any information spread, proximity approaches, or outreach calls of the firms. In the early stage, information-diffusion and proximity-building attempts and the engagement of crowd, customers, and collaborators are relatively low as firms do not put adequate resources in developing the 6A factors. Firms invite lead catalysts in this stage to test the innovated product and influence early adopters' brand association and collaboration with the firm. Lead users form a small group but act as powerful referrals and brand carriers. Firms spend adequate resources in the growth stage to diffuse product innovation attributes through direct communication on a one-on-one basis to drive intensive effect on the innovation-led products among early adopters. Consumers and crowd in this group are strong followers of the lead users and stand as effective opinion leaders for influencing the early majority of consumers. Most companies deploy enormous resources in advertising, communication, and social media involvement during the late growth and maturity stage to drive the customers who are less affluent and less educated but ready to experiment the innovative products. The "early majority" consumer segment constitutes a relatively larger segment than the previous consumer segments, but it is confined to a niche. However, the following stage is of late majority, which is a very large segment and often represents about half of the total number of consumers in each market area. This consumer segment exhibits high adaptability with the innovative products and derives satisfactory value for money that makes the late majority consumers frequent buyers. Consumers in this segment are sensitive to price and quality. There is a threat of deflection when more attractive substitute products penetrate the market. However, a small number of consumers in each market segment are hard to convince and develop confidence as they are indecisive and difficult to convince. The circular and elliptical elements of social proximity to firms are illustrated in Figure 3.1.

Social proximity to be explored by the customer-centric firms has two broad spiral relationship bands illustrated as circular and elliptical proximity in Figure 3.1. Both relationship bands of social proximity are driven by interpersonal and digital information loops from the origin of information (firm, government, society, or crowd) through the course of information transition from one form to another (exclamation, excitement, empathetic, and experiential). The course of information flow

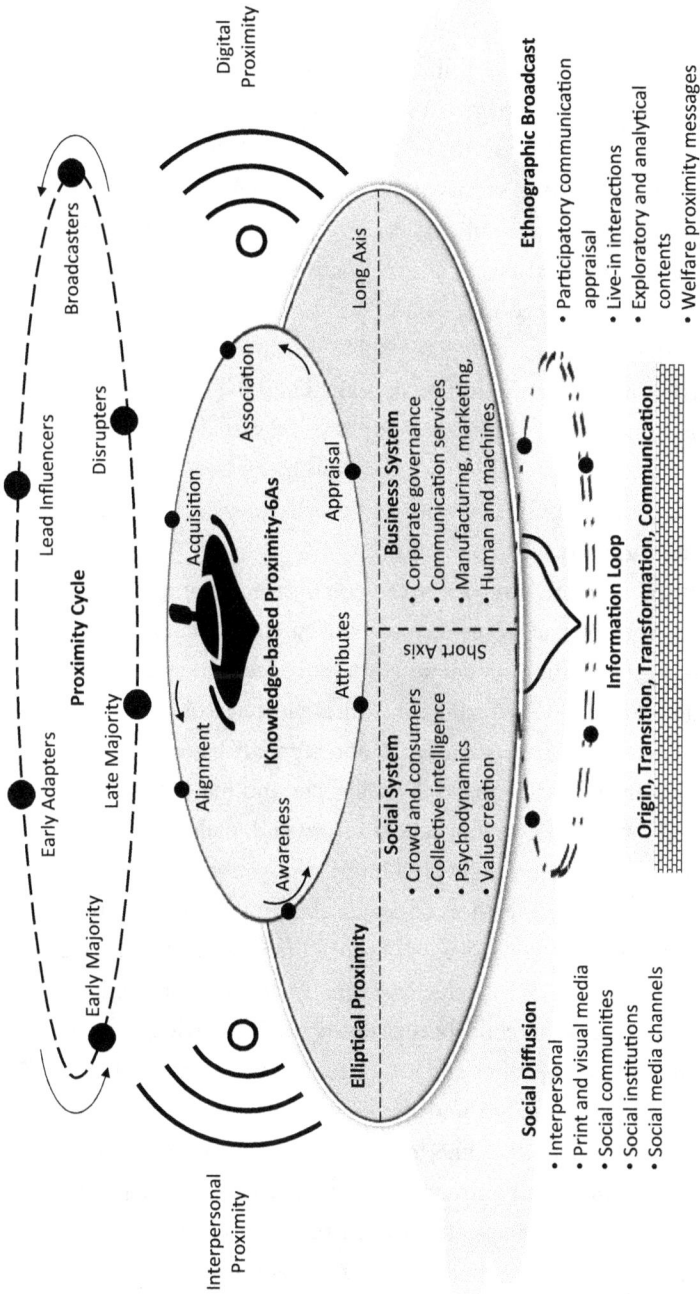

Figure 3.1 *Attributes of circular and elliptical proximity*

Source: Author.

through sociopsychological transitions tends to transform into verbal (readable) and nonverbal (viewable) delivery modes for effective communication. Effective diffusion of information is a significant driver of social penetration for business firms to enhance social proximity and consumer outreach. Firms engaged in social and consumer-product marketing adapt to social diffusion through interpersonal, print and visual media, digital platforms, and social communities. Social institutions such as self-help groups, nongovernmental organizations, and neighborhood communities besides social media channels also significantly contribute to the social diffusion processes of information. In the semiurban and rural areas, firms can focus on ethnographic broadcast of information through participatory communication appraisals and live-in interactions following an ethnographic approach to explore and analyze. The ethnographic broadcast can help in developing possible user-generated contents aiming at co-creating messages for welfare and well-being of consumers to strengthen the corporate social proximity.

The elliptical proximity to society can be constructed and measured on the long axis of business ecosystem as illustrated in Figure 3.1. The business system embedding corporate governance, communication services, manufacturing, and marketing constitutes the long axis of the social proximity as often firms have slow, short, and segment-based proximity. However, the convergence of artificial intelligence and machine learning has accelerated the proximity approaches of firms and made them attractive to the people. The short axis of elliptical proximity in society is a dynamic measure as the preferences of people change rapidly with crowd and consumer cognition, collective intelligence, interpersonal and social psychodynamics, and needs for value creation. The circular proximity of firms in society is based on contributing to the social knowledge on the innovation, technology, benefits, and value-creation programs of the firm across stakeholders, consumers, and the crowd in general. The knowledge-based circular proximity is knotted around the 6A approach in generating value, proximity, and outreach of the firm. The 6A is a sequential approach to enhance proximity of a firm in the society, which consists of generating **awareness** (A1) about the aims and approaches of the firm among the members of the society by emphasizing the **attributes** (A2) of actions and programs to allow the people to **appraise** (A3) the corporate action and match self-congruence to develop **association** (A4) with the firm. Moving forward from these stages, a firm will gain confidence in customer **acquisition** (A5) within the society using the proximity leverage of the firm and frame **alignment** (A6) of consumers and social leaders with the corporate policies. Unilever in India has followed the 6A approach to acquire, align, and empower rural women in Shakti program not only to enhance brand market but also to widen the social proximity of the firm. Similarly, ITC Agribusiness Division of Indian Tobacco Company has penetrated the society and enhanced proximity through *e-choupal* (community meetings on digital platform), which helped the company to adapt to the 6A strategy for proximity marketing of their brands in rural areas of India.

The information loop comprising elliptical and circular proximity concepts is part of proximity cycle, which begins with information broadcasters who can be the employees of the firm, customers, stakeholders, or the crowd as shown in Figure 3.1. Social media platforms are commonly used to broadcast the news about innovation and technology, consumer experience, government interventions, and competitive moves. Broadcasters instigate communication through lead influencers, often known as corporate voices or brand ambassadors, who promote the information and relationship programs of the firm to early adapters. This segment influences early and late majority of people in society to the social moves of the firm over time, and the firm holistically succeeds in enhancing its social proximity. However, in society, a section of disruptors also exists, which can be critical to the current proximity policies but may offer critical lead to the broadcasters to reform relationship programs, communications, and actions of proximity marketing.

Comprehensive knowledge dissemination and trust play a pivotal role in creating customer value, in the absence of which knowledge barriers may limit the size of the market to a subset of customers in the short term. Exploring the synergy between online and offline channels in general reveals that a financial services institute typically delivers standardized, low-value-added transactions such as bill payments, product enquiries, mobile marketing, and credit transactions through the inexpensive Internet channel and specialized, high-value-added transactions such as small business lending, personal trust services, and investment banking through the more expensive branch channel. By providing more service options to its customers, an improved technology adoption will enable the retailers to retain their most profitable customers and generate more revenue from cross-selling. Many know Google for taking a developer-centric focus around the products it builds. It has encompassed this philosophy in the knowledge-dissemination vision of the company to figure out the challenge around social product design within the organization. Accordingly, Google proceeded to create a new network Google+ to get the entire organization reveal the real relationships their users have. It emerged as a product design strategy of the company. Such integrated platform has also facelifted the Google product line and its application. Other companies should also be considering this approach in their organization and may go beyond the role of a corporate social strategist. This generation of the Internet provides wide opportunity for consumers and companies toward the use of blogging tools to better engage the consumer in the cocreation, delivery, and dissemination of marketing messages to the target segments (Singh et al. 2008).

Proximity and market strategies can be implemented effectively by the firms understanding consumer preferences in the changing social and political perspectives. Toyota Motor's success with Prius developed brand awareness on sustainability consciousness and enhanced proximity with people by generating interest in environmentally friendly products. Unilever's innovative product offerings in developing countries, such as its Wheel detergent brand in India, have derived high response to the unmet needs of bottom-of-the-pyramid consumer segments, which has quadrupled the brand proximity through interactions on social media among the consumers in the society. The effectiveness of social media depends on the extent of the participation of consumers on the network platforms and the degree of corporate involvement. Most companies become aware of the risks on social media manipulations and proximity advantage in business; ignoring such risks may damage the stakeholders' value and corporate image in the long term. An understanding of the influence of various groups, their agendas, and their level of activism should be vital to a company to choose the right partners for involving sociopolitical networks in developing the business strategy. Firms should aggregate this information to identify the high-risk plots and need-action areas in the business administration of the firm. It is also necessary to develop potential future scenarios that can consider the reaction of competitors and shifts in consumer patterns. Increased success on corporate and customers' sides has laid the foundation for cocreating business models in which companies and social networks become the key parts of each other's capacity to deliver value (Burgmann and Prahalad 2007). Convergence of technology with customer value provides higher competitive advantage to the business to interact frequently with the complex market players and customers in achieving success in business. Convergence marketing is woven around the five Cs comprising customization, community, channels, competitive value, and choice that drive the "fusion" in the corporate marketing strategies (Wind and Mahajan 2001).

Most of the emerging firms are working hard in developing online social marketing programs and brand campaigns to reach consumers where they "live" virtually. However, the challenge faced by many companies is apparently the way to be active in social media as most firms do not have a clear understanding of how to manage the social networks effectively and what performance indicators should they be measuring and how. Furthermore, as companies develop social media strategies, platforms such as YouTube, Facebook, and Twitter are too often treated as stand-alone elements rather than a part of an integrated system. Firms should invest in building strategies in a systematic way to understand and conceptualize online social media as an ecosystem of related elements involving both digital and traditional media (Hanna et al. 2011). Firms must establish a process for delivering the voice of truth through right communication in social media platforms by disseminating authentic, trusted, and believable information. This reinforces the idea that social media can be promoted by the firms as a tool to voice ideas and concerns and get accurate and credible solutions on various issues of consumers. Social media and collective intelligence allow information to flow in multiple directions rather than just from the top down. Social media is an important addition to a traditional change management program, one that can dramatically increase the acceptance of change and advance an organization more predictably toward its business goals. Collaboration and social media tools can reduce the time needed by an organization to navigate large-scale change programs and deliver a better solution for consumer-related marketing issues in the future.

Visual effects and economic advantage associated with promotional products in the retail stores often stimulate compulsive buying behavior. The point-of-sales brochures, catalogs, and posters build an assumption on perceived use value and the motivational relevance of buying decisions of product. Emotional visuals exhibited on contextual factors of proximity to consumer segments and stimulus attributes drive positive perception of consumers on perceived satisfaction of the products (Codispoti and De Cesarei 2007). Firms demonstrate higher visual attention and increasing visual stimuli during the point-of-sales promotions. Consumers exhibit a muddled search strategy where economic and perceived use value benefits influence the buying decision process among customers. In addition, a pleasant store ambience where attractive displays, music, hands-on experience facilities, and recreation are integrated helps in maximizing the consumer arousal toward buying. It has been observed that consumers perceive a positive effect during interaction with sales promoters if product attraction is high (Wirtz et al. 2007).

The Spiral Effects

There are many spiral effects of communication moving back and forth from firm and society and vice versa, which significantly affect the corporate efforts to enhance social proximity and customer outreach. The corporate policies on communication set a broad framework of communication design, development, and delivery process, wherein engagement of customers and crowd is subjective to the needs of the firm. Firms driving customer and crowd engagement in cocreating communication for the market, customers, and stakeholders increases the possibility of a wider outreach and redefining the social proximity.

The value of a market communication is always contextually specific and is determined by the customer or the beneficiary. The effects of market communication lie on the communicators and responders to a great extent. Therefore, communication is a perspective of value creation and is virtually effective in driving the consumer perceptions on a particular company or business. The customer-centric strategies define coproduction and cocreation as the phenomena that are key to developing integrated marketing communication. In other words, how companies deal with their customers through customer participation in the joint creation of communication value needs to be understood by the firms (Vargo and Lusch 2004). Cocreation allows companies to continually tap the skills and insights of stakeholders and develop new ways of building value chain. Crowdsourcing platforms (physical and digital forums) are largely interactive for exploring new experiences and connections. The collective intelligence process grows organically in the organization as a system. Social media and the virtual society are growing together with technology and are supporting the *Generation Next* business today. Firms need to explore the sensory consumers and business space (C-suite) cocreation through wisdom of crowds (collective intelligence). The concept of *business model design space* describes the opportunities and constraints of creating and capturing value from niche and frugal technologies. The *Internet of Everything* has taken the firms a step forward by enabling them to connect with people to develop smart operational models in a wide range of industry sectors (Wesseling et al. 2020). The centripetal and centrifugal proximity approaches of the firm are the efforts to develop a convergent synergy of divergent factors that interfere with firm–society relationship to expand its outreach to consumers and stakeholders. These factors have spiral effects on both the ends of a firm and society, which are exhibited in Figure 3.2 (A) and (B) in a combined illustration.

Social proximity has two distinctive domains where information, communication, and relationships converge with divergent factors. These domains of social proximity include centripetal and centrifugal dynamics through which firms penetrate social relationship and society exhibits its behavioral system to firms, respectively. Figure 3.2 (A) and (B) illustrates the attributes of centripetal and centrifugal proximity. In both the domains of communication and relationship, society is the axis. In the centripetal domain, the strategies of the firm driving to the axis tend to nurture and widen the social proximity, while in the centrifugal domain, the sociopsychological behavior illustrates the need, engagement, and trend (NET) demanding the actions of the firm toward society. Figure 3.2 (A) exhibits nine strategy blocks with centripetal force driving toward society (axis) to create social proximity. Firms approach social proximity through information cocreation, communication dissemination, mode of communication, social programs, corporate social

1. Information Cocreation
- Resources
- Technology
- HR Support
- Innovation
- Public finance
- CSR projects

5. Corporate Social Responsibility
- Business democracy
- Social development
- Ethnic proximity
- Public–private partnership
- Empowerment
- Engagement

9. People
- Crowd cognition
- Randomization
- Collective intelligence
- Brainstorming
- Icebreaking

6. Gender Proximity
- Women and children
- Gender education and skills
- Leadership and social mobility

2. Communication Dissemination
- Brand ambassadors
  - Social and ethnic
- Social action teams
- Social institutions
- Self-help groups
- Nongovernmental organization
- Link public programs
- Corporate alliance
- Orientation programs
  - Society
  - Crowd (Open system)
  - Customers
  - Stakeholders

4. Social Programs
- Community clubs
- Women forums
- LMX programs
- Team thinking
- Goal-oriented proximity

8. Research
- Socioeconomic
- Ethnographic
- Challenge-based
- Business strategy
  - Design-to-market
  - Design-to-society
  - Design-to-value

7. Integration
- Public policies
- Coordination
- Corporate–local governance
- Reverse accountability
- Industry–society interface

3. Modes of Communication
- Verbal
- Nonverbal
  - Exhibits and videos
- Participatory Social Appraisals

Firm

Society

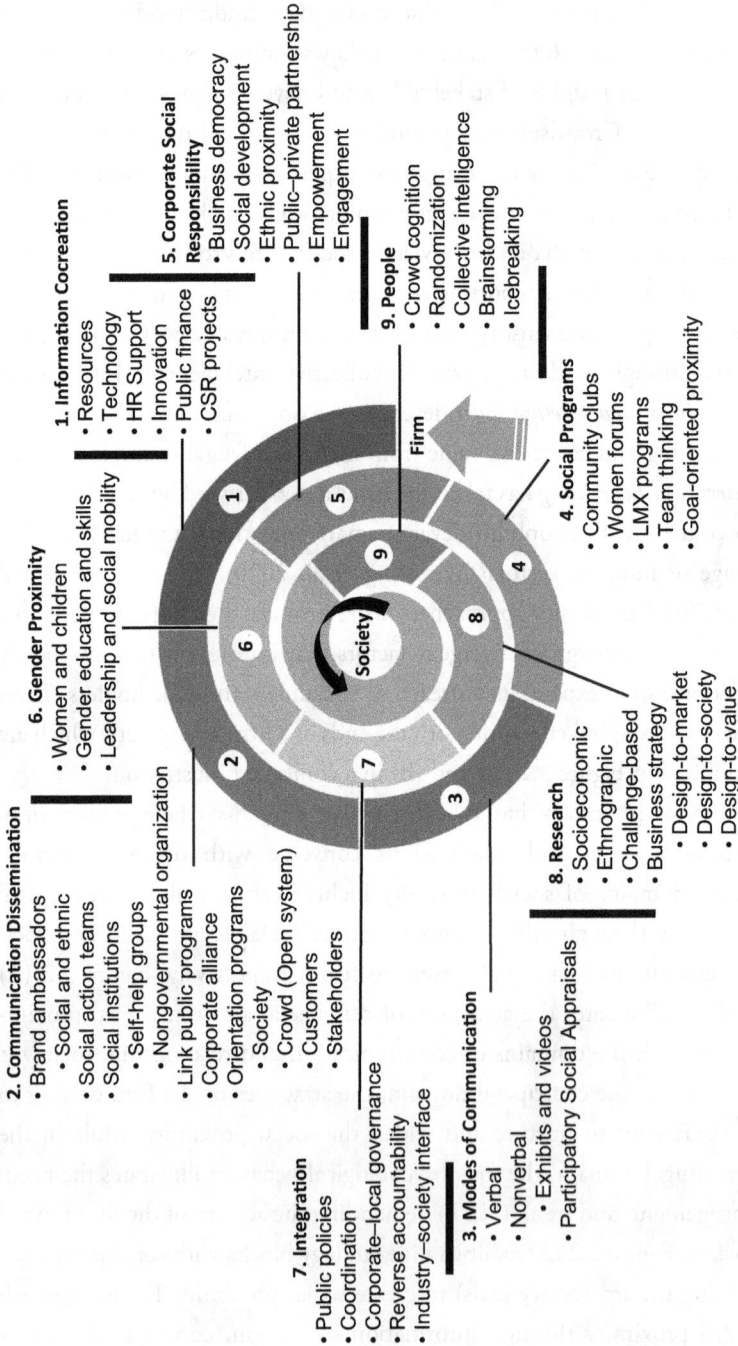

Figure 3.2 (A) Centripetal proximity

Source: Author.

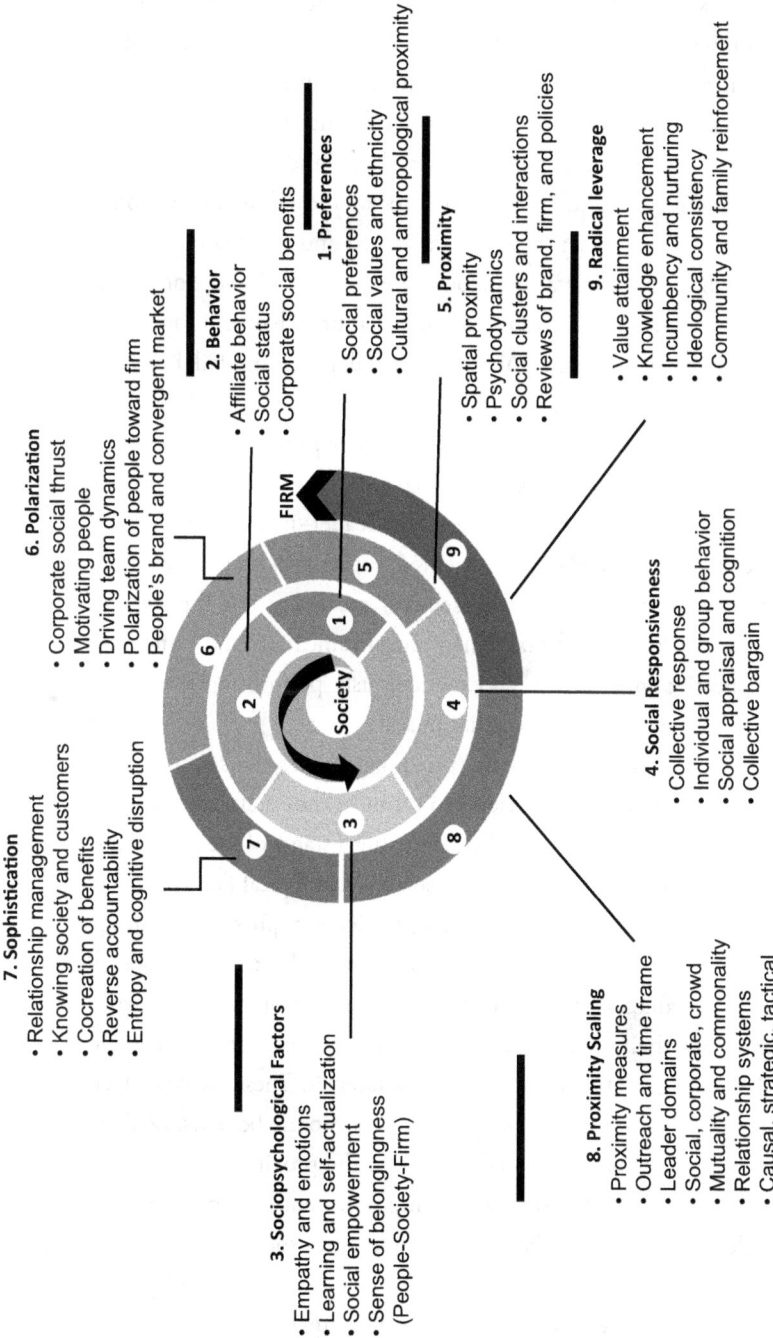

6. Polarization
· Corporate social thrust
· Motivating people
· Driving team dynamics
· Polarization of people toward firm
· People's brand and convergent market

2. Behavior
· Affiliate behavior
· Social status
· Corporate social benefits

1. Preferences
· Social preferences
· Social values and ethnicity
· Cultural and anthropological proximity

5. Proximity
· Spatial proximity
· Psychodynamics
· Social clusters and interactions
· Reviews of brand, firm, and policies

9. Radical leverage
· Value attainment
· Knowledge enhancement
· Incumbency and nurturing
· Ideological consistency
· Community and family reinforcement

7. Sophistication
· Relationship management
· Knowing society and customers
· Cocreation of benefits
· Reverse accountability
· Entropy and cognitive disruption

3. Sociopsychological Factors
· Empathy and emotions
· Learning and self-actualization
· Social empowerment
· Sense of belongingness
(People-Society-Firm)

4. Social Responsiveness
· Collective response
· Individual and group behavior
· Social appraisal and cognition
· Collective bargain

8. Proximity Scaling
· Proximity measures
· Outreach and time frame
· Leader domains
· Social, corporate, crowd
· Mutuality and commonality
· Relationship systems
· Causal, strategic, tactical

Figure 3.2 (B) Centrifugal proximity

Source: Author.

responsibility, gender proximity, integration, research, and people as the strategy blocks for centripetal proximity. Rapid advancement in ICT, human resources support, and innovative corporate social responsibility projects significantly encourage cocreation of communication through user-generated and technical contents. Public finance in social ICT projects helps firms to develop congruence with NET and move deeper into the social proximity. Brand ambassadors, social and ethnic institutions, customers, and crowd disseminate the cocreated and corporate communication down to the societal grassroots. Besides verbal and nonverbal modes of communication, participatory social approach on ethnographic and challenge-based research guides the social proximity-led business strategy. Such a strategy has a triadic focus encompassing design-to-market, design-to-society, and design-to-value perspectives. Accordingly, the centripetal approach of firms to social proximity touches sensitive pathways including women empowerment, leader–member exchanges (LMX), team thinking, and goal-oriented social proximity. However, the head-on challenges at the axis (society) are many not limiting to the crowd cognition, randomization of communication and concepts, filtering collective intelligence, and meticulously performing the social ice-breaking exercise in complex situations.

The centrifugal domain of social proximity moves the sociopsychological factors out of the axis (society) to business ecosystem anticipating stronger firm–society relationship. The centrifugal stages of social proximity include social preferences, behavior, sociopsychological factors, social responsiveness, proximity, polarization, sophistication, proximity scaling, and radical leverage as exhibited in Figure 3.2 (B). The changing social preferences and values, and the transforming ethnicity, often restrict firms from expanding their social proximity to enhance consumer outreach and implementing relationship marketing strategies. These factors affect the social affiliate behavior and adaptation to corporate benefits. Society anticipates empathy and emotional balance in the proximity approaches of the firms, which could ensure social empowerment and inculcate the sense of belongingness triangulating the people–firm–society relationship. With the strong standing of social media channels, collective intelligence, individual and group behaviors, and collective bargain, the society–firm relationships are becoming crowd dominated to a large extent. However, social appraisal of the role of a specific firm or an industry significantly contributes to the social perspectives on proximity approaches of the firm. Various centrifugal factors discussed earlier affect the society–firm convergence on spatial proximity, psychodynamics, and the implementation of a firm's relationship strategies across the social clusters. Most companies with strategic (long term) social thrust invest in motivating people and driving team dynamics to cocreate brands and develop ethnic brand ambassadors to polarize rural and semiurban consumers. Unilever and Procter and Gamble in India have developed rural brand ambassadors to promote affordable sachets of hair-care products within the rural social proximity. Engaging and empowering people to cocreate brand benefits have strengthened social proximity of multinational firms in the developing economies. Empowering people has not only given boost to the empowerment of gender and voice of customers but also inculcated the reverse accountability (stakeholder control) in the management of rural product distribution and promotion systems. Such bottom-up proximity approach of customer-centric firms has significantly improved the scope for firms to observe social, cultural, and anthropological proximity by knowing society and people. Consequently, firms have revised their vision toward social proximity as *think local–act local*.

As society tends to move the centrifugal energy to develop congruence between social needs and implementation of corporate strategies, most firms are eyeing meticulously to work with the proximity scaling by measuring the proximity and outreach time frame and influence of local leaders. The socially dominated firms such as May Kay Cosmetics (United States), AMUL (India), LEGO (Denmark), and IKEA (Sweden) often take radical leverage of social proximity by exploring new geodemographic clusters and serving the incumbency. These companies strengthen their social proximity approaches through ideological consistency and reinforcement of brand values in community and family environment.

The existing interpersonal communication theories describe word-of-mouth behavior in reference to the focus on face-to-face interaction, which illustrates that the communicators are in close proximity and can significantly influence the buying behavior of consumers in a marketplace (Knapp and Daly 2002). The informal communication theories based on the principles of social cognition and interpersonal relationship development from social psychology suggest that given enough time to develop peer interactions, individuals can create fully formed impressions of others based solely on the verbal content on Internet portals. It is imperative that marketers understand how these impressions affect the assessment and use of word-of-mouth information about products, brands, and firms and the consequential consumer behavior both spatially and temporally through the virtual platforms (Brown et al. 2007). Successful cocreation of innovations has a major challenge of commercialization, which has driven the cocreated products and services to evolve ambidextrously with society and corporations. Employee engagement and customer involvement are the pillars of the coevolution process, besides resource pooling, distribution, and managing marketing-mix (product, price, place, promotion, and psychodynamics) functions. Social business design is largely based on the psychosocial drivers that affect the cocreation of innovations and strategies and the commercialization process. Customer and stakeholder participation in cocreating innovation and marketing strategies is effective in exploring the solutions to social problems and determining the needs. Participation in a social purpose is being interactive and emotional as compared to the involvement of customers and stakeholders in an absolute commercial project. The social, cultural, and ethnic foundations nurture belief, trust, and loyalty perceptions during the collective efforts in innovation and developing marketing strategies. Companies carrying out the cocreation process gain societal insights from the knowledge, attitude, and practices (conventional of intermediate) toward finding the social solutions. Most social entrepreneurs join cocreation projects and set mutual benefit goals with the business corporations. In addition, companies benefit from cocreation process in socializing their existing and upcoming brands by developing referrals and brand gatekeepers in the societal niche, which helps in enhancing the customer outreach. Societal engagement of business corporations opens up avenues to enter the downstream markets alongside the mass and premium market segments, driving them to conquer the universe of market (comprising premium, upper mass, regular mass, lower mass, and bottom-of-the-pyramid market segment). In an interactive social and business environment, coevolution of businesses with the societal values provides competitive leverage to the companies and helps in achieving corporate social identity. The intrinsic factors within the social ecosystem that stimulate the cocreation process of social entrepreneurs, customers, and stakeholders include social responsibility-led self-esteem, voluntary behavior, social leadership, and active involvement in social media. The extrinsic factors of the business ecosystem that attract cocreation and coevolution processes with social stakeholders include social governance, public policies, public–private partnership, and the leverage of empowering social stakeholders toward promoting social businesses (Rajagopal 2021).

Firms with consumer orientation deliberate technological and new product interventions in the market that increase the level of communication, collaboration, proximity, and competitive leverage. Firms with descending or zero social proximity typically face consumer deflections, rising tensions, declining collaboration, helplessness, passivity, and profit denial in the long run. Therefore, social proximity is a survival tool for customer-centric firms today. To survive such social dynamics, successful firms such as LEGO, 3M, Samsung, Unilever, Procter and Gamble, and Colgate Palmolive apply certain sociopsychological interventions and establish dialogue with less-known consumers in the society, empower them, and engage them in the cocreation initiative. On the other side, Gillette, Invensys, and the BBC used such interventions to survive the corporate free fall and secure a more productive path by stating social and enhancing the social proximity (Kanter 2003).

The market access competence includes management of brand development, sales and marketing, distribution and logistics, technical support, and so on. All these skills help to put a firm near its customers. The attributes associated with competence such as quality, cycle time management, just-in-time inventory management, and so on, which allow a company to do things more quickly, flexibly, or with a higher degree of reliability than competitors, constitute the integrity-related competence of a firm. The functionality-related competence leads to the skills that enable the company to invest its services or products with unique functionality, which invest the product with distinctive customer benefits rather than merely making it incrementally better. The functionality-related competence is becoming more important as a source of competitive differentiation, relative to the other two competence types. Collective intelligence is also explorative as it is able to connect firms with isolated business ideas with the success of such local experiments. The innovations developed in local markets are based on consumer needs and are marketed within a niche at an affordable price to the consumers. These enterprises do not adapt to "design-to-market" innovation approach. However, the innovations with utilitarian values tend to drive high demand in local markets as they match with the sociocultural and ethnic values. For example, in 2016, an engineer entrepreneur of India designed a low-cost clay refrigerator, which requires no electricity and keeps the cooked food fresh and safe for five days uninterruptedly. This innovative product was branded as "*mittikool*" (clay-cool). It continued to function even in the event of irregular power supplies in the rural areas. The concept of this innovation has been later adapted to the "design-to-market" strategy by a Chinese global giant Haier, which manufactured and commercialized noncompressor refrigerator. Instead of relying on a refrigerant, compressor, and evaporator to maintain cooling, it simply uses water and carbon dioxide (CO_2) plus a unique solid-state cooler. The product claims to save a significant amount of energy, provide more even cooling, eliminate all noises and vibrations, and offer more usable space (Rajagopal 2020).

The technological innovations have percolated down to the consumers from the business-to-business platforms. The 21st century has shown a great potential for designing and developing marketing communications for delivering via mobile devices, personal data assistants, and the evolution of near-field communication technologies. In developing and disseminating marketing information, most firms have considered the factors influencing consumers' acceptance of social platforms such as Facebook, Twitter, and so on, supported by the outreach of technology. Growing market competition has induced consumers to adopt mobile marketing across three influential regions—the United States, China, and Europe. Firms need to examine the extent to which the usefulness of mobile programs and individual characteristics—namely innovativeness, personal attachment, and risk avoidance—jointly influence attitudes toward mobile marketing, and how the latter influences consumers' mobile marketing communication activity across three large and influential markets. The efforts of prominent international companies have shown that perceived usefulness, consumer innovativeness, and personal attachment directly influence attitudes toward mobile marketing communication not only in the markets of developed countries but also in the emerging markets. Marketers seeking to build and maintain customer relationships via mobile platforms should view these individual characteristics as the levers to amplify consumers' acceptance of mobile marketing (Rohm et al. 2012). Comprehensive knowledge dissemination and trust play a pivotal role in creating customer value, in the absence of which knowledge barriers may limit the size of the market to a subset of customers in the short term. Therefore, once a bank has taken the decision to adopt new technology for improving its services and optimizing profit, retailers will lean to depend on market-specific demand characteristics. Exploring the synergy between online and offline channels in general reveals that a bank typically delivers standardized, low-value-added transactions such as bill payments, product enquiries, mobile marketing, and credit transactions through the inexpensive Internet channel while delivering specialized, high-value-added transactions such as small business lending, personal trust services, and investment banking through the more expensive branch channel. By providing more service options to its customers, an improved technology adoption will enable the retailers to retain their most profitable customers and generate more revenue from cross-selling.

Sustainability and innovation are widely affected by the macro factors comprising public policy, investment attractiveness, market environment, and cooperation among stakeholders, consumers, state, and companies. Public policies in developing countries support sustainability projects through funding, accessibility and adaptability to technology, and initial marketing. Public policies encourage cocreation of innovation and public–private partnership in the management of sustainability projects. These policies focus on improving the sociocultural conditions of social and higher economic gains in managing social innovation and sustainability projects. Such public policies emphasize cooperation strategies and encourage social and business organizations to explore different types of alliances that combine productivity, spontaneity, and tangible outcomes in the context of managing sustainability projects, eco-innovations, management, and marketing. In this process, relationships among society, entrepreneurs, and companies contribute significantly to promoting cooperation networks, which are characterized as an attractive strategy leading to a better performance (Lin and Jin 2016). Economic growth and proactive public policies tend to encourage the adaptation of greener and cleaner technologies in environmentally sustainable areas, which necessitates building proactive institutions and developing cooperation. The quality requirements in sustainable and eco-innovation projects encompass rigorous environmental standards, legal systems, property rights, eliminating socioeconomic and political corruption, stakeholder education, removing cultural barriers, and improving the quality of financial information. In addition, the provision of incentives and subsidies to manufacturing firms undertaking technological innovations needs to be clearly drafted and implemented to help social and business organizations to comply with the environmental standards (Sethi et al. 2020).

Proximity Marketing Stages

Consumer behavior is becoming multifaceted in the global marketplace due to a rapid increase in competition, innovation, and technology in products and services. Hence, architecting sustainable companies is not getting any easier. A longitudinal growth of brands across the firms has rapidly altered the perception, attitude, and behavior of consumers over time. Thus, companies are engaging consumers in building confidence in brands and the company by developing symbiotic relationship between consumers and market for sustainable growth. Companies build consumer perceptions of the product and services by disseminating continuous and sustainable communication through various cable channels to the Internet, product placement in movies, and even mobile phone display screens. The first order of business is to take a hard look at the sustainable consumer segment that has long-term profit potential for delivering the right brands for segments and to plan for required investment in building the customer-centric markets. While no good company ignores shifts that are clearly under way, they traditionally segment markets in reference to the size, income, age, and ethnicity of various target populations; estimates of their consumption and loyalty; and information about their locations, lifestyles, needs, and attitudes. Well-managed companies have moved from emphasizing customized items to offering globally standardized products that are advanced, functional, reliable, and low priced. They benefit from enormous economies of scale in production, distribution, marketing, and management. Such dynamism in business and related activities portrays the functional concepts of globalization (Rajagopal 2008).

Consumer behavior is a continuous process and is improved time and again with experience. Trial and error constitute a part of the experimental consumer behavior, which is refined by sharing experience and improving social proximity of firms and brands based on collective intelligence. Consumers often make mistakes while making decisions due to ad hoc reasoning and influences. A stream of experimental evidence in recent years has evidenced that human elements contribute significantly to the right or wrong decisions. However, at the same time, companies also have the role of managers in decision making in consumer business and financial markets (Fox 2015). Consumer preference and value placed on designer apparel is largely influenced by the social differentiation of products and self-esteem of the consumer. These attributes are likely to vary depending on the consumers' cultural orientation. The cultural dimensions of individualism, uncertainty avoidance, power distance, and masculinity should be a useful framework to explain cross-cultural differences in customer acceptance of designer products. Consumers use destination brands for their symbolic value, reflecting the personality and status of the user. Destination brands are perceived as an ostentatious display of wealth. Thus, consumers are motivated by a desire to impress others with their ability to pay particularly high prices for prestigious products (Rajagopal 2011). Consumption patterns are largely governed by the social value of the product, which determines the purchasing intentions, consumer attitudes, or perceptions on brand or advertising slogan. Consumer experience with high socioeconomic power perceptions creates distinct psychological motives toward new products that develop unique consumption patterns (Rucker and Galinsky 2009).

Firms are engaged in various stages of proximity marketing, which include divergent factors that affect the process of outreaching firms to different socioeconomic segments within the social ecosystem. These stages in the context of multiple ecosystems operating in the social environment are exhibited in Figure 3.3.

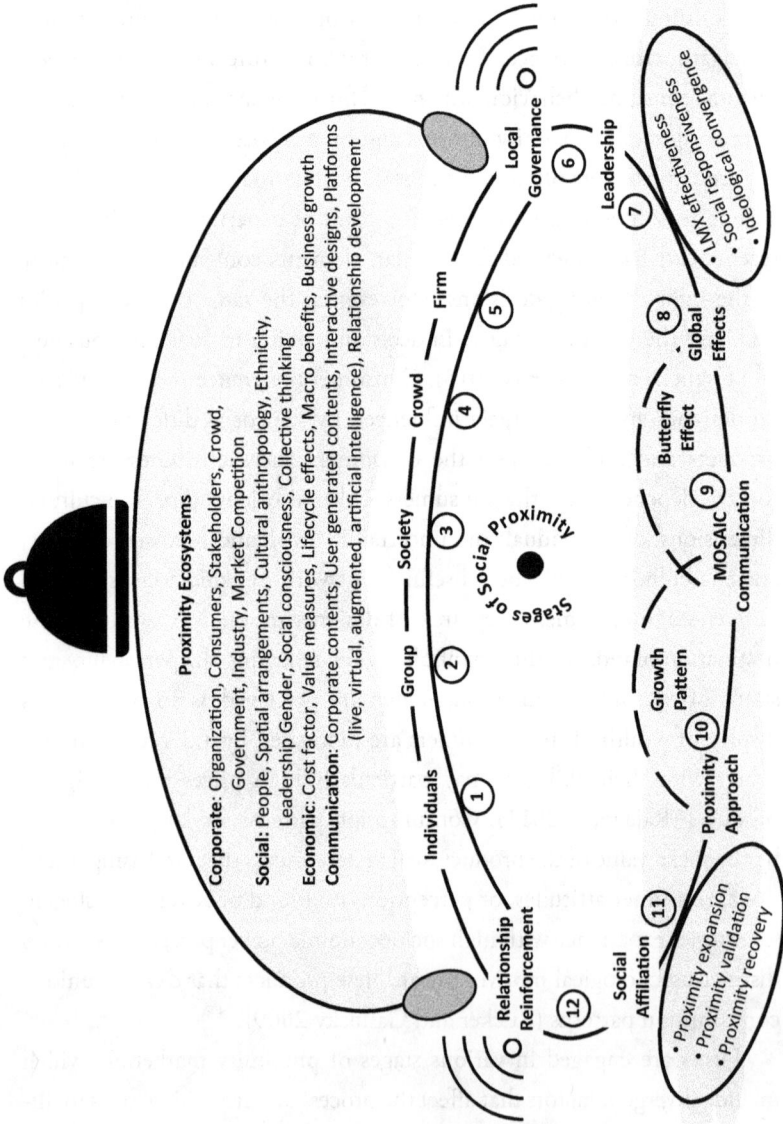

Proximity Ecosystems

Corporate: Organization, Consumers, Stakeholders, Crowd, Government, Industry, Market Competition

Social: People, Spatial arrangements, Cultural anthropology, Ethnicity, Leadership Gender, Social consciousness, Collective thinking

Economic: Cost factor, Value measures, Lifecycle effects, Macro benefits, Business growth

Communication: Corporate contents, User generated contents, Interactive designs, Platforms (live, virtual, augmented, artificial intelligence), Relationship development

Stages of Social Proximity

Individuals ① Group ② Society ③ Crowd ④ Firm ⑤ Local Governance ⑥ Leadership ⑦

- LMX effectiveness
- Social responsiveness
- Ideological convergence

Global Effects ⑧ Butterfly Effect MOSAIC ⑨ Communication

Growth Pattern Proximity ⑩ Approach

Relationship Reinforcement Social Affiliation ⑪ ⑫

- Proximity expansion
- Proximity validation
- Proximity recovery

Figure 3.3 Stages in social proximity to firms

Source: Author.

Though the stages of social proximity appear simple and streamlined, firms often face social alignment problems with their policies. While moving through these stages, firms face enormous challenges, ambiguity, and transitional complexities because of the inconsistency in the social cognition and individual and group behaviors. There are broadly 12 stages involved in developing an effective social proximity by the customer-centric companies as illustrated in Figure 3.3. The social proximity journey begins with the accessibility of individuals to the firm in the first place, which influences group behavior and constructs a peer community. The conglomeration of such micro and niche communities forms a large society, which, in a liberated form, explodes over time as a crowd with boundaryless interactions. These stages are categorical and critical for the firms to nurture and integrate within their corporate policies and strategies. Firms such as LEGO (creative toys—Denmark), TOMS (cause marketing—United States), Ben & Jerry (social equality and well-being—United States), Dr. Bronner's (organic and environmental-driven cosmetics—United States), AMUL (dairy farmers organization—India), and Grameen Bank (microfinance—Bangladesh) have high social proximity and largely depend on social collaboration to grow a socially effective business. These companies encourage cocreation and local governance and develop local leadership skills to reach social proximity and business performance in local markets and have a global effect. Macro effects on the proximity of firms can be achieved through Massive Open and Socially Accessible Interactive Communication (MOSAIC) approaches. Socially responsive firms adapt to MOASIC environments using physical and digital proximity to outreach consumers in all clusters. Based on the MOSAIC performance of the firm on cocreation and diffusion of communication, most firms choose their strategy for effective social proximity, which determines the strategic growth pattern of the firm. Some ideas contributed by the society, such as *reverse accountability* in Grameen Bank experience, TOMS *buy-one-give-one* concept in marketing (shoes), and *Shakti experiment* of Unilever in India (women's empowerment), often have far-reached effects across the globe, which can be termed as *butterfly effect* of the firm–society proximity. These factors build social affiliation and reinforce firm–society proximity for mutual benefit. The proximity ecosystem consists of corporate, social, economic, and communication subdomains as exhibited in Figure 3.3. Besides people, government, and industry in the corporate ecosystem of proximity, the social arrangements, cultural anthropology, leadership, and collective thinking broadly constitute the social ecosystem of proximity to firms. The economic ecosystem of proximity envelops cost factors (investment), value measures (value for money), life-cycle effects (longevity of relationship and proximity), and the extent of mutual benefits. The communication ecosystem has a blend of corporate and user-generated contents besides digital platforms and interactive communication designs.

With the advancement and outreach of information technology to millions of social network users in developing nations, there is an influx of applications and tools that help people to connect on various crowd platforms to manifest their ideas and experiences. The popular crowd interaction tools range from Facebook to YouTube to Instagram that endorses new paradigms of social and commercial innovations, which has emerged as cocreation and coevolution. Services cocreation in suburban and rural geographies has emerged as a new approach of hearing people on finding innovative solutions for chronic, casual, or predetermined social problems. It is the process by which services are developed jointly by companies through user-generated contents. While the cocreation of services is in process, customers and stakeholders tend to create value by opening up in the niche, regional, national, and global markets. Start-up, small, and medium enterprises largely rely on the cocreating process for designing new services and cultivate a cocreative engagement platform based on brainstorming, discussions on ecosystem elements, innovations dialogue, accessibility of innovated and improved services, risk assessment, and transparency in disseminating the user-generated contents (Ramaswamy 2009).

Social engagement is a socially responsive approach in managing tasks and socioeconomic practices with expected outcomes. Social engagement aligns with individual, community, civic, and institutional benefits including leverages from business and economy. While social scholarship focuses on the individual and community attributes as a state of engagement, the social perspective of engagement endorses collective impact on cocreated businesses through a socially determined process. The design-to-society philosophy is, therefore, aligned with the social engagement theory and social presence maxim, which refers to the degree of presence perceived by the community participants in generating and disseminating communication. Social presence theory argues that social media (physical and digital interactions) should align with psychological perception of involvement (presence) and transmit visual and verbal cues. Social presence broadly includes the activities of sharing ideas and experiences, communicating social postures, social brand expressions, social needs, upholding customer voice, and monitoring checks and balances on business to society value transfers (Calefato and Lanubile 2010).

Crowdsourcing has attained global focus as many social issues such as sustainability, public health, organic cultivation, and regional development have congregated as civic and corporate social responsibility. Integrating people with business to achieve profit-with-purpose and social values has encouraged service-led growth through practical techniques. The collective intelligence has encouraged low-cost service innovation integrating the following elements of *services ecosystem*:

4As: Awareness (collective intelligence), attributes (need-based design), affordability (cost-effective services), and adaptability (social and economic stimuli to consume services)

4Cs: Cost to customer (tangible and intangible costs), convenience (availability and perceived ease of use), communication (transparency and clarity in user-generated contents), and conflict resolution (customer relationship management)

4Vs: Value (customer and social values), validity (collective decision), venue (social marketing of services), and vogue (value and lifestyle)

4Es: Exportability (crowd-based innovation), expansion (improvements in services and processes), experience (sharing with community), and emotions (sense of belongingness with crowd-based services design)

4Is: Interest (public interest), information (crowd-based, recurring, and strategic), image (social and personal congruence), and implementation (people-led growth)

4Ms: Marketing of services (strategic and tactical focus), mobility (geo-demographic fit), management (crowd- and social-governance), and maintenance (public–private partnership)

Services are intangible and dynamic, which need periodic user intervention to improve in real time using affordable technology and design driven by the crowd. Most product innovations unlike services focus on partial dynamic attributes like pricing and promotion, which affect the commercialization of the innovated products. The product designs are relatively static with predetermined physical properties. Services are largely driven by experience and emotion. Therefore, perceived values for services are vulnerable unlike products and need frequent interventions of users to improve the service attributes in collaboration with the service providers. Service blueprinting is a process for designing new and improving services based on the changing customer preferences and is securely grounded in the customer's experience, which allows value-based dynamic service processes (Bitner et al. 2008).

Crowdsourcing is an open innovation approach to solve problems, create new products, and improve consumer experiences. Upstream and mainstream consumer brands adapt to grow as crowd brands for achieving quick success in the competitive markets. Crowdsourcing provides a strategic pool of collective intelligence by engaging consumers as a part of a brainstorming exercise and action. It delivers interesting and dynamic marketing opportunities for services brands such as Netflix, Amazon Prime, and Disney Channel through effective consumer engagement (Bal et al. 2017). Crowdsourcing has emerged as a powerful tool to promote service brands by empowering service-brand communities within the social and ethnic ecosystem. Brand communities segmented from a larger crowd enable customer-centric firms to make decisions that influence the image of services brands and product offerings in a controlled and planned way. Such a move in managing crowd-motivated service brands reveals powerfully positive effects as the campaign of Ryan Air, a low-cost airline of Ireland, was endorsed by the crowd as an economic value-based services in Europe. Crowdsourcing offers mutual benefit for firms and consumers as users receive benefits of value for money, social comfort, and comparative self-esteem among peers. The crowdsourcing firm benefits from collective intelligence to build future collaboration with people and gain confidence on its services brands. McDonald's Twitter hashtag campaign in 2012, #McDStories, was designed to impart information about the restaurant chain's suppliers and allow customers to share their own McDonald's stories publicly (Estellés-Arolas and González-Ladron-de-Guevara 2012).

The design-to-society approach is founded on value-based business thinking, which explains the concepts of "competing with social purpose" and "performance with purpose" underlying in the welfare marketing business school of thought. The combination of design-to-society and design-to-market business philosophies connects social aspirations including the customer values to persuade market-growth needs of the companies. An effective social strategy tagged with the brand value fortifies the business goals and means. Nonetheless, it mitigates the risk of passive social associations and radical conceptualization of means to achieve performance and poses threats to stakeholder acceptance of society-linked business models. The stakeholder value can be created for all stakeholders, customers, the company, and the community at large through strategic pursuit of brand marketing and corporate goals (Rodriguez-Vila and Bharadwaj 2017).

A social media activist may have a mix of experience with product design, marketing, software applications, and the extended reach of communication. Companies should analyze customer experience centered on social interactions to develop community-linked marketing approaches. Such customer connectivity helps the managers to stay on social media platforms like Facebook page and work with social media account management, social advertising, and social media campaign management, which are the typical customer-centric marketing tasks for a company. As social networks are growing fast and gaining psychodynamics, there emerges a need for a new executive-level social marketing strategist, who can fully embrace the focus on social marketing. Social consciousness and business are growing simultaneously among the customers and stakeholders because of the ease of use of technology and transformation of communication systems from conventional wisdom to digital networks. Corporate social responsibility has become the tool to generate social consciousness and value streams to support social marketing perspectives of business. Public policies and the media have become proficient to stimulate the companies to take initiatives in developing social markets and inculcating the social consequences in the future business modeling to grow their business with the social outlooks. Consequently, the social face of business has emerged as an inescapable priority for the customer-centric companies to gain competitive leverage. Some successful business-to-customer companies like Amazon discovered Whole Foods as a social business place to generate social values and drive business growth faster. Similarly, Toyota and Volvo have found design-to-society approaches in business more as source of innovation and competitive advantage than a path of smooth transition of technology-oriented business in the society. Companies, while developing social imperatives in business, need to identify the social consequences of their actions and discover opportunities to benefit society and themselves by strengthening the competitive benefits. The design-to-society business modeling has, therefore, emerged as a collective thinking mindset for strategic growth of business through the social value stream (Porter and Kramer 2006).

Companies should develop social media strategies based on *Hub and Spoke model*, where a hub is located around social media. The *hub* may be led by the corporate social strategist to monitor the core communication movements within the networks and draw a framework of marketing strategy integrating customer attributes and corporate policy. The hub marketing framework needs to be further converged with the functionaries accountable in various departments of the company that denotes *spokes* in the model. New applications for the mobile social networking platforms are constantly appearing in the market, which have tempted many companies to tap the social network activities also from the mobile devices. A mobile device is a tool that allows access to a ubiquitous network beyond one specific access gate. The most common example of mobile devices is mobile phone, but a netbook also counts if it can access different types of wireless networks such as WLAN and 3G (Kaplan 2012). Design-to-society is a community approach in developing market ecosystem on the social foundation. Most companies invest in creating social value by cocreating corporate social responsibility and developing public–private partnership by working on a social cause. Though the corporate investment in design-to-society has a long-run payback, it could be a tactical approach in managing market competition through the social value inputs of the business. Costs and benefits of the social investment of business, from the perspective of targeted growth in the marketplace, often pose many challenges. Design-to-society approach to targeted community provides a significant benefit to the customers and stakeholders over the conventional for-profit marketing methods. However, in some cases, such as in sustainability projects, the social investment involves high cost in terms of either money or intangible measure (difficulty, for instance, in quitting smoking); it becomes harder for the company to connect the payback to the existing revenue streams. Social marketers face their greatest challenge in converging the intangible social benefits with business growth and performance with purpose (Rangan et al. 1996).

Cause Marketing and Social Proximity

Social marketing platforms have driven the consumers to get increasingly involved in active roles not only in communicating among peers but also in cocreating marketing content with companies and their respective brands. Many social media consumer groups have become strategic partners to the companies in building their brand; for example, Bimbo bread company in Mexico has been using social media platforms to promote its brands since long; in the recent past, it has created a social media platform for the football fans using the celebrity players to promote its sandwich bread brands. Most consumer-oriented companies are also looking to develop online social marketing programs and campaigns to reach consumers on *where is as is* basis to give the shopping experience "live" online. However, most companies do not truly understand how to get involved with the consumer actively through the social media as platforms such as YouTube, Facebook, and Twitter are too often treated as stand-alone elements rather than part of an integrated system (Horppu et al. 2008).

Social media applications including collaborative projects, microblogs, blogs, content communities, social networking sites, and virtual worlds have become part of the standard communication repertoire for many companies. The creation of powerful mobile devices has elevated the growth opportunities for numerous social media applications to go mobile. Most companies have developed a parallel communication channel around social media along with their business propositions. Hence, the emerging firms feel that there should be a social marketing strategist who is responsible for stimulating discussion in the media, filtering communications, picking new ideas, and analyzing opportunities for cocreation of strategies with the consumers. The role of social media strategist should be to develop customer-centric approaches for the company and integrate social experiences into products and services. The role of social media strategists should be to figure out the current relationships of customers, determine the ways to bring out those relationships into the experiences of every product and service of the company, build new social experiences and embrace the existing experiences with the company, and make the customers stay on the network platforms with their friends and family.

Direct marketing and retailing companies largely view sales networks in terms of direct contacts and often depend on the social networks. However, those companies intensively involved with customers like financial services may not necessarily have an effective network because networks often pay off their value through indirect contacts. Moreover, a thumb rule in customer-centric companies is to adopt relevant social networks and let them grow with the support of the company so that it can embark on such platforms to gain competitive advantage in the marketplace. Hence, the density of the connections in a network is important. However, thin networks are also better for generating unique information. Managers can use three levers comprising direct marketing structure, compensation, and skills development to encourage front-liners to adopt a network-based view and make the best possible use of social webs. For instance, the sales force can be restructured to delink lead generation from other tasks, because some people are very good at building diverse ties but not so good at maintaining other kinds of networks. Companies that take steps of this kind to help their marketing and sales teams build better networks will reap competitive advantages (Ustuner and Godes 2006).

Case Studies

TOMS: *Social Proximity Program*

Companies are increasingly integrating social proximity programs through cause-marketing sensitivity among consumers and align business by pursuing the need-based social movements. Social proximity initiatives can look different for different companies, but it typically entails programs around charitable fundraising, workplace conditions, social benefits such as volunteerism and environmentalism. People-oriented companies including cooperatives adapt to social proximity programs in collaboration with the stakeholders and customers. International companies such as JP Morgan, Goldman Sachs, and Amazon are also inclined to fulfill their commitments to social justice and sustainability, which makes the trend clear to work with customers, stakeholders, and society at large. An American TOMS shoe company has experimented the cause marketing as one of the tools to get deeper into the social proximity and stay as social brand ahead of total commodity companies.

The purchasing perspective of consumers across generations has shifted consumer focus to social sustainability and conscious consumption. According to a Nielsen poll in 2018, about 85 percent millennials and 80 percent of generation-Z consumers rank sustainability and social consciousness at the top to develop their engagement with the brand and company.[1] Based on the changing socioeconomic concerns and technology disruption in the upstream markets, consumers remain cautious with spending, collaborating, and action-planning with companies to overcome socioeconomic barriers. In the increasing consumer-packaged goods retail scape, the rise in costs and corporate markups has resulted in the burden of rising prices but the impact varied dramatically across the socioeconomic clusters. As financial situations and social proximity polarize further in changing global scenarios, the insecurity of social firms and the secure flexibility of high-end technology firms will grow simultaneously in the social ecosystem over time.

TOMS shoes invented the *buy-one-give-one* model in 2006, but socially conscious consumers are attracted to cause marketing concept to get association with the company in the form of embedded giving. This company called for volunteers to give an old pair of shoes for a social cause while buying a new pair of shoes from TOMS. This program has significantly impacted the social proximity drive of the company for over a decade. In 2019, this company could not continue with this program due to threatening losses. For most consumers, the great appeal of TOMS was the apparent simplicity of the offering as described by the company "you buy a pair of shoes, we give a pair to a person in need." This corporate

---

[1] For details, see *Consumer Outlook 2023: The Unsettled State of Global Consumers* (New York, NY: A C Nielsen Company).

mission was portrayed by this company based in Los Angeles to make society realize that giving away old shoes on a mass level was small but a simple way to penetrate the social clusters and raise the brand consciousness. During the early years when the TOMS story took off like a rocket and its cause-marketing story mesmerized millions of consumers, the company faced tremendous difficulty in giving away as many shoes as it was selling. The TOMS team discovered that giving is harder than acquiring. The company conducted research on giving (social distribution of shoes to needy) and attempted to better understand how to improve the social impact of the firm. TOMS is now engaged in cocreating a workable model for TOMS including overhauled product design and the new giving model. The pandemic's negative impact on brick-and-mortar retail sales has adversely affected the company although it reportedly had a record year for online sales. The company is cocreating a workable model including revamped product design and the new giving model. Covid-19 pandemic had a negative impact on brick-and-mortar retail sales that had a setback but those were the record years for online sales.

Summary

Social proximity has both circular and elliptical patterns that affect business evolution with a wider outreach in society. Business information flows from a firm to society and vice versa through the hybrid techniques including physical interface as a conventional path of information and simultaneously adapts to digitization ecosystem for an effective social media and ethnographic broadcast. This chapter argues that proximity circles have a lot of locus points on a social platform equidistant from all geodemographic segments comprising social clusters, neighborhoods, socioeconomic levels, gender, age, preferences, social consciousness, social media, and consumption. There are many spiral effects of communication moving back and forth from firm and society and vice versa, which significantly affect the corporate efforts to enhance social proximity and customer outreach. The elliptical proximity to society can be constructed and measured on the long axis of business ecosystem. Besides the circular and elliptical proximity patterns, this chapter discusses a new concept of knowledge-based proximity marketing model in a circular system built around 6A factors comprising awareness, attributes, appraisal, acquaintance, acquisition, and alignment. Furthermore, a new concept of centripetal and centrifugal dynamics of social proximity is discussed in this chapter, which illustrates that the centrifugal domain of social proximity moves the sociopsychological factors out of the axis (society) to the business ecosystem anticipating a stronger firm–society relationship. The centrifugal energy in society tends to develop congruence between social needs and implementation of corporate strategies, and most firms are eyeing meticulously to work with the proximity scaling by measuring the proximity and outreach time frame and influence of local leaders.

Proximity and market strategies can be implemented effectively by the firms for understanding the consumer preferences in the changing social and political perspectives. The concept of *business model design space* describes the opportunities and constraints of creating and capturing value from niche and frugal technologies. This chapter delineates that most firms approach social proximity through information cocreation, communication dissemination, mode of communication, social programs, corporate social responsibility, gender proximity, integration, research, and people as the strategy blocks for centripetal proximity. The stages of social proximity appear simple and streamlined. While moving through these stages, firms face enormous challenges, ambiguity, and transitional complexities because of the inconsistency in the social cognition and individual and group behaviors. It is also argued in the chapter that the design-to-society approach is founded on value-based business thinking, which explains the concepts of "competing with social purpose" and "performance with purpose" underlying in the welfare marketing business school of thought. Direct marketing and retailing companies largely view sales networks in terms of direct contacts and often depend on the social networks.

References

Bal, A.S., K. Weidner, R. Hanna, and A.J. Mills. 2017. "Crowdsourcing and Brand Control." *Business Horizons* 60, no. 2, pp. 219–228.

Bitner, M. J., A.L. Ostrom, and F.N. Morgan. 2008. "Service Blueprinting: A Practical Technique for Service Innovation." *California Management Review* 50, no. 3, pp. 66–94.

Brown, J., A.J. Broderick, and N. Lee. 2007. "Word of Mouth Communication Within Online Communities: Conceptualizing the Online Social Network." *Journal of Interactive Marketing* 21, no. 3, pp. 2–20.

Burgmann, J. and C.K. Prahalad. 2007. "Co-creating Business's New Social Compact." *Harvard Business Review* 85, no. 2, pp. 80–90.

Calefato, F. and F. Lanubile. 2010. "Communication Media Selection for Remote Interaction of Ad Hoc Groups." *Advances in Computers* 78, pp. 271–313. Elsevier.

Codispoti, M. and A. de Cesarei. 2007. "Arousal and Attention: Picture Size and Emotional Reactions." *Psychophysiology* 44, no. 5, pp. 680–686.

Estellés-Arolas, E. and F. González-Ladron-de-Guevara. 2012. "Towards an Integrated Crowdsourcing Definition." *Journal of Information Science* 38, no. 2, pp. 189–200.

Fox, J. 2015. "From 'Economic Man' to Behavioral Economics." *Harvard Business Review* 93, no. 5, pp. 78–85.

Hanna, R.C., A. Rohm, and V.L. Crittenden. 2011, "We're All Connected: The Power of the Social Media Ecosystem." *Business Horizons* 54, no. 3, pp. 265–273.

Hansen, M.T., N. Nohria, and T. Tierney. 1999. "What's Your Strategy for Managing Knowledge?" *Harvard Business Review* 77, no. 2, pp. 106–116.

Horppu, M., O. Kuivalainen, A. Tarkiainen, and E. Hanna-Kaisa. 2008. "Online Satisfaction, Trust and Loyalty, and the Impact of the Offline Parent Brand." *Journal of Product and Brand Management* 17, no. 6, pp. 403–413.

Kanter, R.M. 2003. "Leadership and the Psychology of Turnarounds." *Harvard Business Review* 81, no. 6, pp. 58–69.

Kaplan, A.M. 2012. "If You Love Something, Let It Go Mobile: Mobile Marketing and Mobile Social Media 4x4." *Business Horizons* 55, no. 2, pp. 129–139

Knapp, M.L. and J.A. Daly. 2002. "Handbook of Interpersonal Communication." Thousand Oaks: California, CA: SAGE Publications.

Lin, F.J. and Y.H. Jin. 2016. "The Effect of Network Relationship on the Performance of SMEs." *Journal of Business Research* 69, pp. 1780–1784.

Porter, M.E. and M.R. Kramer. 2006. "Strategy and Society: The Link Between Competitive Advantage and Corporate Social Responsibility." *Harvard Business Review* 84, no. 12, pp. 78–92.

Rajagopal. 2008. "Measuring Brand Performance Through Metrics Application." *Measuring Business Excellence* 12, no. 1, pp. 29–38.

Rajagopal. 2011. "Impact of Radio Advertisements on Buying Behaviour of Urban Commuters." *International Journal of Retail and Distribution Management* 39, no. 7, pp. 480–503.

Rajagopal. 2020. *Sustainable Businesses in Developing Economies—Socio-Economic and Governance Perspectives.* New York, NY: Palgrave Macmillan.

Rajagopal. 2021. *Crowd-Based Business Models: Using Collective Intelligence for Market Competitiveness*. Cham, Switzerland: Springer, A Palgrave Macmillan Imprint.

Ramaswamy, V. 2009. "Are You Ready for the Co-Creation Movement?" *IESE Insights, Third Quarter*, no. 2, pp. 29–35.

Rangan, V.K., S. Karim, and S.K. Sandberg. 1996. "Do Better at Doing Good." *Harvard Business Review* 74, no. 3, pp. 42–54.

Rodriguez-Vila, O. and S. Bharadwaj. 2017. "Competing on Social Purpose." *Harvard Business Review* 95, no. 5, pp. 94–104.

Rohm, A.J., T. Gao, F. Sultan, and M. Pagani. 2012. "Brand in Hand: A Cross Market Investigation of Consumer Acceptance of Mobile Marketing." *Business Horizons* 55, no. 5, pp. 485–493.

Rucker, D.D. and A.D. Galinsky. 2009. "Conspicuous Consumption Versus Utilitarian Ideals: How Different Levels of Power Shape Consumer Behavior." *Journal of Experimental Social Psychology* 45, no. 3, pp. 549–555.

Sethi, P., D. Chakrabarti, and S. Bhattacharjee. 2020. "Globalization, Financial Development and Economic Growth: Perils on the Environmental Sustainability of an Emerging Economy." *Journal of Policy Modeling* 43, no. 3, pp. 520–535.

Singh, T., L.V. Jackson, and J. Cullinane. 2008. "Blogging: A New Play in Your Marketing Game Plan." *Business Horizons* 51, no. 4, pp. 281–292.

Vargo, S.L. and R.F. Lusch. 2004. "Evolving to a New Dominant Logic for Marketing." *Journal of Marketing* 68, no. 1, pp. 1–17.

Wesseling, J.H., C. Bidmon, and R. Bohnsack. 2020. "Business Model Design-Spaces in Socio-technical Transitions: The Case of Electric Driving in the Netherlands." *Technological Forecasting and Social Change* 154. https://doi.org/10.1016/j.techfore.2020.119950.

Wind, Y. and V. Mahajan. 2001. *Convergence Marketing: Strategies for Reaching the New Hybrid Consumer*. New York, NY: Free Press.

Wirtz, J., A.S. Mattila, and M.O. Lwin. 2007. "How Effective Are Loyalty Reward Programs in Driving Share of Wallet?" *Journal of Service Research* 9, pp. 327–334.

CHAPTER 4

Social Steering Strategy

Overview

This chapter discusses social steering strategy emphasizing various approaches of consumer engagement. The PMA has been explained in the context of experience sharing and cocreation of marketing strategies by engaging customers. The chapter argues that action research and community problem-solving through interactive communication, experience and ideas sharing, and exploring collective decisions help firms in strengthening consumer outreach, satisfaction, and loyalty. Therefore, the PMA serves as a collective approach to communicate, cocreate, and coevolve the customer-centric firms with stakeholders to address PNS factors collectively (Chambers 1994). Participatory business appraisal has been discussed as a new concept, a continuous learning tool by engaging customers, stakeholders, and crowd within the business ecosystem. Participatory appraisal is used as a driver to actions research in resolving social issues and analyzing the cultural, biological, and legal perspectives to promote customer-centric businesses on a social scale. Companies that market sustainable products used to design a participatory appraisal workshop to analyze the situation from a cultural, biological, and legal perspective to social consciousness about green products on a human scale (Lara et al. 2018). This chapter also discusses the role of social marketing and public organizations including self-help groups, cooperatives, and crowd partnering in managing the proximity approach to expand consumer outreach and experience. In fact, crowdsourcing has led to the emergence of entirely new business models. Such crowd-based business models (CBBMs) can lead to an important competitive advantage while simultaneously presenting new challenges to entrepreneurs and executives (Täuscher 2017). The case studies on the practices of social proximity marketing strengthen the discussion on social approach to proximity marketing in this chapter.

Participatory Market Appraisal

PMA is a qualitative approach used by firms to understand consumer behavior, brand consciousness, preferences, and perceived value. This approach is based on community participation to document knowledge and opinions on corporate communications, brands, marketing strategies, and competitive leverages in planning social and business proximity programs. PMA engages the total population, irrespective of defined demographic clusters and geographic distribution of population. Firms develop concept maps using the PMA approach of consumer research to develop both tactical and strategic proximity marketing plans. Since PMA is a community-based marketing approach, it tends to eliminate the individual biases and validate the populist opinions and motivate crowd cognition, which helps firms in developing the customer-centric social proximity with the socioethnographic ecosystem. In this market information analytics, cognitive appraisal of consumers is shared in social events and on the social media platforms by spreading digital word-of-mouth. Proximity research through PMA therefore leads to the development of customer-centric strategies and programs that are creative, productive, and sustainable in the competitive marketplace. PMA engages people in society holistically in participatory learning methods (PALM) to implement the suggested proximity plan.

PMA approach is described as a social learning tool that enables people within the community to share, enhance, and analyze their knowledge and living conditions to plan and act. PMA has evolved within social research and ethnographic methods in social sciences. This approach embeds direct learning from local people offsetting biases, optimizing opinion trade-offs, triangulating information, and seeking diversity. Firms can facilitate content analysis in two phases—by the subjects (unfiltered) and systematically using coding and analysis (filtered). Firms in the PMA process should be able to ensure critical self-awareness and responsibility and share the true and contextual (evidence-based) information with the consumers. Some major attributes of PMA are summarized as follows:

- Evidence mapping and interpretation
- Sociocultural considerations in fieldwork design
- Individual *vs* society, content analysis of qualitative research, triangulation
- Styles of participation and observation
- Ethics in proximity—conduct of corporate leaders, social influencers, and consumers

PMA allows all entities in society irrespective of gender and income differentiation to practice participatory mapping and modeling, transect-walks, and matrix scoring. In PMA exercise, consumers are engaged in mapping their PNS factors, and well-being expectations, and ranking CSR and social infrastructure. Consumers and crowds in the PMA process also explore the existing gaps and try to cocreate concept maps for developing design-to-market, design-to-society, and design-to-value strategies. Such social research of a firm also motivates subjects to develop institutional maps indicating the involvement of a firm in social proximity projects, and their role and performance. Institutional maps are useful in analyzing the perceptions of people not only to measure social proximity but also to evaluate CSR projects. In addition, PMA encourages consumers and crowds to develop perceptual maps, trend, and change analysis and suggest pathways of corporate involvement in enhancing social proximity through value creation. In the PMA, sharing of information and content analysis are based on open discussions through social interactions. PMA has been widely used by the firms to drive social marketing, explore business opportunities, and enhance social proximity of firms in rural and semiurban geodemographic segments. The participatory approach has been useful in exploring the ways in which businesses use and create diverse forms of rural and social capital. This approach helps people (crowd) describe the attributes of manufacturers, marketers, and consumers distinctively marketing with social value creation. Therefore, PMA triggers the debate about whether society proximity alone is a sufficient parameter to define remote outreach and understanding the dynamics of social change driven by local business development (Bosworth and Turner 2018). An effective participatory appraisal requires greater empowerment of the subjects. Sometimes, the information paths are complex and chronologically discrete in PMA compared to the other qualitative social interventions approaches and tools. Therefore, it is not possible to establish standardized methods and tools in PMA, because each process of participatory research must be tailored for the specific community where subjects express their views and construct maps (Menconi et al. 2017). The convergence of PMA and social proximity depends on various factors as illustrated in Figure 4.1.

PMA and social proximity are the people's approach used by the firms to enhance their proximity to the society and customer outreach to build relationships. PMA and social proximity are driven by the six broad domains comprising sociopsychological factors, visibility in community, inner layers of society, participatory actions, information analysis, and action mapping as illustrated in Figure 4.1. PMA has emerged as an institutional tool for concept mapping by attracting people's participation with niche or a larger social conglomerate. Social participation in PMA through corporate social campaigns, sociopolitical moves, and "social commons" help firms in developing cocreated strategies with people's engagement and social consciousness. PMA encourages analyzing collective opinion on products, brands, promotions, social proximity, and individual and group behavior. Collective discussions on social media and business forums reinforce filters to eliminate innate and acquired biases on social or personal context. Such balanced opinion sharing in PMA helps firms in optimizing views of the society within the context of market ecosystem. Besides these sociopsychological factors, visibility in community is largely affected by crowd transparency, open forum interactions, and multicluster social participation in the PMA exercise. However, culture (learned, acquired, and interrelated), anthropomorphic cognition, and ethnographic KAP attributes comprising knowledge, attention, and perceptions often affects the visibility in society. A visible community participation encourages continuity in social learning, diffusion of knowledge, and streamlines the process of knowing, doing, and being. Such state-of-the-art social participation within social proximity helps

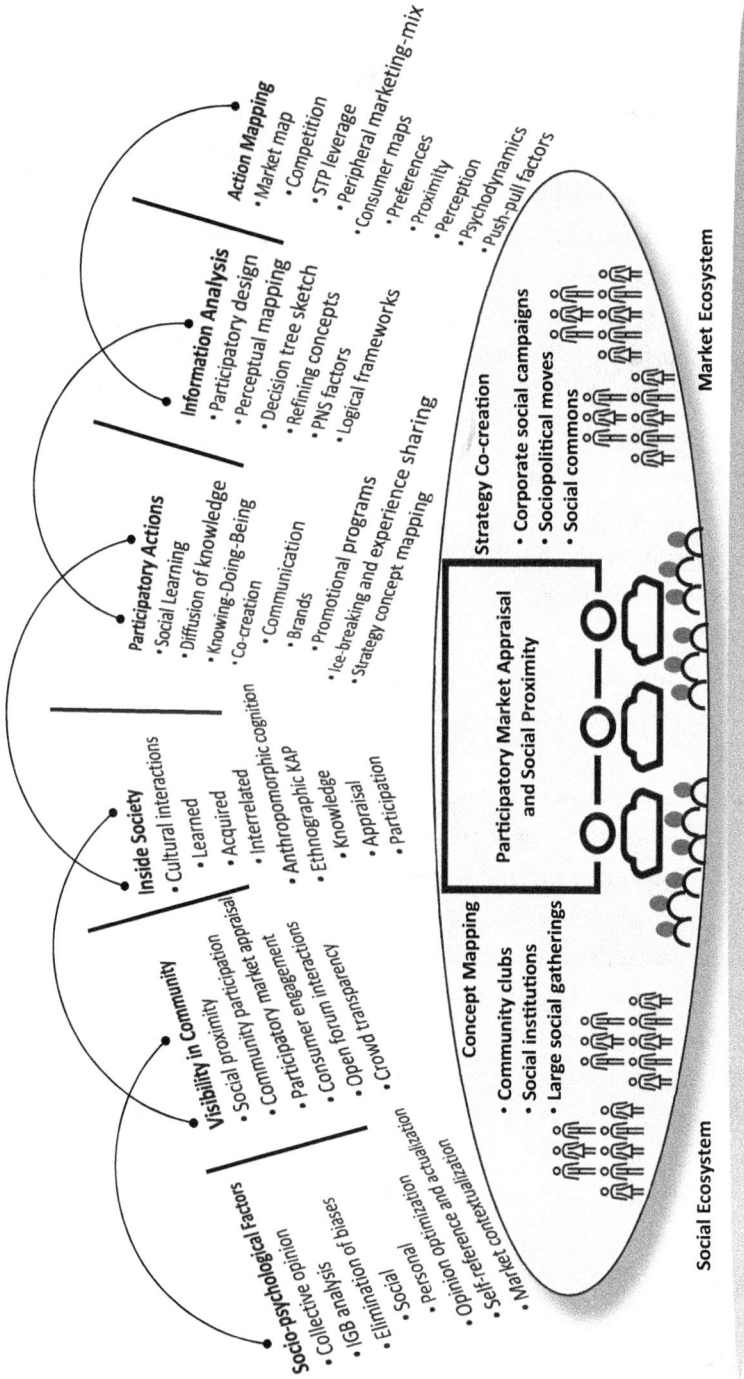

Figure 4.1 Convergence of participatory market appraisal and social proximity

Source: Author.

firms in encouraging crowd, consumers, and stakeholders in cocreation brands, communication, and promotional programs. A major challenge in the PMA exercise is to systematically manage icebreaking, brainstorming, and experience mapping activities, as these factors have high bearing on the development of customer-centric strategies. Based on participatory actions and information analysis firms can cocreate perceptual mapping, decision tree model, and logistics framework by refining concepts related to PNS factors. In addition, PMA also helps firms to understand the market awareness among consumers as in this process participants are engaged in mapping competition, STP leverage (segmentation, targeting, and positioning strategy benefits) and evaluate the fit of peripheral marketing-mix elements. The outer ecosystem of marketing mix includes the following elements that are debated by the participants in PMA:

- 4As: Awareness, Attributes, Availability, and Affordability
- 4Cs: Cost-to-customer, Convenience, Communication, and Conflicts
- 4Vs: Validity, Value, Venue, and Vogue
- 4Es: Expansion, Exploitability, Emotions, and Experience

Consumer maps can be developed during the PMA process to plot preferences, proximity, perceptions, psychodynamics, and push–pull factors by products, demographic segments, and utilitarian or hedonic values.

The experimental designs in building social proximity and customer relations are characterized by a systematic interaction of firm and people on thematic objectives such as new product development, pricing, promotion, and knowledge-transfer programs for a long period. Random selection of people from social cluster to administer a predetermined relationship program might not be effective over the long run. The PMA, therefore, is an experimental design for the firms to develop social proximity, customer relationship, and customer outreach by engaging them in a psychodynamic exercise of common interest. Social proximity programs with focus on social and economic development employ PMA to the rural, semiurban, or urban consumers to explore their consumption perspectives, needs, and the desired solutions to existing problems, which reveal the latent demand. Most firms conduct experimental research to enhance proximity effects by revealing the results of controlled-group experiments by moderating the extraneous variables. Dynamic research designs are developed with variations in the dependent and independent variables woven around the broad research theme. The dynamic proximity enhancement research designs are developed using brainstorming sessions and causal loop diagrams derived out of these sessions. Such research design is used for the subjects (respondents) who have multiple dimensions to express the final output. An example to explain dynamic research design is conducting qualitative research in the health sector with an objective to know the satisfaction of patients on a chronic ailment. In this case, the casual loop diagrams drawn during the preliminary round of conversations with the consumers and stakeholders determine what is important for them to get social health. The community indicators may include cost of treatment (low), abilities of doctors (high), auxiliary support such as nursing (affordable), insurance support (high), or life-expectancy (prolonged). Different respondents may have different focuses on carrying out conversation. Accordingly, the dependent variable will change in reference to the subjects. Such qualitative research is largely consolidated as case studies in a thematic research volume. Virtual platforms such as blogs and vlogs have also become the major resources of ethnographic text mining and virtual interactions. Digital platforms have become the new field for qualitative inquiry and emerged as rich assets for carrying out participatory behaviors that unveil information about interesting lifestyle of people and deliver information about emerging subcultural in contemporary society. The participatory methodology encourages reflexive behavior among the subjects to share inside information, which could not be obtained through quantitative research (Gibson et al. 2004).

In qualitative studies, the ongoing process of mapping consumer perceptions, semantics (interconnected and contextual ideas), and PNS factors often prompts firms to revise the relationship programs. In PMA, firms benefit from the CI where participants are invited to collaborate in participatory action research in designated social laboratories. Such events call for a larger interactive process wherein the primary premises of qualitative inquiry are more fully realized (Stringer 2007). Experimenting

PMA embeds the synchronization of tasks that include identifying research problems, setting social objectives, conceptualization of PNS factors, and seeking ethnographic approach. Content cocreation within the existing social and business situation can be developed through customer interviews, participatory maps, and flowcharts to document the cause-and-effect relationships, and business interactions. PMA has evolved over time within the broad context of evidence-based programs on communication in planning social and business.

Exploring Consumer Insights

Zaltman metaphor elicitation technique (ZMET) is a milestone in measuring the cognitive moves of people on personality development perspectives. ZMET explores both conscious and unconscious thoughts, to understand people from inside at the deepest level possible. Ethnographers, who are involved in mapping the subconscious thoughts of their subjects, use this technique extensively. Firms enhancing social proximity and customer outreach observe, and interact with, people in their most emotionally relevant environments, and combine metaphor elicitation methodology for deeper, more nuanced understanding of the perceptions of all members in a society. By applying the ZMET, firms can determine how effectively people's unconscious emotional drivers identify the meaning people cocreate on the social or personal development standpoints. In this methodology, subjects collect a handful of images representing their thoughts and feelings about a particular topic, and each participant is interviewed using their images as a jumping-off point for discussion. This method is like PMAs, in which subjects map their resources, identify problems, and suggest solutions (Rajagopal 2019).

The ZMET methodology involves the following key elements for cognitive analysis of information:

- Contextual stimuli
- Sensory cognition
- Episodic memory
- Rationale, metaphor, and anthropomorphism
- Emotional consequences

- Physio-psychological response
- Consumer traits and values
- Storytelling and storyboard analysis
- Verbal- and nonverbal communication
- Controlled gestures, voice analytics, and neuroimagery analysis

Contextual stimulus is a situation-based motivation given to the subject during the interview process in qualitative research. The situations are assessed in reference to behavioral status and their expected consequence on the subject. Therefore, opinions of the subjects on pictures widely vary and affect the real-time responses. For instance, a picture of a person who is looking at a food store might stimulate the subject contextually to reveal whether he had passed through such a money crunch situation. The consequence of such contextual stimuli may be either positive or depressing, which might affect the real-time response of the subject. Hence, researchers should understand the behavior of the subject before introducing any contextual stimuli.

Sensory cognition is a process, which moves from senses to the brain, to carry out cognitive analysis. The upstream sectors of synaptic hierarchy in the brain develop unimodal association with the features of sensation such as color, motion, form, and pitch, and encode them for cognitive analytics. However, complex sensory experiences such as objects, faces, word forms, spatial locations, and sound sequences are encoded within downstream sectors of unimodal areas. Hence, colors and physical objects do drive the sensory cognition of the consumers, stakeholders, and business partners during the PMA exercise. Inflexible bonds between sensation and action lead to instinctual and automatic behaviors that are often resistant to change, even when faced with negative consequences (Mesulam 1998). Such sensory cognition helps researchers explore the experiences-led responses over space and time.

Rural PMA in Southeast Asia

HUL studied ethnographically the needs of rural women in India and engaged them in revealing their social and economic perceptions explicitly through both participatory rural and market appraisals. Understanding the need for economic empowerment of rural women has helped HUL in developing the strategy blueprint of *Shakti program* (*Shakti* meaning Power in Hindi language). A participatory move to this program has driven triadic effects on HUL brands in the rural markets in India, which encompassed the corporate drive to enhance social proximity, empowerment, and brand identity. In this way, HUL laid the foundation of *Shakti program*, which pioneered the concept of training local women as rural sales agents who sell Unilever products door to door in their communities. HUL has grown its women-empowerment project Shakti by 50 percent during the period 2019 to 2022. Over 1,60,000 women participate in this women's empowerment and social proximity program, a project that was introduced in the early 2000s. These women are called *Shakti Ammas* and are present in 18 states in the country. These women participants were provided with smartphones, which give them access to the program application. HUL has decided to transfer the commission to participating women directly to their account and each get their money every month (Ahmed 2023). A perennial earning has not only economically empowered rural women but also strengthened their purchasing power and zeal for cocreation and coevolving with the company by sharing their experience, ideas, and ways of business expansion through periodical PMAs.

To attract rural population and enhance social proximity, the company has created audio entertainment for rural areas that can be accessed via smart phones, adapting a common practice among frugal cellphone users: the missed call (giving prematurity call rings). The missed call concept is to send an alert to the contact so that a call back can be generated. This is an economical approach to manage the phone call tolls and save time. To conserve talk time, mobile phone users dial a number, then hang up before they are charged, although the other person can see who called. It's a way of letting someone know you want to reach them. In 2011, HUL exploited this social practice in a pilot promotion for its Active Wheel detergent in some of India's poorest and most rural areas. People were asked to call a number that was cut off after two rings, so it cost them nothing. An automatic free callback provided some comic dialogue from Bollywood star Salman Khan and ads for Wheel. In four months, HUL got 16 million calls and Wheel sales tripled in the region. This strategy has enhanced the social proximity of the company enormously and HUL has become a strong corporate brand icon in rural and semiurban areas.

The company has created variations in Bangladesh, Vietnam, Sri Lanka, Egypt, and other countries. Philippines has abundant micro stores with small volume holding variety of retailers, called *sari-sari* stores that sell as many as 200 different items every day. These stores account for over 36 percent of the sales of fast-moving consumer goods in the country. As distributing goods to these *sari-sari* stores is complicated and expensive, Unilever Philippines proposed to recruit some of the larger stores to serve as subdistributors alongside their regular operations after conducting a quick PMA exercise with these retailer communities. Unilever offered the superstores discounts on it brands, while the *sari-sari* stores get better access to more brands of the company. The superstores also serve as the venues for social stimulation, called *fiestas*, which combine product demonstrations and giveaways with games and entertainment. Unilever organizes about 500 fiestas annually to promote prime brands, which contribute to a leap of 30–80 percent of sales during fiesta weeks. Similarly, Unilever Thailand launched Platinum store initiative to transform urban shopping experience to rural customers by restructuring stores with limited offerings in rural areas. Sitting with the rural store owners in a PMA and participatory learning exercises, Unilever helps them design their layouts, develop promotions, and bring in partner companies for services such as ATMs. However, these stores must meet certain requirements, including assuring strong visual merchandising of Unilever products. The redesigned Platinum stores attract more customer traffic and revenue (Mahajan 2016).

Social Proximity and Social Marketing

Social marketing is an approach to develop socially beneficial behavior for community-oriented products and services. In this context, social marketing is a concept of cocreation, and has been explored in several social marketing examples from marketing of birth-control contraceptives to renewable energy and water conservation products for social benefit.

Cocreation is the process of customers and producers determining value together, where customers are engaged at all levels of value proposition and market transaction. Value, cocreated in the social products and their marketing to customers, relies on the belief that customers are proactive to the social innovations and their applications (Desai 2008).

Social networks are growing rapidly, and they engage people in expressing their viewpoints on different genres of topics including business and innovation. Customers and stakeholders of customer-centric companies share their opinions or ideas on social media sites such as Facebook, Twitter, or Instagram. The acquired information is subjected to analyzing contributors' preferences, backgrounds, task-related information, and social relationships to match corporate goals and contributors for crowdsourcing tasks (Li et al. 2021). As the competition is increasing in the global marketplace, most firms are reorienting their marketing communication strategies through customer-to-customer networking, as customer-driven communication is found more trustworthy and decisive. Consequently, consumers are adopting increasingly active roles in cocreating marketing communication with companies and their respective brands. Most of the emerging firms are working hard in developing online social marketing programs and brand campaigns to reach consumers where they "live" virtually. However, the challenge faced by many companies is apparently the way to be active in social media, as most firms do not have clear understanding of how to manage the social networks effectively, and what performance indicators they should be measuring and how. Further, as companies develop social media strategies, platforms such as YouTube, Facebook, and Twitter are too often treated as stand-alone elements rather than the part of an integrated system. Firms should invest in building strategies in a systematic way to understand and conceptualize online social media as an ecosystem of related elements involving both digital and traditional media (Hanna et al. 2011).

The collaboration and networking platforms empower employees, customers, and partners to be active participants in global conversation. Social media tools and platforms provide an effective communications channel for customer-centric business communication and as a transparent knowledge-sharing initiative across the organization. Firms must establish a process for delivering the voice of truth through right communication in social media platforms by disseminating authentic, trusted, and believable information. This reinforces the idea that social media can be promoted by the firms as a tool not only to voice ideas and concerns but also to get accurate and credible solutions on various issues of consumers. Social media and CI allow information to flow in multiple directions rather than just from the top down. The convergence of communication helps firms in managing crowdsourced information and sharing experiences on innovations, improvements, and temporary setbacks. People with common interests, or related role players can form communities to learn from and support one another on social media platforms. Social media can also help firms in cases where there is a need for creating a more collaborative culture and drive the change initiatives (Rajagopal 2013).

Social marketing strategies are effective tools to align business goals with social development and value-generation perspectives. Social innovations, sustainable development, green marketing, and implementing CSR programs stimulate the enhancement of performance with social purpose. This linear path bridging the gap between society and business validates the design-to-society and design-to-market philosophies. Social validation of marketing programs by sharing customer experiences on digital platforms and generating user-driven contents creates the scope of cocreation of products and services effectively within the society and the market. Sustainable customer products companies such as IKEA, GE Energy, and Unilever focus on inducing corporate social leadership in managing the CSR. However, while implementing society-linked business models, companies tend to develop community hubs for customer and stakeholder interactions on face-to-face, digital, or hybrid communication models. The interactions of customers on these platforms help companies document the voice-of-customers to support strategy designs. In addition, public policies, public–private partnerships, and social psychodynamics leverage companies in designing programs to evolve in vulnerable social sectors (health, education, housing, agriculture, and nonfarm economic production) with meticulous business strategies. Social business is a value-led function involving customers, stakeholders, and entrepreneurs. The initiatives of involving the social entities in cocreating products and services help firms in driving quickly to cocreate and strengthen social business due to wider acceptability among customers. Social businesses are more effective in reaching bottom-of-the pyramid customer segment and transforming demand for innovative products. Therefore, building a social base for innovative products ensures reaping of higher gains as compared to the market-oriented competitive strategies. Cocreation is an upcoming phenomenon in business ecosystem, which involves society and business in sharing and adapting experiences of people respectively. It is a bidirectional dynamic of exchanging ideas, experiences, innovation concepts, developing prototypes, and commercializing generic thought into the business avenues. Experiencing cocreation is an art, which is portrayed by the business communities with the support of personal and digital interfaces to know the insights of all players, including customers, in the market operations. Cocreation of business models with the underlying customer and stakeholder experiences has emerged as a new paradigm of strategy innovation. Customer-centric companies such as Nestlé, Conagra, Amazon, Unilever, and Tata India can explore the public domain holistically today to innovate products and services with compelling value propositions through cocreating the strategy with effective employee engagement (Ramaswamy and Gouillart 2008). The core and peripheral factors affecting business proximity with society to create value through PMA and social engagement are illustrated in Figure 4.2.

Business proximity to society and market is governed by the four principal domains comprising social marketing, consumer creativity, social technology, and corporate connect with the social and corporate ecosystem as exhibited in Figure 4.2. However, at the core PMA, behavioral portfolios of consumers, PNS factors, and ACCA as collective approach nurture the design thinking at the core of business proximity to society. With the advancement of ICT, social media channels have grown digital by disseminating the community contents emerged through the active and radical psychodynamics. These factors significantly diffuse the effects of social proximity of firms and encourage consumer creativity through crowd dynamics comprising crowdsourcing, crowdfunding, and crowd cognition. Crowd engagement in consumer well-being and business promotion ambidextrously and significantly contributes to CI. Consequently, there is a need to develop soft community infrastructure

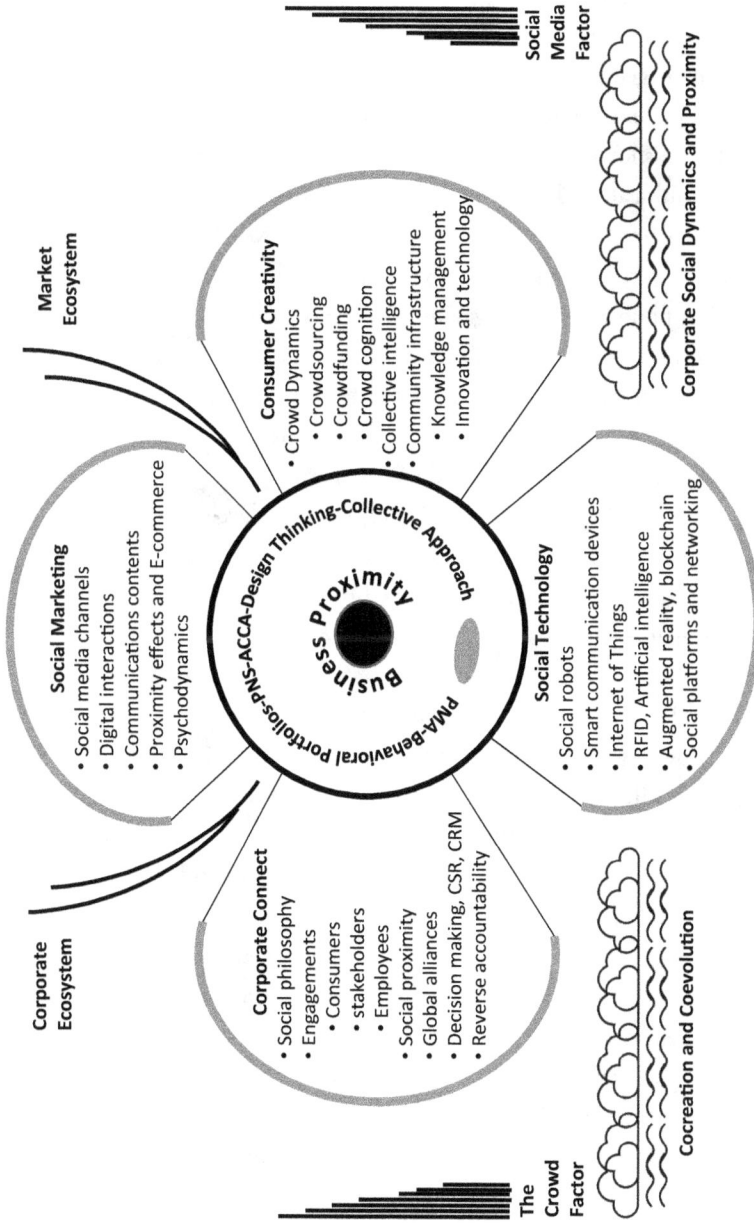

Figure 4.2 Business proximity to society and market: a holistic view

Source: Author.

on knowledge management, innovation, and technology. Besides these challenges, technology-driven firms are engaged in providing social robots to exchange social information supported by the AI, smart communication devices such as smartphones and notebooks, Internet of Things, and a combination of geographic positioning system and communication. Radio frequency identification (RFID) and blockchain communication technologies have shown an integrated effect in developing social proximity by the health care industry in rural and semiurban areas. A perfect blend of social marketing, consumer creativity, and social technology has helped firms to redefine and reinforce corporate connect as a changing relationship philosophy by engaging all players in business, society, and marketing in a holistic manner. Accordingly, global alliances with social institutions in the developing countries has significantly impacted the social proximity of firms through reverse accountability, CSR, and customer relationship management in the 21st century.

Often, firms growing with crowdfunding tend to develop alliances with social networks and engage in media advocacy to complement a social marketing program. Commonly, crowd-based businesses operated through social marketing programs are intervened by the social conventions, local politics, and community organizations to gain social support. For example, a health care company may involve social networks to disseminate knowledge about breast cancer, and the diagnosis and treatments associated with it. Though this issue might be raised by the health care company as a social marketing debate, it also appears to be an issue to be addressed by the local nongovernmental organizations and the local politics. Hence, this product of crowdfunded social health clinics in a social network could attract any of these behaviors—getting an annual mammogram as a mix of social–commercial issue, seeing a physician each year for a breast exam as a matter of social health care programs offered by the local public governance, and performing monthly breast self-exams as an issue associated with social education. As social media activities achieve scale of returns over a period, the challenges of the company may center less around justifying funding and more on organizational issues such as developing the right processes and governance structure and identifying clear roles for all involved in social media strategy.

At the core of every company, there exists crowd-based group of varied sizes consisting of customers, investors (emerging out of crows, regular, and potential investors), and key partners who raise the voice on design, process, performance, and profit goals and achievements. Broadly, the voice of customers is critical to design quality and marketing strategies. Firms need to nurture these groups as the think tank of knowledge and provide liberal space to share their emotions, experience, and egalitarian values. They contribute to the CI over time, which encourages firms to adapt to the organizational behavior of knowing (acquiring and analyzing information), doing (adapting to practical recommendations of the group), and being (growing as customer-centric company with competitive differentiation). Long-standing crowd communities (such as Microsoft user communities, Kindle self-publishing communities, and Amazon prime communities) grow like an institution, which comprises the people whose perceived interests and needs are considered, as decisions are made throughout the organization. In the large customer-centric organizations, the core group constituted out of larger segment of stakeholders and customers (may be defined as crowd segment) is supported by the organization to grow as a CI resource). The members of the core group share unique values and knowledge that support corporate decisions toward new designs, product development, and developing competitive marketing strategies; and induce independence, creativity, and power, across the employees of the company. Such behavior of key partners, stakeholders, and customers create sustainable value, and boost-up the practice of taking collective decisions and adapting to bottom-up organizational strategies in developing new innovations and managing strategies (Kleiner 2003). The business environment today is hierarchically arrayed within industry with transitional multimodal business system across large firms. Large firms within industries (such as pharmaceuticals) develop business consortiums and focus on collaborative strategizing and expanding the key partners geographically. The changing business ecosystems today drive greater flexibility in strategic partnership by allowing firms to develop collaborations contextual to the CI, social values, and benefit—spread across the stakeholders (Reeves et al. 2015). Such a shift in the business philosophy has encouraged the role of CI in building customer-centric strategies and cocreating customer-centric innovations to develop stand-alone posture in the competitive marketplace. The growth of virtual commerce (electronic and mobile commerce) has emerged as the most popular outgrowth of marketing-with-customer philosophy.

It is observed that if individualism–collectivism in business is adequately balanced, they serve as a good source of intercultural fit while building shared leadership to protect mutual values. Such managerial perspectives help firms in reconfiguring individual and cultural orientations and styles of persons of different origin in the design of management teams to build high levels of social effectiveness in the work environment (Carlos 2005). However, managing the cross-cultural challenges in the workplace may be made easy by developing a strategic fit of values in the organization with flexibility in individual values and shared personality traits. In the low-trust cultures, the interpersonal relationship remains obscure and business dealings are largely bureaucratized and tagged with evidence. Such negotiation approaches slow down the process of getting the work done and may cause retrenchment from the business scenario over time. Thus, it is necessary to identify the right and responsive people, who can be relied upon and who qualify on organizational parameters, to build future relationship continuum.

Firms may find effective ways in working with social media applications to deliver personalized learning experiences to the consumers related to the brand equity, promotions, and comparative advantages. Firms should not use social media just for general broadcasts of information. Business organizations should use social media linked innovative collaboration platforms in a variety of ways to encourage effective company–consumers–suppliers coordination in information-sharing and knowledge-building opportunities. Social media and collaboration solutions allow information to flow in multiple directions rather than only from the top down. For example, using wikis and microblogs applications for sharing short bursts of information, marketing firms can crowd-source ideas and involve employees more directly in innovative strategies. Firms can build greater internal loyalty by actively soliciting continuous feedback on issues related to the change. Social media is an important addition to a traditional change management program, one that can dramatically increase the acceptance of change and advance an organization more predictably toward its business goals. Collaboration and social media tools can reduce the time an organization needs to navigate large-scale change programs and deliver a better solution for consumer-related marketing issues in the future. The exponential growth of social media has been observed from the beginning of the 21st century with manifold channels booming around the world. Besides, independent and company-led blogs have also been able to attract stakeholder interactions and build categorical resources (society, technology, sustainability, innovation, green consumerism, and consumer electronics). The increasing contribution of CI also percolates from video informatics and journalism published on the Facebook, Twitter, LinkedIn, Instagram, and YouTube, which offers firms to explore the user-generated contents in creating customer-centric communication and stay competitive. Both the extensive and intensive use of social media channels by the customers and stakeholders has thrusted companies to use it as a tool for mass customization by motivating crowd-based design thinking for their own products in a democratic way, manifesting the philosophy of "by the people and for the people." Consequently, social media has nearly democratized most businesses by empowering people not only to gain stakeholder and customer confidence but also to focus the company's business explicitly to the target customers (Hildebrand et al. 2013).

Consumer Creativity and Business Proximity

Cocreation has emerged as an outgrowth of crowdsourcing and crowdfunding practices in most firms engaged in commercialization of innovative customer-centric products and services. Collective brainstorming to generate new ideas and coevolving the business with the innovative products, which have the potential for market disruptions, often provide competitive leverage to crowd-based businesses. Stimulating ideation process in crowd is effectively channelized through the social networks by creating portfolio-based groups to allow conscious participation. Crowdsourcing has become a dynamic tool in the business ecosystem today, which stimulates collective ideation, critical thinking, and investor prospects. The crowd-based ideas are largely customer centric and based on cost-effective technologies. However, there are many challenges in branding crowd-based products and developing competitive marketing strategies to commercialize them. Often, crowd-based business ideas portray strong disruptive attributes and drive product attractiveness against the existing brands. The CI embeds social emotions and strong psychodynamics that have the potential to disrupt the demand of existing brands in the competitive marketplace. Crowd-based ideation supports companies in cocreation and coevolution processes with stakeholders through social interaction, social innovations, and social governance. In the context of crowd-based businesses ecosystem, customer and potential investors constitute the core of crowd to contribute ideas and resources. Social entrepreneurship is therefore a community comprising various levels of interdependent innovation-driven business projects, which coevolve in an ongoing business cycle and constantly renew their crowd configurations. The business ecosystem of crowd-based firms is affected by extrinsic factors comprising political, economic, social, technological, environmental, and legal subsystems in a given region. The coevolution process of business models based on crowd-sourced ideas enclose collective vision, codesigning inputs, and cocreation potential as the triadic activities in a business domain (Liu and Rong 2015). Public policies encourage cocreation of social innovation and potential competitive business projects through crowdsourcing, crowdfunding, and public–private partnership in developing countries. However, the crowdfunding regulations are yet to take a mature shape in many emerging markets. In India, crowdfunds can be raised for a social cause to support public health, education, ecological housing, and rural transport in the form of donations. Equity crowdfunding in India is illegal. To issue equity shares in India, companies need to comply with the provisions of The Companies Act, 2013. The Act provides detailed provisions and rules regarding the issue of equity shares through public and private placement. The crowdfunding policies focus on improving the sociocultural conditions by ensuring higher social and economic gains in managing social innovation and sustainability projects. Such public policies emphasize pooling of crowd capital resources within the approved financial outlay of the business projects, develop cooperation strategies, and encourage community business governance or proportionate share in the firm's governing board. Crowd-based companies tend to explore different types of alliances that combine productivity, spontaneity, and tangible outcomes in the context of managing sustainability projects, eco-innovations, management, and marketing. In this process, relationships among the customers, potential crowd-investors, social entrepreneurs, and firms contribute significantly in promoting cooperative networks engaged in developing attractive strategy for improving performance (Lin and Jin 2016).

Collective information boosts social values in various layers. At the bottom of the pyramid, the values of CI (ideation, reviews, and investment proposals) not only pool information but also inculcate emotions, esteem, and commitment among the people and entrepreneurs. These factors positively influence the value-creation process. The crowd-based businesses rely on value creation to develop and strengthen relationships with the customers, stakeholders, and potential investors (donors) that enables cocreation, and coevolution of social innovation and business projects. The crowd investors, donors, and equity holders have a sense of belongingness in crowdfunded firms, and they intend to have community governance of such firms. In addition, collaborative projects promoting stakeholder engagements in managing sustainable projects, innovations, and technologies contribute to the social value creation (Liu et al. 2020). B-to-C and B-to-B markets are driven by consumer demands because they are perceived as more value oriented and of added benefits. Locally integrated strategies of business-to-consumer companies of micro-, small-, and medium sizes exhibit the current trends of consumer engagements and cocreation. Such crowd-based business model explains the current trends from economic perspectives, and the new crowd-based organizational theory is beginning to examine the organizing principles of such firms at the bottom of the pyramid (Tallman and Fladmoe-Lindquist 2002). In the customer-centric business models, firms often assure product quality and services, and tend to overcome the administrative complexities on cost control, environmental technologies, and chaotic social issues. The cocreation and codesigning approaches of customer-centric companies such as IKEA have established business philosophy of connecting with consumers and developing an emotion-based relationship with them as the key to leveraging loyalty and advocacy behavior (Rajagopal 2019).

Entrepreneurs in crowdfunded firms are engaged mostly in developing social innovations by exploring the social resources including social capital, skills, capabilities and competencies, stakeholders' values, and expected returns. These firms are engaged with their crowd-based collaborators in improving existing business practices and acquired competencies to integrate crowdsourced ideas and corporate goals to codesign and cocreate business models for niche segments (Arena et al. 2020). Effective social innovators stimulate external stakeholders to meet the existing social needs and build strategies for business initially focused around the bottom-of-the-pyramid market segment with a scope to penetrate the mass market. Creating social businesses and sustainable innovation, therefore, are aimed at delivering cost-effective and long-term solutions through social marketing approaches. Most multinational firms are targeting bottom-of-the-pyramid market segments to acquire higher market share in the mass market, and these firms are fostering to develop a sustainable value chain. These firms, in association with small and medium enterprises, tend to build local markets and augment the scope of markets considering the 4A elements comprising awareness, acceptance, adaptability, and affordability toward the crowdfunded social brands. Firms growing with the collective business approaches also invest in educating local market players and alliance partners, developing infrastructure, and providing value-added community services. The alliance firms also create shared value by improving products and reorganizing market segments, redefining productivity in the value chain, and enabling local cluster development.

In crowd-based firms, consumers and potential investors are considered as the valuable source of innovation. They effectively engage in cocreation activities such as the generation, design, refinement, and testing of ideas, and building new product concepts. Crowd collaboration helps firms in developing new products and services with customer focus. The voice of customers, projections on investments, and crowd-based business strategies help firms to provide effective solutions to decrease the high failure rates among new products. Crowd-based firms not only explore the opinions, desires, and needs of consumers, potential investors, and social leaders but also motivate them to contribute their creativity and problem-solving skills to design, develop, and deliver (3D) the disruptive products (Rajagopal 2021). Consequently, consumers serve as cocreators. Crowdsourcing has also become a common practice among the large multinational companies to increase the proximity with customers and inculcate brand value. With the growing success of crowdsourcing contribution, most companies have developed virtual platforms to collect information. However, the transfer of tacit knowledge that enables consumers to innovate with the firms needs a high level of stimulation focused on returning benefits. Competitively strong customer-centric companies have focused on the development of superior crowdsourcing tools for concept evaluation through virtual prototypes and product testing (Füller 2014).

In 2012, Heineken, a Dutch beer company, asked designers in different destinations about how the future of night clubs in Europe should be. Many volunteer product designers, customers, and product critiques joined the campaign, and their semantically mapped opinions were presented at Milan's Design Week in 2012, with a live recreation of the space. Apart from being a cocreation success story, the cocreation initiative of the company has attracted considerable media impact and it has also become a reference campaign in terms of advertising and marketing. In addition, Heineken launched its cocreation platform in 2012, asking game lovers, beer drinkers, and environmentally conscious consumers for ideas that would make its packaging more sustainable. Similarly, Threadless, a fashion e-commerce company that manages and sells crowd-sourced T-shirt designs, built a sustainable model by producing high-quality shirts in limited quantities to create the sense of a premium brand. The company pushed cocreation by inviting users to suggest designs and buying preferences. Consumers posted their design in the website while other users voted on the design options and the creations that received the most support from the community were produced. Threadless is an artistic creation and has become a profitable business. Crowdsourcing, therefore, raises an evident example of sustainable payoff among large, small, and start-up ventures (Boghin 2014).

Companies engage consumers in knowledge cocreation and collaborative knowledge diffusion processes to support an interpretive model of the consumer knowledge. The knowledge cocreation process encourages diffusion of customer-generated contents on social media and helps in strengthening the community learning design. Consumers learn about products, services, and new consumption patterns through community resources. The community learning process prompts coshopping and coviewing of brands in the marketplace, and stimulates consumers to review the referrals and conform to community decisions. Hence, most referral programs of consumer products companies focus on diffusing brand awareness among the family or community as a source of knowledge hub of consumers (Rajagopal 2019). Most social-centric companies develop new products as "design-to-value" by involving consumers in cocreation process. Such consumer and stakeholder engagements in new product development help companies effectively manage seasonality of products in the marketplace and develop sustainable consumer attitude and consumption behavior. Therefore, it is observed that like social needs, consumer behavior also turns value oriented over time. The consumer value chain often supports sustainability and social consciousness.

Cocreation with customers has evidenced a wide success among some brands of customer-centric companies. However, the challenges that practitioners need to overcome in building and sustaining online collaboration in design and product development process include hypothetical ideas, high project costs, market risks, and the expected time to prepare market in adapting to the products based on the CI. Since 2001, Procter and Gamble (P&G) has successfully been bringing outsiders into its research and development process and motivating them to speak out their ideas on new product development. The company has also targeted senior citizens with specific skill sets, ex-employees, and retired technical specialists of airline companies. The cocreation platform of the company—"Connect + Develop"—has supported many products across portfolios, improved product development process, and effectively doubled the number of employees engaged in the research and development area of the company without adding to payroll costs, though incentives were given to external collaborators (Boghin 2014).

Successful innovation leads to customer involvement and profits, which can be achieved through cocreation by aligning consumers and market players in the innovation process. Some multinational companies have invested in sustainability projects by taking advantage of social media to diffuse new ideas and stimulating cocreation of innovative products and services. For example, the role of cocreation has become central to sustainability management in the social initiatives of the 21st century. Energy market transition, which is enabled by new affordable energy technologies and digitalization, opens novel opportunities for developing innovative energy solutions through CI and public–private cocreations. The new technologies emerging through cocreation enable stakeholders to buy low-cost renewable energy. The process of coinnovation is stretching the ideation process through extensive use of digital platforms and stakeholder involvement. Coinnovation is an ecosystem-wide activity that involves multiple stakeholders who collaborate toward a shared social goal and explore niche strategies to commercialize eco-innovations. However, in active societies such as Chinese sociological and business culture, the co-innovators simultaneously compete with one another across geo-demographic segments to market their innovative products and services (Kotilainen et al. 2019).

Consumer Emotions, Socialization, and Proximity

Consumer emotions are largely set through verbal and nonverbal market communications extended by the companies. Advertisements play a critical role in stimulating consumer emotions. Since the late 20th century, as the usage of computers has rapidly grown, the Internet has been the prime anchor of marketing communications and stimulant of consumer emotions. Compared to offline media communications, social network platforms possess unique characteristics that affect the likelihood of generating emotions and reactions to the experience on the brand among fellow customers and employees of the firm. The emotions online are largely driven by the vividness of social networks, interactivity, challenge, interaction speed, machine memory, and allowable social interactions. Depending on how a social network platform performs on these dimensions, positive or negative emotions on the products, services, or on the image of the company may emerge. For example, using machine memory to automatically generate purchase recommendations based on prior consumption patterns may be perceived as pleasantly surprising, while a firm sending unsolicited e-mails based on a user's cookie trail may be annoying. Such feelings generated and shared by the consumers get attached to the brand and build its equity in the market. Thus, the challenge for brand managers is to get consumers to develop positive emotions with a brand, and to manage company sponsors' social network websites by understanding the consumer emotions and their ramifications (Jones et al. 2008).

Driving arousal and merriment among consumers as a major influencing factor in making buying decisions is a recent strategy and an innovative concern of retailers, as these factors reveal personalized enjoyment during shopping. Arousal during shopping may be seeded through multifaceted activity that may be performed in various ways and embodies different consumer feelings. However, firms at times fail to recognize that what influences buyers' satisfaction is not the same as what engenders store loyalty, and consequently does not effectively develop the retail ambience to stimulate buying decisions. Hence, they need to vigilantly manage the quality of arousal and merriment by developing adequate customer involvement in the buying process and retain young consumers (Miranda et al. 2005). The three distinct dimensions of emotions including pleasantness, arousal and merriment, and dominance have been identified as major drivers for making buying decisions among adolescent consumers. The retail point of purchase is the time and place at which all the elements of a sale—the consumer, the money, and the product—converge. Marketers must make the most of the communication possibilities at this point to increase their sales (Rajagopal 2006). There are some common strategies adopted by retailers to overcome the problems of fickle consumers, price-slashing competitors, and mood swings in the economy. Such wishful thinking holds that retailers will thrive only if they communicate better with young consumers through in-store amusement, recreation, and collaborative product demonstrations involving consumers, to help their purchase decisions. Most customer-centric firms also offer buying incentives to develop conviction on buying such tried-out products (Berry 2001).

Consumer socialization among peers is driven by the dynamism of social media, which encourages market-based interactions among the peers. The blogs, instant messaging, and social networking sites all provide communication tools that make the socialization process easy and convenient. The virtual communities easily socialize new incumbents into common and special interest groups and help them quickly learn task-related knowledge and skills through their interactions with other members. Besides quick inductions of members in the virtual groups, the inflow of consumers to social media websites is increasing and helping them communicate with others and find information to help them make various consumption-related decisions. The grapevine effect of social media also facilitates education and information analysis among the members, as the socialization agents within the informal groups provide vast product information and evaluations quickly (Taylor et al. 2011). Some studies reveal that peer communications influence consumers to such an extent that they convert others into virtual shoppers, while some retailers also encourage social media communication by setting up tell-a-friend functions on websites.

Besides innovation and social stimulation, consumer behavior is largely driven by personal expectations and associate values. Therefore, customer-centric companies are investing in creating customer value through crowd-based motivation, customer relations, and offering products and services of sustainable utilitarian values. In addition, social health issues have taken a center stage to persuade consumers on well-being, diet, and organic consumption values, which has both crowd-based and individual appeals. Such dual focus of social and business development through value creation drives consumers to alter consumer behavior and ensure not only confidence in the brand and firm but also provide opportunity to firms for expanding the geodemographic outreach. In such marketing approach, brands play a critical role in shifting the consumer behavior to more profitable product portfolios. The social brands today have higher potential to both create and shift consumer behavior by stimulating consumers toward experimentation and value creation, aligning with the corporate goals and strategies, and judging the performance of products and services through CI and perceive values. In addition, partnering with social institutions and creating a crowd movement to validate the corporate strategies on creating value among consumers and markets also play a significant role in determining the consumer behavior today (Sidibe 2020). This approach has allowed Unilever's sustainable living brands such as Dove to help over 35 million young people around the world with self-esteem education since 2005, and Lifebuoy, which has reached over billion consumers with its handwashing campaigns educating social preventive health care measures and created immense consumer value. Similarly, Ben & Jerry's food products, which are followed by the campaigns for social justice and climate change, and Unilever's social strategy of empowering rural women through the Shakti program (*Shakti* meaning Power in Hindi language) have created enormous customer value and sustainable behavior.

The acquired and shared culture among consumers drives awareness about the new trends, which in turn, arouses new consumer preferences. For example, consumer preferences for 3D games, virtual reality products, and trendy consumer electronics influence consumers in the emerging markets as millennial effect. The experience sharing over digital platforms further influences the consumer behavior over a long time. Patterns of consumerism are changing in society, as there are shifts in the consumer demography in the markets. The explosion of mass consumer segment, urbanization, and increase in the size of the population of aging consumers have contributed significantly to the shifts in consumer preferences and overall consumption behavior. Direct-to-customer marketing strategies, convenience shopping, and social media-driven marketing approaches of companies have increased social and cultural influence on developing consumer behavior. However, disruption in technology, and attraction toward local consumption also contribute in driving the consumer behavior dynamic across geodemographic segments. In addition, extended technology life cycle builds positive consumer perceptions on higher value for money. Cocreation and codesigning approaches of customer-centric companies such as IKEA have established the business philosophy of connecting consumers and developing an emotion-based relationship with consumers as the key to leveraging loyalty and advocacy behavior. Cocreation and coevolution appear to be effective processes in building consumer behavior. Firms relying on crowd-based business models and CI, such as IKEA, LEGO, and Starbucks, have experienced that customer engagement with crowd-motivation serves as best strategies to inculcate consumer behavior. Such strategies leverage a company's core capabilities on one hand and help in acquiring customers on the other, by generating emotions and sense of belongingness for the brand. Understanding both self-references-based and induced consumer perceptions plays a significant role behind conscious (self- and crowd-referred) and unconscious (imaginary and unclear choices). Research-oriented firms invest in exploring such consumer behavior in their customers and watch behavioral transitions. Customer-centric companies build cumulative advantage by mining the emotional connection of brands with the customers, such as LEGO explores over time that many people have high satisfaction with the dark colors of building blocks (Lafley et al. 2017).

Case Studies

Social Marketing and Proximity: A Corporate Campaign Mosaic

This section discusses four brief case studies on social and proximity marketing experimented by various customer-centric firms through social campaigns, crowd dynamics, and CI. Most firms have founded their social proximity approach on cause marketing, while some firms followed the public interest as the key to enhance social proximity and outreach to customers. Consumer products and services companies have found that the passage through social media to acquire new customers and enhance social proximity, is most appropriate to create awareness and acquaintances of customers with the brands and corporate policies.

Wendy's, an American fast-food giant, followed proximity marketing approach to radical expansion of its customers against the polarization, defection, and substitution behavior of customers over the years. The company experienced a meteoric rise in 2017, which revealed customer loyalty, brand love, service appreciation, and customer attention of the company. Consequently, this brand has received high popularity amidst the rapid and radically growing competition in the consumer food services industry. The social proximity campaign, driven by the company using the social media platforms with its witty one-liners, sharp comebacks, and savage roasts on Twitter, has upheld the brand image and helped the company in socializing their brand. Twitter users wanted the brand's roasts with pure unadulterated fun of getting roasted (chicken) by Wendy's. The Twitter strategy of the company succeeds in driving the social proximity manifold by embedding the unique sense of humor that they consistently engaged in the social media platforms over time. This is a great example of how a customer-centric company can leverage social media such as Twitter with humor, CI, and consistent brand persuasion to drive the social media campaigns to success at the social core. Wendy's strategy has led to a current Twitter following of over 4 million users.

"Let's talk what people talk" was the inspiration to the National Biscuit Company (Nabisco) to take the brand deeper into society and drive proximity to the product by acquiring new customers and markets across the regions. OREO brand crafted the campaign on power cut in the neighborhood to illustrate the color and texture of the biscuit. The company has followed the social media approach to enhance proximity to their brand and customer outreach to cocreate value. The social media campaign "Dunk in the dark" through Twitter is a thrilling example of clever and spontaneous marketing, which captures the attention of social media participants and elevates the social proximity of the brand by creating awareness and attraction. This idea related contextually to a power outage experienced that left fans literally in the dark in New Orleans during the Super Bowl in 2013. The company has moved this storyline to the reality-based social experience in the rural and semiurban areas in developing countries in Southeast Asia, Africa, and Latin America. As people have experienced both predictable and unpredictable power cuts, relating the color of the biscuits with darkness makes people understand the brand appeal. Meanwhile, the OREO marketing team linked the communication to a social continuum released the tweet as "power out, no problem, you can still dunk in dark." The tweet was shared over 13.8K times, resulting in phenomenal brand reach.

To commemorate 90 years of Mickey Mouse, as well as to support the Make-A-Wish foundation, Disney launched their #ShareYourEars campaign in 2018 on Twitter. This campaign enabled the visitors to cherish the memories and creative art of Mickey character by decorating a pair of Mickey Mouse paper ears and post a picture of them wearing the ears with the hashtag #ShareYourEars. This campaign attracted customers to express their perception, creativity, and emotions on the Mickey Mouse character on social media. A significant social proximity was generated through this campaign as most people could post their favorite pair of Mickey Mouse ears from the Disney parks, or any "creative ears" that resembled Mickey's, to join the campaign and inculcate a sense of belon ingness. The campaign, in return, aimed that Disney would then donate $5 for every post to the Make-A-Wish Foundation, which generated a brand socialization effect through cause marketing. This campaign has received over 1.77 million posts and over 420 million social impressions for Disney, with approximately three-time increase in customer outreach and quintuple increase in engagement for Make-A-Wish.

Xiaomi, the Chinese technology company, has a clear mandate to reach out to people by stimulating social proximity through the social media, and stay in constant contact with its loyal customers on their cocreation community forum MIUI, which is known as Mi User Interface (MIUI, pronounced as "Me You I"), is a customized Android ROM developed by Xiaomi (Mi) for smartphones and tablets based on the Android operating system. The platform has over 10 million registered users and more than 100,000 daily publications where the brand's most hardcore fans meet to discuss gadgets, share knowledge, and generally lay seed of cocreation. Loyal customers also voice their preferences for the next version of mobile phones of the company. Employees of the company monitor the forum, continuously looking for customer feedback and possible improvements. Reward mechanisms such as points for participation, access discounts, and other exclusive benefits are also implemented to drive loyal members in the community.

Summary

PMA is a qualitative approach used by firms to understand consumer behavior, brand consciousness, preferences, and perceived value. This approach is based on community participation to document knowledge and opinions on corporate communications, brands, marketing strategies, and competitive leverages in planning social and business proximity programs. Proximity research through PMA therefore leads to the development of customer-centric strategies and programs that are creative, productive, and sustainable in the competitive marketplace. The chapter argues that PMA engages people in society holistically in a PALM to implement the suggested proximity plan. Consequently, it can be stated that PMA and social proximity are the people's approach used by the firms to enhance their proximity to the society and customer outreach to build relationships. PMA and social proximity are driven by the six broad domains comprising sociopsychological factors, visibility in community, inner layers of society, participatory actions, information analysis, and action mapping.

Social collaborations and use of networking platforms empower employees, customers, and partners to be active participants in global conversation. This chapter delineates that social media tools and platforms provide an effective communications channel for customer-centric business communication and as a transparent knowledge-sharing initiative across the organization. Proximity marketing strategies also strengthen the scope of social marketing to align business goals with customer value-generation perspectives. Collective information boosts social values through various layers. At the bottom of the pyramid, the values of CI (ideation, reviews, and investment proposals) not only pool information but also inculcate emotions, esteem, and commitment among the people and entrepreneurs. Efficiency in social marketing and sustainable innovation, therefore, are aimed at delivering cost-effective, value packed, and long-term solutions. Consumer emotions are largely set through verbal and nonverbal market communications extended by the companies. Advertisements play a critical role in stimulating consumer emotions. In addition, consumer socialization among peers also drives dynamism on social media, which encourages market-based interactions among the peers.

References

Ahmed, A. January 9, 2023. "Hindustan Unilever's Women Empowerment Project Shakti Rises by 50% Over the Last 3 Years." *The Hindu Business Line* (Business Newspaper).

Arena, M., G. Azzone, and G. Piantoni. 2020. "Shared Value Creation During Site Decommissioning: A Case Study From the Energy Sector." *Journal of Cleaner Production* 251, (in press). https:// doi.org/10.1016/j.jclepro.2019.119587.

Berry, L.L. 2001. "The Old Pillars of New Retailing." *Harvard Business Review* 79, no. 4, pp. 131–137.

Boghin, J. 2014. *Three Ways Companies Can Make Co-Creation Payoff.* New York, NY: McKinsey & Company.

Bosworth, G. and R. Turner,. 2018. "Interrogating the Meaning of a Rural Business Through a Rural Capitals Framework." *Journal of Rural Studies* 60, no. 1, pp 1–10.

Carlos, M.R. 2005. "Emergence of a Third Culture-Shared Leadership in International Strategic Alliance." *International Marketing Review* 22, no. 1, pp 67–95.

Chambers, R. 1994. "The Origins and Practice of Participatory Rural Appraisal." *World Development* 22, no. 7, pp. 953–969.

Desai, D. 2008. "Role and Relationship Management and Value Co-Creation in Social Marketing." *Social Marketing Quarterly,* 15, no. 4, pp. 112–125.

Füller, J., K. Hutter, J. Hautz, and K. Matzler. 2014. "User Roles and Contributions in Innovation-Contest Communities." *Journal of Management Information Systems* 31, no. 1, pp. 273–308.

Gibson, G., A. Timlin, S. Curran, and J. Wattis. 2004. "The Scope for Qualitative Methods in Research and Clinical Trials in Dementia." *Age and Ageing* 33, no. 4, pp. 422–426.

Hanna, R.C., A. Rohm, and V.L. Crittenden. 2011. "We're All Connected: The Power of the Social Media Ecosystem." *Business Horizons* 54, no. 3, pp. 265–273.

Hildebrand, C., G. Haubl, A. Herrmann, and J.R. Landwehr. 2013. "Conformity and the Crowd." *Harvard Business Review* 91, no. 4, pp. 23–24.

Jones, M.Y., M.T. Spence, and C. Vallester. 2008. "Creating Emotions Via B to C Websites." *Business Horizons* 51, no. 5, pp. 419–428.

Kleiner, A. 2003. "Are You In With the In Crowd?" *Harvard Business Review* 81, no. 7, pp. 86–92.

Kotilainen, K., U.A. Saari, S.J. Mäkinen, and C.M. Ringle. 2019. "Exploring the Microfoundations of End-User Interests Toward Co-Creating Renewable Energy Technology Innovations." *Journal of Cleaner Production* 229, pp. 203–212.

Lafley, A.G., R. Martin, R.G. McGrath, S. Cook, J.V. Knudstorp, and D. Champion. 2017. *Cumulative Advantage.* Cambridge, MA: Harvard Business School Press.

Lara, C.S., A.F. Crispín, and M.C.L. Téllez. 2018. "Participatory Rural Appraisal as an Educational Tool to Empower Sustainable Community Processes." *Journal of Cleaner Production* 172, pp. 4254–4262.

Li, Y.M., C.Y. Hsieh, L.F. Lin, and C.H. Wei. 2021. "A Social Mechanism for Task-Oriented Crowdsourcing Recommendations." *Decision Support Systems* 141, Art 113449. https://doi.org/10.1016/j.dss.2020.113449.

Lin, F.J. and Y.H. Jin. 2016. "The Effect of Network Relationship on the Performance of SMEs." *Journal of Business Research* 69, pp. 1780–1784.

Liu, G. and K. Rong. 2015. "The Nature of the Co-Evolutionary Process: Complex Product Development in the Mobile Computing Industry's Business Ecosystem." *Group & Organization Management* 40, no. 6, pp. 809–842.

Liu, S., W. Xiao, C. Fang, X. Zhang, and J. Lin. 2020. "Social Support, Belong-ingness, and Value Co-Creation Behaviors in Online Health Communities." *Telematics and Informatics* 50, (in press). https://doi.org/10.1016/j.tele.2020.101398.

Mahajan, V. 2016. "How Unilever Reached Rural Consumers in Emerging Markets." *Harvard Business Review Digital Article*. Cambridge, MA: Harvard Business School Publishing. https://hbr.org/2016/12/how-unilever-reaches-rural-consumers-in-emerging-markets (accessed April 22, 2023).

Menconi, M.E., D. Grohmann, and C. Mancinelli. 2017. "European Farmers and Participatory Rural Appraisal: A Systematic Literature Review on Experiences to Optimize Rural Development." *Land Use Policy* 60, no. 1, pp. 1–11.

Mesulam, M.M. 1998. "From Sensation to Cognition." *Brain* 121, no. 6, pp. 1013–1052.

Miranda, M., L. Konya, and I. Havira. 2005. Shopper's Satisfaction Levels Are Not Only the Key to Store Loyalty." *Marketing Intelligence and Planning* 23, no. 2, pp. 220–232.

Rajagopal. 2006. "Innovation and Business Growth Through Corporate Venturing in Latin America: Analysis of Strategic Fit." *Management Decision* 44, no. 5, pp. 703–718.

Rajagopal. 2013. *Managing Social Media and Consumerism: The Grapevine Effect in Competitive Markets*. Basingstoke, UK: Palgrave Macmillan.

Rajagopal. 2019. *Qualitative Marketing Research: Understanding How Behavioral Complexities Drive Marketing Strategies*. New York, NY: Business Expert Press.

Rajagopal. 2021. "Crowd-Based Business Models—Using Collective Intelligence for Market Competitiveness." New York, NY: Palgrave Macmillan.

Ramaswamy, V. and F.J. Gouillart. 2008. "Co-Creating Strategy With Experience Co-Creation." *Harvard Business School Newsletter* Cambridge: Harvard Business School Press.

Reeves, M., K. Haanaes, and J. Sinha. 2015. "Navigating the Dozens of Different Strategy Options." *Harvard Business Review* 93, no. 6, pp. 1–17.

Sidibe, M. 2020. "Marketing Meets Mission." *Harvard Business Review Digital Article*. Cambridge: Harvard Business School Press.

Stringer, E. 2007. *Action Research*. Los Angeles: Sage.

Tallman, S. and K. Fladmoe-Lindquist. 2002. "Internationalization, Globalization, and Capability-Based Strategy." *California Management Review* 45, no. 1, pp. 116–135.

Täuscher, K. 2017. Leveraging Collective Intelligence: How to Design and Manage Crowd-Based Business Models." *Business Horizons* 60, no. 2, pp. 237–245.

Taylor, D.G., J.E. Lewin and D. Strutton. 2011. "Friends, Fans, and Followers: Do Ads Work on Social Networks?" *Journal of Advertising Research* 51, no. 1, pp. 258–275.

CHAPTER 5

Consumer Advocacy

Overview

This chapter discusses the changing perspectives of consumer advocacy from the point of view of sharing new forms of radical, collaborative, and innovative experiences through proximity marketing approaches. The discussion on advocacy patterns includes the consumer focus on anthropomorphism, follower psychology on digital media, out-of-the-box customer advocacy, and creative semantics. Such models in proximity marketing are used to take advantage of structured semantics, reasoning, or decision-making power (Horkoff et al. 2019). This chapter also discusses the future of shopping using technology and collective consumerism. The growing technology-based retailers such as Amazon (VR kiosks), Alibaba (Buy + mobile VR platform), eBay (VR Department Store app), and IKEA (VR kitchen showroom) have been making efforts to embed VR into their e-commerce services as a tool to drive relationship marketing and proximity effects. These firms are trying to transform the future of the shopping ecosystem through head-mounted displays, haptic devices, body-tracking sensors, motion-tracked controllers to structure future shopping, and smart (omnichannel) retailing ecosystem (Xi and Hamari 2021). This chapter emphasizes how lessons can be drawn from the experiences of success and failure in doing business with people. The pace at which organizations learn may become the only sustainable source of competitive advantage over time (Senge 1990). This chapter also includes a case study on institutional consumer advocacy.

Experiential Marketing

Experiential marketing helps companies to socialize the brands and gain competitive advantage in the marketplace. However, perceptions take a long time to develop into an attitude. However, developing behavior is often more impulsive than judgmental for consumers, as attitude is largely determined by the pressure of consumer needs, available choices, and sustainable consumer perceptions. Impulsive attitudes emerge out of consumer psychodynamics, and peer pressure (Rajagopal 2018). Consumer perceptions are sensitive to their experiences and help in building attitude if sustained for a reasonable period. Most consumer-centric companies ensure that consumers gain favorable and sustainable perception through brand campaigns, digital communications, social media forums, and product- and services trials. In this perceptual-mapping process, the cognitive drivers help consumers in developing consistency in attitude, which not only positions the brand as "top-of-mind" element but also encourages repeat buying behavior. The consistent attitude is reflected in the buying behavior and sharing of brand experience by consumers extensively over the interpersonal and digital platforms. To create positive perceptions among consumers, companies tend to inculcate needs-led perceptions using emotional strategies such as physiological (survival), safety, love, esteem, and self-actualization. By sharing experience on perceptions and attitude, consumers influence fellow consumers as well.

Companies use effective advertising, communications, and informal learning on social media and community platforms, and invest enormous resources in consumer education to develop brand knowledge, product perceptions, and purchase intentions. Consumers today buy solutions, not products per se. Therefore, consumer-centric companies employ resources on consumer research to periodically understand and refresh consumer needs and preferences. Accordingly, companies offer consumer-marketing solutions with competitive advantage to encourage acquisition and retention of profitable customers. A successful company manages customers individually, demonstrating how its products or services help in solving problems of buyers and develop higher perceived value. Brand awareness, quality referrals, and brand-experience sharing earn enormous benefits to develop individual relationships with customers. To achieve these goals, companies must become aware of the different types of benefits they offer and convey their value to the appropriate executives in customer-centric company. Loyal customers show predictable behaviors such as growing the relationship between consumer experiences and providing word-of-mouth endorsements that help the company in acquiring new customers (Narayandas 2005). Consumer behavior is governed by the following synchronized, linear path of cognitive–materialistic–utilitarian relationship among other attributes as discussed in the following:

- Knowledge, perception, attitude, and behavior
- Awareness, attributes, affordability, and adaptability
- Validity, value, venue, and vogue
- Engagement, explorative, emotions, and consumption experience

The process of mapping the perceptions of consumers on various value-generating elements to support decision-making process is complex. However, most companies tend to develop constructing customer value through various interpersonal communications and cognitive building-blocks exercise. Such efforts help companies in generating opportunities to improve their performance in existing markets or break into new markets. If the marketing mix is blended rightly, the brands pay off in stronger customer loyalty, greater consumer willingness to try a particular brand, and sustained revenue growth. Companies need to consider the elements of functional-, emotional-, and lifetime value, and social impact of mapping the consumer perception and improving mass-market brands (Almquist et al. 2016).

The variety of goods, and the range of sales channels offering them, have also grown beyond dimensions due to the success of virtual stores. Simultaneously, the product quality has also steadily improved. E-commerce companies such as Amazon are expanding their portfolios from virtual to brick-and-mortar businesses. Acquisition of Whole Foods Market, a retail giant in the United States, by Amazon shows the reversal of trend from virtual to brick-and-mortar retailing. Many companies are streamlining their systems for providing goods and services by making it easier for customers to buy and use ambidextrously from online and in a physical store. Such a strategy is helping them to build consumer loyalty on one channel and disseminate consumer experience on the rest of their business channels. A growing number of companies is lowering costs, strengthening consumer loyalty, and attracting new customers who are defecting from less user-friendly competitors (Womack and Jones 2005). Value-based perception of consumers develops consumption attitude by evaluating value for money, competitive benefits, and utilitarian satisfaction. Often, a positive consumption experience guarantees satisfaction, and develops brand loyalty and sustainable behavior among consumers over time. Consumers, who are active on social media, also develop knowledge, perceptions, and motivations through the user-generated contents and experience sharing. As social media is dynamic, it is attributed to variable consumer behavior.

Client relations play a significant role in acquiring new clients and retaining them. Industrial marketing companies extend care for customers through client-specific key accounts managers. The managers and frontline employees get engaged with the clients for various portfolios of products and services. The proclient relations of industrial marketers emphasize listening to client's needs and problems empathetically and provide solutions on real time. Client relationship is also extended to create awareness on products and services through destination training, simulations, and experience sharing to match with rapidly changing innovations and technology trends. Like low-profile B-to-C companies, most industrial marketing firms also aim at reducing costs primarily by staying opaque to their clients. Such an approach not only makes companies less competitive in the market but also develops a pool of inadequately served and increasingly frustrated clients. An equally damaging effect of poor client relations is the resulting estrangement of employees from clients. Technology-led B-to-B marketing companies affirm their commitment of active and empathetic involvement with customers to understand the ways in which business interactions can be cocreated. The deployment of social networks and digital client-services technologies help clients and stakeholders in experience sharing, and construct a common workplace (Gorry and Westbrook 2009). The convergence of experience-led proximity marketing approach of a firm with diffusion, adaptation, responsiveness, and transformation (DART) is exhibited in Figure 5.1.

Convergence of DART in proximity marketing by diffusing experiences of customers and stakeholders to drive social proximity of the

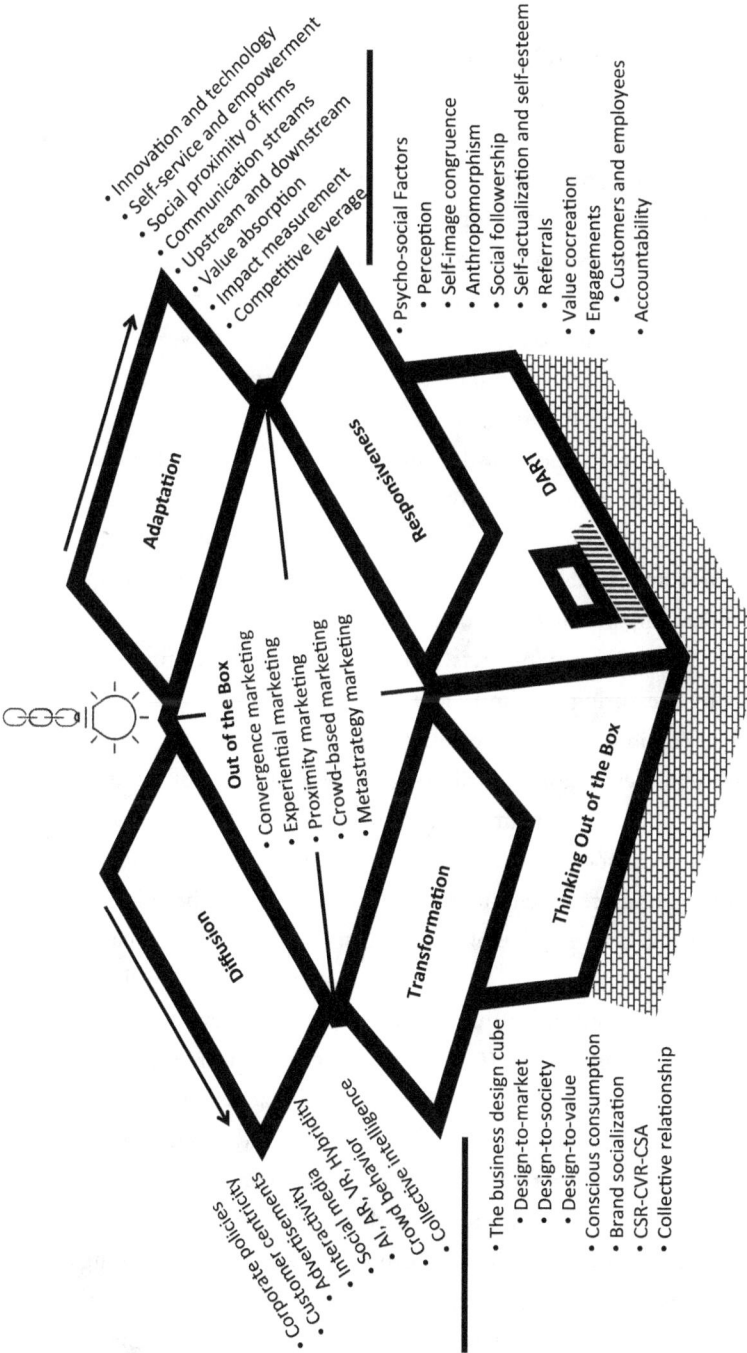

Figure 5.1 The DART factors affecting the proximity strategy

Source: Author.

firms is one of the major challenges as illustrated in Figure 5.1. The crowd-based and meta-marketing strategies by engaging customer communities and social institutions help firms in enhancing the proximity of a firm in the society. The design-to-marketing approaches of firms such as LEGO and IKEA has significantly contributed in increasing their social proximity and customer outreach with specific segmentation–targeting–positioning strategies in a predetermined market or geodemographic segment. Proximity to the society of a firm can be stimulated through effective advertising strategies on social media to engage people on interactive communication and crowd activities. The corporate policies to drive customer engagement through augmented reality and VR embedded with artificial intelligence and hybridity significantly contribute to the crowd behavior and CI. These elements constitute the diffusion domain of the DART conglomerate. Successful diffusion of corporate communication to drive social proximity encourages customers and stakeholders to adapt innovation and technology in communication, product deliveries, and value cocreation in both upstream and downstream markets. Firms can gain the competitive advantages by measuring the impact of adaptation of such individual and group perceptions and behavior in managing the proximity marketing activities. Besides, factors contributing to the adaptation of diffused corporate communication, many psychosocial factors as illustrated in Figure 5.1 affect the social responsiveness of the firms, which stimulate value cocreation and accountability toward socializations of brands and image of the firm. Convergence of design-to-market, design-to-society, and design-to-value strategies of the firm strengthens the meta-business approaches of CSR, corporate value regeneration (CVR), and corporate and stakeholder accountability (CSA) over time in a given region or geodemographic segment. A blend of these factors across the DART domains help firms to build collective relationships and promote conscious consumption and brand socialization at the grassroots.

Companies aiming to gain high market share amidst competition drive client involvement through experience sharing like making industrial clients share test drive experience of automobiles, quality of broadband Internet, interactive product websites, and so on. Client involvement commonly builds a positive attitude toward the products and services. Industrial clients may have low or high involvement with frugal innovative products to perceive the value and competitive advantage and develop an attitude toward buying them. Bottled water is a low-involvement product for a workplace of a company, on which purchase decision is made without an extensive or intensive market research or emotional involvement. Contrary to hiring suppliers for bottled water, leasing of printing and scanning machines is a high-involvement product that requires industrial clients to review technology opinions and economic viability. Analysis of attitudinal metrics of industrial clients indicates that liking, market attractions, and price make substantial impact on developing the buying attitude among industrial clients. As industrial clients are largely driven by the product attractiveness and marketing tactics of competitors, the product's use value and price appear to have the highest elasticity.

Customer Advocacy Patterns

Large companies prefer to stay with customers and analyze information on their perception and preferences to identify the latent and expressed needs. However, implementing the relationship programs are complex, as they incur high cost and employee commitment to reach out the customers and ensure the satisfaction and value propositions. In addition, data mining requires investment in digital infrastructure, data warehouse management, and periodic analysis of consumer data. Consequently, relationship programs need strategic designing to develop community–customer value and customized selling in mass consumer segment.[1] Firms have been relying in the past on push marketing strategies to sell their products and services. The emphasis of these firms has shifted to relationship marketing, which unveiled the customer-centric philosophy. This became the pivotal strategy for many firms. The innovative phase of relationship marketing includes the social concept of 4C's comprising convergence (customer needs and marketing strategies), connectivity (between customer perceptions and corporate actions), content

---

[1] G. Dowling. 2002. "Customer Relationship Management: In B2C Markets, Often Less Is More," *California Management Review* 44, no. 3, pp. 87–104.

creation (experience sharing and implementation of applied strategies), and cocreation (building relationship with customer engagement). However, these tactics tended to show low effectiveness, particularly as the power of customers continues to grow with heavy inflow of tactical communications and personalized promotions. In response, innovative companies are now trying a different approach such as providing customers with open, honest, and complete information, and then finding the best products for them even if those offerings are from competitors. Such efforts of companies are truly representing customers' best interests and are essentially becoming corporate advocacy for them. If a company advocates for its customers, they will reciprocate with their trust, loyalty, and purchases either now or in the future.

The positive emotions of customers are leveraged by the corporate goals to deliver probrand customer advocacy. The employee commitment and one-on-one customer marketing strategies also help companies in developing positive relationship marketing with customers (Rajagopal 2022). In addition, the divergent factors of value streams are spread across the customer engagement (emotional association), role of influencer (transfer of knowledge and decision making), and motivation through referrals (customer advocacy), all of which play significant role in implementing the customer relationship programs. Most customers conceive the benefits of customer relationship programs as a social drive and get motivated through crowd behavior. The digital attraction, visual merchandizing, and video displays on the virtual store platforms create stimuli and emotions among the consumers to develop buying intentions on social media. The social emotions, crowd behavior, and CI have increased the possibility of buying on social media and encouraged brand advocacy due to the ease of purchase.[2] Most customer-centric companies aim at providing desired value and lifestyle, self-actualization, and comparative self-esteem in the value creation process. Patterns of consumerism are changing in society, as there are shifts in the customer demography in the markets. The explosion of mass

---

[2] J. Lindsey-Mullikin and N. Borin. 2017. "Why Strategy Is Key for Successful Social Media Sales," *Business Horizons* 60, no. 4, pp. 473–482.

customer segments, urbanization, and increase in the size of the population of aging customers have contributed significantly to the shifts in customer preferences and overall consumption behavior. Cocreation and codesigning approaches of customer-centric companies like IKEA have established business philosophy of connecting customers and developing an emotion-based relationship with customers as the key to leveraging loyalty and advocacy behavior.[3]

Crowdsourcing generates psychodynamics and helps in cocreating crowd-based business models that aim at doing business in consumer products in closed or open niche markets. Positive psychodynamics among consumers creates pull-effect for specific brands in the market. The pull-effect generates high consumer demand, which benefits companies in increasing market share and profit by reducing the marketing costs. Such costs for brands are spread across advertisements, in-store promotions, price discounts, and point-of-sales incentives to the consumers. Psychodynamics also generates referrals and brand advocacy behavior among consumers, which helps companies acquire new consumers at relatively low cost. The consumer networks and advocacy have also been discussed in the context of crowd-based business modeling.[4] Driving disruptive innovation in large companies requires firms to be ambidextrous to compete in mature markets where efficiency, control, and incremental improvement are essential to exploit the available market potential. Disruptive strategies help companies simultaneously compete with new technologies in emerging markets, which need agile business strategies, salesforce autonomy, and understanding shifts in consumer behavior.[5]

---

[3] Rajagopal. 2021. *Crowd-Based Business Models—Using Collective Intelligence for Market Competitiveness* (New York, NY: Palgrave Macmillan).

[4] Rajagopal. 2019. *Contemporary Marketing Strategy: Analyzing Consumer Behavior to Drive Managerial Decision Making* (New York, NY: Palgrave Macmillan), pp. 3–33.

[5] C.A. O'Reilly, III and M.L. Tushman. 2013. "Organizational Ambidexterity: Past, Present, and Future," *Academy of Management Perspectives* 27, no. 4, pp. 324–338.

Anthropomorphism

The taxonomy of consumer behavior includes individual and group behavior, and social consumption behavior. Consumer emotions contribute significantly to the neurobehavioral dynamics, which reflects in consumer perceptions, attitude, and actions.[6] Emotions, personality, self-concepts, self-image congruence, and anthropomorphism significantly affect the buying–decision making and consumption practices. In addition, external factors (social behavior, market trends, and technology) and shifts in preferences (personal, health, organic, and sustainability) influence consumer behavior over the long term. The external influence is acquired by individuals across geodemographic segments and market behavior. The principal behavioral drivers include intention toward experimenting innovative products, sharing experience, and exhibiting neurotic attitude. These factors lead to various psychological determinants such as self-actualization (leading to supremacy), anthropomorphism, individualism driven by introvert tendencies, and collectivism. Individual behavior is also driven by peer comparison of common perceptions, practices, and pragmatic thinking, which leads to inculcating competitiveness within individual behavior.

Customer relations evolve around the social concepts, self-perceptions, crowd behavior, anthropomorphic appeal, etiological interpretation to consumption, and personal and public meanings of brand for customers. Neurological effects are intensively associated with human cognition, emotions, and anthropomorphic expressions within the society. The extreme or hedonic neurological response to emotions is seen as arousal and merriment, experience sharing, and psychophysical mood manifestations, while negative neurological perceptions illustrate melancholic state of neurobehavioral projections such as isolation, indifference, and dejection from the social and personal attractions. Consumers experience such neurobehavioral changes during in-store or online shopping, as they encounter sensory attributes such as visual

---

[6] Q. Xu, S. Gregor, Q. Shen, Q. Ma, W. Zhang, and A. Riaz. 2020. "The Power of Emotions in Online Decision Making: A Study of Seller Reputation Using fMRI," *Decision Support System* 131, pp. 1–11.

merchandizing, audiovisual programs, and interpersonal communication, and attain "do-it-yourself" experiences.

Follower Psychology

A flexible followership psychology is embedded in human evolution, which enables people to select their leaders in different contexts depending on their perceptions, objectives, and needs. Follower psychology has become a crowd movement after social media has grown into prominence as communication drivers. Following a leader in social media helps consumers to acquire knowledge in a shared direction, understanding the crowd behavior, and develop contextual perceptions. Consumers have evolved with social media leadership psychology that has prompted them to explore new concepts and opportunities to enhance social proximity with the firms and brands. People are more positive about promising leaders who meet their needs (Waal-Andrews and Vugt 2020). The rapid advancement of leaders, followers, and influencers in marketing today has played significant contributions in the digitalization era. The influencers have led firms to partner with social media influencers to lay the foundation of consumer opinions on social media channels. Usually, influencers with large numbers of followers have wide outreach and proximity to the market. According to the recent Influencer Marketing Benchmark Report, the influencer marketing industry is set to grow to approximately $16.4 billion in 2022. In 2021 alone, the global number of influencer marketing-related service offerings grew by 26 percent with most brands using the same influencers across different campaigns (Zhou et al. 2023).

Social media users tend to follow social media influencers spontaneously if their activities are congruent to each other. As influencers endeavor to enhance their social outreach and proximity, followers significantly contribute to the commercial value of the brands led by the influencers. Over time, such influencer-followers conglomerate results into a potential proximity marketing nexus focusing on improving social well-being and cocreating consumer value. Influencer characteristics such as physical attractiveness, social attractiveness, experience sharing, and self-presence; and followers' participation foster social engagement of consumers and stakeholders through the prosocial relationship and sense of belongingness (Young et al. 2004). Crowd behavior, corporate motivation, and positive thinking among consumers significantly influence society–firm relationships through social media. Influencers offer useful insights to gauge consumer engagement and cocreate proximity marketing benefits. Social media addiction leverages the leader-member following tendency on social sites, which cocreates social values by promoting cross-sectional social proximity and driving the consumer consciousness and well-being. Social media influences the gatekeepers of crowd behavior who participate in discussions and activities and form virtual communities around the consumers (Farivar et al. 2022).

Semantics

Semantics exhibits connectivity of thoughts, perceptions, and values among customers on any given object, situation, or within an existing business ecosystem. Cognitive semantics is the continuity of thought process that occurs in the human mind. Cognitive semantics emerges as a process of thoughts and communication that connects to a core thought or mental state addressing a specific ecosystem (Brandt 2005). Customers tend to develop compositions of contextual meaning and senses of a given word, phrases, situations, concepts, or acquired information that affects the processing of complex thoughts, perceptions, and emotions. However, research on embodied cognition demonstrates that perceptual semantics is more than just synchronization of thoughts on lexical meanings rather than perceptual experience. Semantic thoughts are extensions of a principal thought leading to contextual interpretations and decisions. Therefore, perception-based information such as key terms in communication, advertisements, social media messages, and corporate announcements need to be meticulously drafted and posted. Customers who are sensitive to the critical appraisals of words and their meaning engage in wooing perceptual semantics to arrive at cognitive synthesis and decisions. Consequently, market communications including word-of-mouth conversations need a transparent and noncomplex array to encourage positive semantic exercise on concepts and embedded meaning of market communication (Günther et al. 2020).

The notion of semantics has evolved over variations in the use of language, which enables to determine a contextual meaning or its ecosystem. Using cognitive semantics, customers tend to bread contextual meaning of words and perceptions on specific communication keywords. For example, the word "green" might have the semantic expansion to explore the contextual terms such as sustainable, organic, fertilizer, permaculture, natural cultivation, renewal sources, energy, public policy, social consciousness, and the like. Necessarily, perceptual semantics play as decision drivers in developing the ACCA paradigm. However, the question of how the meanings of words is represented in the mind is complex, as the development of semantics to a specific word or concept relates to the existing knowledge and experience of the customers in building semantics. Customers may lean toward positive or negative trail of semantic thoughts based on their repository of knowledge and experience. The earliest views of word meaning in conjunction with the efficiency of cognitive process assume that words represent sets of embedded features and theories, which hold magnanimous potential to explain several phenomena and contextual comprehension, and build a logical framework of relative concepts, perceptions, and guided decisions. Perceptual semantics also inculcates emotions, impulse, and conscious or unconscious cognitive biasness toward specific context. Consequently, the cognitive semantics-based lexicon ecosystem affects customer values with biased, distorted, or develop negativity in thoughts. Commonly, the meaning of words does not depend just on how words are defined, but words, phrases, and sentences in which they appear stimulate the cognitive process (Sanford 2006). Growing concepts in social psychology and neuromarketing experiments endorse that cognitive semantics has been vibrant among the customers today due to updated knowledge and analytical vigor to build appropriate perceptions and buying intentions. The cognitive process, neural network, and social behavior moderate the cognitive semantics process among customers in making buying decisions. One of the critical theoretical perspectives of cognitive neuroscience in recent years is the controlled semantic cognition (CSC) framework. This framework proposes that a network of brain areas provides access to sematic information and its appropriate usage. The CSC theory and associated models have been applied to explain a wide range of evidence on positive and negative notions of customer neurological effects in decision making by analyzing the available information. The CSC protagonists use the term "semantic cognition" to describe a set of supramodal processes that explain the ecosystems of thoughts woven around the information (keywords and concepts). These processes include the refinement of verbal and nonverbal experiences to form a coherent knowledge base by steering the thoughts within a specific ecosystem of market information (Adolph 2010).

Semantics is more frequently associated with language skill, which comprehends cognitive thought process and perceptual manifestation, and portrays nonverbal behaviors including action perception, object inter-action, and a range of sociocognitive processes. The nonverbal behavior is expressed as empathy, emotions, and communications, which broadly constitute semantic representational system within hub (desire and need)- and-spoke (perceptual semantics) architecture. This model plays an essen-tial role in acquiring and analyzing information from personal sources and public domain through various social networks, and reviews affective experiences. Broadly, such "embodiment" of connected thoughts is shared among various episodes of semantic memory (Binney and Ramsey 2020).

Semantics is concerned with interconnected words, and their mean-ing and contextual relevance in the research. Formal semantics is the study of logical aspects of meaning such as sense, reference, and implication within the context of the research study. Logical and lexical semantics studies the word meanings and their etymological relations within the research domain, while conceptual semantics studies the cognitive struc-ture of meaning. Firms engaged in social marketing and developing prox-imity to the society can follow any of the suitable semantics methods to develop a semantic map during the interviews and interpret the semantics during the information analysis of qualitative inquiry. Prior to beginning the qualitative inquiry, researchers need to be well acquainted with the study area by understanding the basic dispositions of people around, and their ethnic, social, and cultural values. Making judgments based on self-reference or invalidated referrals may cause bias among researchers toward respondents and their responses. The problem defined for qualita-tive research can further be supported by socioeconomic, ethnocultural, and cognitive semantics. Semantics is the linguistic and logical expression of the meaning of the research problem interrelated with a variety of variables determining causes and effects. The semantics can be predetermined, or formal semantics can be developed during the initial study process. The semantics of the problem describes logical aspects of derived meaning, such as sense, reference, implication, and logical form, to justify the research problem and choose appropriate study design. Qualitative researchers commonly organize focus group sessions with consumers to explain the objectives of the research, and to acquire firsthand opinions on the research problem.

The underlying challenge in market research is to understand the consumer who is the nucleus of the business ecosystem, and is intertwined with the psychosocial, economic, political, technological, and legal complexities. The consumer acts as the pivot of business and overpowers the markets across regions. Understanding the consumer is as complex as knowing the human mind, as neuroscientists claim that only about 10 percent of its total potential has been discovered as of today. Learning from consumers is a grassroots expedition for researchers to explore the emotions, perception, attitude, and behavior that lead to the semantics of decision making within the dynamic of business ecosystem. Interacting with consumers to learn their emotions is central to qualitative inquiries, and mapping cognitive analytics to guide the market research for an organization is the foundation of qualitative research. Qualitative inquiries are founded on reasoning and thematic connectivity of arguments entwined in a research domain. Such inquiries are held through in-depth interviews, perceptual mapping, cognitive semantics, and sharing of experiences across spatial and temporal dimensions. Social outreach of firms is driven through an informal scenario, which is comfortable to the respondents and researcher. As the qualitative inquiry is based on sharing experiences and forethoughts, and mapping semantics of perceptions, it needs to be organized in a place that respects privacy and personality. Creating an exhibitionistic setup may distract the respondents and restrict the flow of thoughts in a construed ambience. The most suitable ambience for qualitative research is the place, which is dependable, relaxing, and free from external interventions. In qualitative research, the focus is mainly on verbal elucidations, facial interpretations, and the researcher's observation. Design-to-society approach involves an interpretive, naturalistic approach to explore research themes, which demands qualitative researchers to explore research in the natural settings. Therefore, implementing proximity marketing strategy in the natural setting of communities would benefit both the firm and the stakeholders. It would enable them to interpret phenomena in terms of the meanings embedded in the responses of the consumers and stakeholders.

Several ideas, responses, and observations emerge during the in-depth interviews with respondents; so, a skilled researcher should engage in carrying out perceptual mapping and semantics during the proximity drive. Perceptual mapping would help the researcher map the flow of responses against the principal and interrelated questions. Joining several responses to the related questions on perceptual map can guide the firms in determining the state of emotions (such as happiness, sadness, anger, commanding, aggressive, defensive, and submissiveness). Interpreting emotions in qualitative research leads to establish the thrust of responses—vertical (self-image congruity) and horizontal (social-image congruity). The thrust in responses reinforces the respondents' involvement in the research and the commitment in responses.

Customer-centric firms develop semantic maps on the interconnecting words outgrowing from the responses during the in-depth interviews in the qualitative research process. These firms develop unique social concepts for specific geodemographic segments and analyze consumer information through PMA. The ecosystem of qualitative research embeds grounded theory, and sociocultural and political environment at the background, while the research setting, development of research instrument, quality of information, arguments and validations, audiovisual aides, and the observation of researcher form the foreground of research. The proximity approach embedding design-to-society relationship model encourages explorative instead of experimental strategies.

Design-to-Proximity

The design-to-society attributes today are transforming from conventional wisdom to digital tools to socialize brands and deliver social values. The digital interactions among customers help companies socialize the brands and create brand value for competitive leverage. Socialization of marketing strategies, innovations, and brands drives collective impact among customers, which strengthens the competitive positions of companies in the marketplace. The collective impact has enabled many successful collaborations in social health, education, small enterprises, energy, and agricultural sector by guiding businesses and blending the ecosystems to deliver solutions and create value. In the process, companies explored economic opportunities to ride over the competitive hurdles. The collective impact is generated with a common agenda between the society and the companies to align design-to-market approaches within the social ecosystems, which helps in aligning business operations and commitments. Creating and delivering values from business to society needs a shared measurement system that reinforces activities among the stakeholders, customers, and the company. In addition, user-generated content derived from the social platform requires appropriate filters to highlight consistent and value-based communication, which builds trust and ensures establishing the mutual goals. Nonetheless, linking society with business operations needs dedicated support of the employees, corporate management, stakeholders, customers, suppliers, and other players in business operations. Involving society with business is a synchronized process of communication transfers, resource sharing, public-will creation, integrating social and business infrastructure, and aligning corporate social objectives with the public policies (Kramer and Pfitzer 2016). Consequently, companies develop competitive strategies aligning social purposes, and coevolve business to deliver the social business solutions. In this process, companies widely benefit from the social knowledge pool and CI.

The business and society convergence are supported by transformational (change in social thinking) and transactional (value-based philosophy) thinking by cocreating solutions to the societal problems related to business sector. Social marketing strategies are the effective tools to align business goals with social development and value generation perspectives. Social innovations, sustainable development, green marketing, and implementing CSR programs stimulate the enhancement of performance with social purpose. This linear path bridging the gap between society and business validates the design-to-society and design-to-market philosophies. Social validation of marketing programs by sharing customer experiences on the digital platforms and generating user-driven contents develop scope of cocreation of products and services effectively within the society and market. Sustainable customer products companies such as IKEA, GE Energy, and Unilever focus on inducing corporate social leadership in managing the CSR. However, while implementing society-linked business models, companies tend to develop community hubs for customer and stakeholder interactions on face-to-face, digital, or hybrid communication models. The interactions of customers on these platforms help companies document the VoCs to support strategy designs. In addition, public policies, public–private partnerships, and social psychodynamics leverage companies in designing programs to evolve in vulnerable social sectors (health, education, housing, agriculture, and nonfarm economic production), with meticulous business strategies.

A good social strategy for a company requires an analysis of all internal marketing and sales assets. In this way, the company can gather up all customer/client-facing online content, including policy papers, published reports, presentations, messaging, online videos, and mobile applications. To get close involvement with social media, a company needs to list all relevant contents appearing on blogs, any on-site communities, Facebook, and Twitter to inculcate an active discussion. To have an effective and hassle-free involvement with social networks, a company should assess what has been communicated (content types, length, and messaging per target), and how and how often it has been communicated with the network users. To work with social media platforms, business-driving keywords need to be identified and set onto the search engines by the company. There are many reasons social media can be a productive marketing channel or platform. Rather than employing it as a tactic, the purpose should dictate the strategy and the tactics used for reaching desired goals.

A company can run many customer surveys online, but some most interesting and progressive market research can be found within the social communities where customers interact, share information, and make recommendations. Monitoring and analyzing various social media streams and engaging into active dialogues with customers are more challenging for firms. To stay engaged in effective social participation and portray the corporate image of the company to generate awareness about the brands, companies believe in developing design-to-society strategies. In the global marketplace, markets are open, and customers interact without boundaries about a company's products, brands, and services across the network platforms. Thus, companies should intervene in social media and participate in conversations about its products, brands, and services, and streamline the discussions. It would be a good idea for the companies to provide adequate information to educate customers about products and services in the formats and media types they prefer. The relationship of a company with social networks can go a long way toward building business sensitivity that results in strengthening the status of the company against its competitors. Becoming a user of homogeneous social community involves consistently contributing quality content and rewarding those who respond positively on the posting, and growing large base followers through attractive initiatives. Such base of concurring connections can serve as an effective distribution channel for unique and interesting contents, which drives traffic to ad-supported blogs that host the content. Companies that would like to use the social media actively may also consider turning on *link bait strategy* (advertisements that have perennial links). The link bait not only attracts links but also attracts traffic. However, many sites supported by advertisements report that traffic from social media sites is disreputable for not clicking on links. The link bait strategy includes creating visuals with website links, focusing on core functions of the company, listing social media links (forums, communities, and blogs) for providing quick customer solutions, website layout optimization, and capitalizing on voice of customers (reviews and feedback).

Effective social networking on digital and face-to-face interactions enables companies to design network marketing. Engaging customers in the marketing process drives psychodynamics and enhances the scope of peer-review-led brand building. Direct marketing and retailing companies largely view sales networks in terms of direct contacts, and often depend on the social networks. However, companies intensively involved with customers, such as financial services, may not necessarily have an effective network because networks often pay off their value through indirect contacts. Moreover, A thumb rule in customer-centric companies is to adopt relevant social networks and let them grow with the support of the company, so that it can embark on such platforms to gain competitive advantage in the marketplace. Hence, the density of the connections in a network is important. However, thin networks are also better for generating unique information. By increasing investment in social media through network marketing, companies such as Mary Kay Cosmetics engage customers also as sellers, both in the face-to-face and digital forums. With the growing interest of mobile marketing among customers, the digital networks such as Facebook have become widely used forums and exhibit real transactional emotions in the virtual marketplace. However, social networks have yet to emerge as a fully functional vehicle for building customer loyalty, and as a cognitive platform to create brand awareness. Marketing through Facebook helps in increasing loyalty by integrating personal beliefs and trust with public opinions to reinforce customer satisfaction, perceived value, and commitment toward a brand. Such experiment has been a success for the high-value fashion brands in apparel, cosmetics, and perfumes. Such personal–public blend in brand relations is growing strong for followers of the brand, which inculcates loyalty over time among customers in the society (Gamboa and Goncalves 2014).

Managers can use three controls: Direct marketing structure, compensation, and skills development to encourage, monitor, and evaluate enthusiastic customer-sellers to adopt a network-based view for effectively using the social network platforms. For instance, the sales force can be restructured to delink lead generation from other tasks because some people are very good at building diverse ties, but not so good at maintaining other kinds of networks. Companies that take steps of this kind to help their marketing and sales teams build better networks and reap competitive advantages (Ustuner and Godes 2006). In view of the several successful efforts of the virtual-platform companies such as Google and Amazon, the emerging business organizations should start considering the role of social product strategist into their organizations' social media strategy. Companies should seek out product-focused managers who demonstrate strong experience in building social user experiences into the products they work with, and are able to manage the up-front social networks such as Facebook and Twitter applications and experiences. The social media strategist should also have a proven understanding of the benefits of social design for a company's products. The design-to-society philosophy lays foundation for design-to-market and design-to-value thinking. However, companies face a major challenge in screening, classifying, and responding to public opinions in the process of socializing the business. Many companies, which explore marketing and business opportunities through the digital community platforms, are often unable to exploit the information to a full extent. Social media impacts entrepreneurial, financial, operational, and corporate social performance. Interactions within social channels develop social capital, disseminate customer preferences, and help social marketing. Broadly, social networking drives the companies in building appropriate society-driven business model. On social media, the number of "followers" and volume of "likes" positively influence shared values of the company and attract critical masses toward the shared and user-generated contents (Paniagua and Sapena 2014).

Social networks also help firms in becoming sustainable by building loyalty and trust corporate policies. Successful sustainable enterprises in developing countries often involve informal networks that include businesses, nonprofit organizations, and local communities. These networks prompt the firms to go for investments in the financial, social, human, and ecological capital areas. Successful sustainable networks require business enterprises to sponsor for ensuring the network's financial sustainability and serve as the anchor of the company. Multinational corporations sometimes support social networks to anchor with specific operational objectives (Wheeler et al. 2005). Google has done this well; it has tried to embrace social media. Many know Google for taking a developer-centric focus around the products it builds. It has encompassed this philosophy in the knowledge dissemination vision of the company to figure out the challenges around social product design within the organization. Accordingly, Google proceeded to create a new network Google+ to get the entire organization reveal the real relationships their users have. Such integrated platform has also facelifted the Google product line and its application. It has emerged as a product-design strategy of the company.

Summary

This chapter focuses on experiential marketing and customer advocacy patterns. Experiential marketing helps companies to socialize their brands and gain competitive advantage in the marketplace. Most consumer-centric companies ensure that consumers gain favorable and sustainable perception through brand campaigns, digital communications, social media forums, and product- and services trials. Customer advocacy is influenced by the anthropomorphism, follower strategy, perceptual semantics, and design-to-proximity approaches of a firm. Value-based perception of consumers develops consumption attitude by evaluating value for money, competitive benefits, and utilitarian satisfaction. Convergence of DART attributes significantly affect the proximity marketing. Proximity of firms can be enhanced by diffusing experiences of customers and stakeholders to drive social consciousness about the firm. However, it is one of the major challenges, as the process of mapping the perceptions of consumers on various value-generating elements to support decision-making process is complex. Discussions in this chapter argue that the customer-centric policies often drive customer engagement through augmented and CI, real-time experiences, and artificial intelligence. These attributes constitute the diffusion domain of the DART conglomerate. Successful diffusion of corporate communication to drive social proximity encourages customers and stakeholders to adapt innovation and technology in communication, product deliveries, and value cocreation in both upstream and downstream markets.

This chapter delineates that the convergence of design-to-market, design-to-society, and design-to-value strategies of the firm strengthens the meta-business approaches of CSR, CVR, and CSA over time in a given region or geodemographic segment. Customer-centric firms develop semantic maps on the interconnecting words outgrowing from the responses during the in-depth interviews in the qualitative research process. The design-to-society attributes today are transforming from conventional wisdom to digital tools to socialize brands and deliver social values. A blend of these factors across the DART domains helps firms to build collective relationships and promote conscious consumption and brand socialization at the grassroots. Consumer networks and advocacy have also been discussed in the context of crowd-based business modeling. Emotions, personality, self-concepts, self-image congruence, and anthropomorphism significantly affect the buying-decision making and consumption practices. In addition, external factors (social behavior, market trends, and technology) and shifts in preferences (personal, health, organic, and sustainability) influence consumer behavior over the long term.

It is argued in the chapter that a flexible followership psychology in human evolution enables people to select their leaders in different contexts depending on their perceptions, objectives, and needs. Follower psychology has become a crowd movement after social media grew into prominence as communication drivers. Social media users tend to follow social media influencers spontaneously if their activities are congruent to each other. As influencers endeavor to enhance their social outreach and proximity, followers significantly contribute to the commercial value of the brands led by the influencers. Nonetheless, semantics exhibits connectivity of thoughts, perceptions, and values among customers on any given object, situation, or within an existing business ecosystem. Cognitive semantics is the continuity of thought process that occurs in the human mind. Semantics is concerned with interconnected words, and their meaning and contextual relevance in the research. It is the linguistic and logical expression of the meaning of the research problem interrelated with a variety of variables determining causes and effects.

References

Adolphs, R. 2010. "Conceptual Challenges and Directions for Social Neuroscience." *Neuron* 65, pp. 752–76.

Almquist, E., J. Senior, and N. Bloch. 2016. "The Elements of Value." *Harvard Business Review* 94, no. 9, pp. 47–53.

Binney, R.J. and R. Ramsey. 2020. "Social Semantics: The Role of Conceptual Knowledge and Cognitive Control in a Neurobiological Model of the Social Brain." *Neuroscience and Biobehavioral Reviews* 112, no. 1, pp. 28–38.

Brandt, P.A. 2005. "Mental Spaces and Cognitive Semantics: A Critical Comment." *Journal of Pragmatics* 37, no. 10, pp. 1578–1594.

Farivar, S., F. Wang, and O. Turel. 2022. "Followers' Problematic Engagement With Influencers on Social Media: An Attachment Theory Perspective." *Computers in Human Behavior* 113, (in press). https://doi.org/10.1016/j.chb.2022.107288.

Gamboa, A.M. and H.M. Goncalves. 2014. "Customer Loyalty Through Social Networks: Lessons From Zara on Facebook." *Business Horizons* 57, no. 6, pp. 709–717.

Gorry, G.A. and R.A. Westbrook. 2009. "Winning the Internet Confidence Game." *Corporate Reputation Review* 12, no. 3, pp. 195–203.

Günther, F., M.A. Petilli, and M. Marelli. 2020. "Semantic Transparency Is Not Invisibility: A Computational Model of Perceptually-Grounded Conceptual Combination in Word Processing." *Journal of Memory and Language* 112, pp. 1–16.

Horkoff, J., N.A. Maiden, and D. Asboth. 2019. "Creative Goal Modeling for Innovative Requirements." *Information and Software Technology* 106, pp. 85–100.

Kramer, M.R. and M. Pfitzer. 2016. "The Ecosystem of Shared Value." *Harvard Business Review* 94, no. 10, pp. 80–89.

Narayandas, D. 2005. "Building Loyalty in Business Markets." *Harvard Business Review* 83, no. 9, pp. 131–139.

Paniagua, J. and J. Sapena. 2014. "Business Performance and Social Media: Love or Hate?" *Business Horizons* 57, no. 6, pp. 719–728.

Rajagopal. 2018. *Consumer Behavior Theories: Convergence of Divergent Perspectives With Applications to Marketing and Management*. New York, NY: Business Expert Press.

Rajagopal. 2022. *Agile Marketing Strategies—New Approaches to Engaging Consumer Behavior*. Cham: Springer.

Sanford, A.J. 2006. "Semantics in Psychology." In *Encyclopedia of Language & Linguistics*, ed. K. Brown, 152–158. 2nd ed. Amsterdam: Elsevier.

Senge, P.M. 1990. "Leader's New Work: Building Learning Organizations." *MIT Sloan Management Review* 32, no. 1, pp. 7–23.

Ustuner, T. and D.B. Godes. 2006. "Better Sales Networks." *Harvard Business Review* 84, no. 7, pp. 102–112.

Waal-Andrews, W. and M. Vugt. 2020. "The Triad Model of Follower Needs—Theory and Review." *Current Opinion in Psychology* 33, pp. 142–147.

Wheeler, D., K. McKague, J. Thomson, R. Davies, J. Medalye, and M. Prada. 2005. "Creating Sustainable Local Enterprise Networks." *Sloan Management Review* 47, no. 1, pp. 33–40.

Womack, J.P. and D.T. Jones. 2005. "Lean Consumption." *Harvard Business Review* 83, no. 3, pp. 58–68.

Xi, N. and J. Hamari. 2021. "Shopping in Virtual Reality: A Literature Review and Future Agenda." *Journal of Business Research* 134, pp. 37–58.

Young, A.F., A. Russell, and J.R. Powers. 2004. "The Sense of Belonging to a Neighborhood: Can It Be Measured and Is It Related to Health and Wellbeing in Older Women?" *Social Science and Medicine* 59, no. 12, pp. 2627–2637.

Zhou, L., F. Jin, B. Wu, Z. Chen, and C.L. Wang. 2023. "Do Fake Followers Mitigate Influencers' Perceived Influencing Power on Social Media Platforms? The Mere Number Effect and Boundary Conditions." *Journal of Business Research* 158. https://doi.org/10.1016/j.jbusres.2022.113589.

About the Author

Dr. Rajagopal is Professor of Marketing at EGADE Business School of Tecnologico de Monterrey (ITESM) at Mexico City Campus and fellow of the Royal Society for Encouragement of Arts, Manufacture, and Commerce, London. He is also fellow of the Chartered Management Institute and fellow of the Institute of Operations Management, United Kingdom. He is a visiting professor at the Boston University, Boston, Massachusetts, since 2013. Dr. Rajagopal is also visiting professor since August 2020 at the UFV India Global Education of the University at the Fraser Valley, Canada, and teaches marketing-related courses. He has been listed with biography in various international directories.

Dr. Rajagopal holds postgraduate and doctoral degrees in Economics and Marketing, respectively, from Pandit Ravishankar Shukla University in India. His specialization is in the field of Marketing Management. He has to his credit 71 books on marketing management and rural development themes and over 400 research contributions that include published research papers in national and international refereed journals. He is Editor-in-Chief of International Journal of Leisure and Tourism Marketing and International Journal of Business Competition and Growth. Dr. Rajagopal was Associate Editor of Emerald Emerging Markets Case Studies (2012–2019), published by Emerald Publishers, United Kingdom. He is on the editorial board of various journals of international repute.

Dr. Rajagopal has been conferred the honor of Distinguished Professor by the EGADE Business School, Mexico, in 2020. His research contributions have been recognized by the National Council of Science and Technology (CONACyT), Government of Mexico, by awarding him the highest level of National Researcher-SNI Level-III in 2013. He has been awarded United Kingdom–Mexico Visiting Chair 2016–2017 for collaborative research on "Global–Local Innovation Convergence" with University of Sheffield, United Kingdom, instituted by the Consortium of Higher Education Institutes of Mexico and United Kingdom.

Dr. Rajagopal has been conferred the Overseas Indian Award (*Pravasi Bhartiya Samman Award*) in January 2023 for his outstanding contribution in the field of Education. This is the highest honor conferred by the President of India. This award has been conferred in acknowledgment of the outstanding achievement in the field of Education in India, USA, and Mexico.

Index

Note: Page numbers followed by f and t refers to figures and tables respectively. Page numbers followed by "n" refer to foot notes.

Concise and Applied Business Books

www.ingramcontent.com/pod-product-compliance
Lightning Source LLC
Chambersburg PA
CBHW061213220326
41599CB00025B/4631